Illusory Freedoms:
Liberalism, Education and the Market

Other books in this series:

Illusory Freedoms:
Liberalism, Education and the Market

RUTH JONATHAN

The Journal of the Philosophy of Education Society of Great Britain

Blackwell Publishers
108 Cowley Road, Oxford OX4 1JF, UK

350 Main Street, Malden, MA 02148, USA

British Library Cataloguing-in-Publication Data
Data applied for

Library of Congress Cataloguing-in-Publication Data
Data applied for

Printed in Great Britain by Redwood Books, Trowbridge.
This book is printed on acid-free paper

Contents

Preface

Ruth Jonathan, like her predecessors in this series, deals with matters of great current importance. The application of market mechanisms to education is found increasingly throughout the world. In the UK, for example, such mechanisms extend from the introduction of vouchers for nursery schooling to new funding arrangements being contemplated for higher education. These, it seems likely, will abandon the principle that university education is a good for the community as a whole rather than just for the individual—who will therefore be expected to pay for his or her benefits, as for any other consumer good.

Ruth Jonathan shows how these important educational matters are bound up with a range of fundamental issues in political and social philosophy. Such issues involve disputes, for example, 'over whether the self is or is not prior to its ends, over whether autonomy is to be construed as an individual value or as a social good, over where the boundaries lie between the public and private domains, over whether the state can or should stand neutral between competing ideas of the good' (p. 3). These questions are both fundamental for our understanding of education and they are themselves significantly affected by that understanding. For education is 'a uniquely significant site for studying how our beliefs and commitments about human possibility and defensible social principles cash out in the real world' (*ibid.*).

Philosophy of education thus engages in dialogue, profitable to all sides, with other disciplines. Ruth Jonathan here contributes significantly to that dialogue. The *Journal of Philosophy of Education* is grateful to her for publishing her work in its series of Special Issues.

Richard Smith

Introduction

Over the past two decades the public provision of education has undergone a significant change in many liberal democracies.[1] At the beginning of this period of change, shifts in attitude and policy seemed from each local vantage point to be just a particularly strong swing of the pendulum of opinion and direction which characterises adversarial political systems. However, as each set of local commentators became increasingly aware of similar changes taking place in societies whose declared political complexion differed markedly from their own, as similar kinds of radical change affected other areas of social practice and public provision, and as the 'radical' rhetoric of the early 1980s evolved into the common currency of discourse in the mid 1990s, it became evident that this was no mere pendulum swing. The buzz words 'privatisation', 'consumer-democracy', 'the triumph of the market', 'globalisation', etc. had become accepted currency, but these served as slogans or labels rather than as explanatory concepts.

A primary purpose of this analysis is to offer an explanatory framework for the sea-change which has taken place over the last twenty years in the ways in which we understand, conduct and direct education—that social practice which is most central to the evolution of value and of circumstance. The case-study setting to which reference will be made happens to be the UK but could, *mutatis mutandis*, have been any one of several western liberal democracies. That said, the phenomenon in question has been starkly evident in the UK, where a resurgent neo-liberalism took on a triumphalist zeal in its mission to reverse an earlier consensus course of social development which had aimed at enhanced baselines of public provision. The point of the analysis which follows, however, is not simply to add to a growing debate which either celebrates or deplores recent changes in ethos, practice and policy. It does not set out merely to weigh the pros and cons of contrasting approaches in terms of their likely impact on levels of social equality, national economic competitiveness, cultural ambience, social cohesion, or whatever (often conflicting) criteria of judgement are brought into play in contemporary dialogues of the deaf about suitable policies for ensuring a 'better' provision and distribution of education. The point of the analysis is rather to take seriously the insight that education is a society's most central social practice, to locate within a broader context the changes which have taken place with respect to that practice, and in so doing to enhance our understanding of that broader context.

The context in question, of course, is undeniably social and inescapably complex. It consists in a nexus of values, realities and frameworks of interpretation in continuous interaction. In this dynamic, our prevailing social theory and our established social practices each reflect and underpin the other in periods of stable consensus, and each challenge and highlight points of weakness in the other in periods of social contestation. Uncomfortable though they are, it is thus through such periods of contestation that developments in our understanding, as well as modifications of our circumstance, take place. It would therefore be a missed opportunity if philosophers of education were to confine themselves at this time to a study of only the immediate educational implications of far-reaching change. For the climate of public debate today tends to represent and treat education on the one hand as a private consumer good, best produced and distributed by the mechanism of free market exchange considered appropriate for such goods in a liberal democracy, and on the other hand as the public site for the production of those skills thought exchangeable to advantage in the global market. And this changed vision of education, with all its internal contradictions, has a provenance with much deeper roots than the often-instanced 'oil recession' of the mid 1970s and the demonised legacy of 1960s progressivism, and more extensive consequences than the foreseeable reversal of gains in social equity previously achieved through enhanced educational opportunity.

There are of course many strictly educational questions there which can and should be addressed. These are unarguably within the remit of philosophers of education, just as applied philosophers might properly examine the ethical implications of the recent introduction of market conditions into the provision of health care. This work is clearly both useful and urgent, but it is also limited in scope. It addresses the symptoms and damaging consequences of the course on which social change now seems set but it has little to say about, and even less effect on, the underlying engine of that course. It might reasonably be claimed that that is the task of political and social philosophy. Indeed it is, and the revitalisation of these fields of inquiry over the same two decades is testimony to the fact that social theory and social practice are in constant mutual interaction and modification. For liberalism itself is currently under renewed and intensive theoretical scrutiny at the same time as one of its more fundamentalist variants is changing the nature of our social practices and altering the distributions of our social goods.

However, recognising the power of theory and practice to test and modify each other, it is a basic premise of this monograph that a significant contribution to current debates within social and political philosophy can be made by a focus on the practice and theory of education. For example, inquiry into the presuppositions and implications of moves to direct public education according to neo-liberal principles (principles which in their extreme form Gray has aptly labelled "paleo-liberalism"[2]), or scrutiny of attempts to defend earlier practice and policy from the standpoint of a neutralist liberal philosophy of education, are each in different ways very germane to the current search for a theoretically coherent and practically defensible form of liberalism. Such analyses are clearly the task of philosophers of education although this is not comfortable work. It demands radical reappraisal not merely of a range of educational practices and policies—business as usual, or the philosopher of education's 'normal science'—but also of the justifying theory against which practice and policy can be weighed in periods of stable consensus. More than this, it requires re-examination of the framework of socio-political theory to which liberal philosophy of education pervasively makes implicit reference—and in which many of the most hallowed aims and procedures of liberal education are based.

At a time when the central tenets of liberalism are the subject of debate, it would be strange if philosophers whose primary object of social interest is education had no part to play in addressing them. In disputes over whether the self is or is not prior to its ends, over whether autonomy is to be construed as an individual value or as a social good, over where the boundaries lie between the public and private domains, over whether the state can or should stand neutral between competing ideas of the good, etc., the connection between these questions and any justifying theory for the *aims, content and processes* of education is undeniable. Similarly, on matters such as the legitimate scope of the state, on whether individuals 'own' their talents and attributes, on how far individual choices in a social context should be considered self-regarding, etc., then any justifying theory for the appropriate *distribution* of education is of crucial relevance. It is evident—and unsurprising—that the contemporary watershed in social theory mirrors and is mirrored by an equivalent watershed in the conduct and direction of our central social practices. Among these, education has a quite unique function which makes analysis of its practice and justifying theory a key component in the reconstruction not only of our social life but also of our social understanding and aspiration.

This, of course, is because education is the one social practice which *both reflects and produces* social circumstance *and* values. Moreover, it is the one 'public service' whose nature and purpose, as will be seen, is inevitably altered by changed mechanisms for its distribution and control. And in turn, with changes in the nature and purpose of education, we create changed parameters for the further evolution of value and circumstance. For these reasons, it is a uniquely significant site for studying how our beliefs and commitments about human possibility and defensible social principles cash out in the real world. As the most fundamental of all social practices, its study is both a key component of, and a fruitful test-bed for, social theory—as thinkers from Plato to Dewey readily understood. We would therefore expect the scope of philosophy of education to broaden in periods of contestation and to intersect with the work of political and social philosophers.

To insist on this broader purpose for educational inquiry is not to suggest that crucial educational questions of content and process be neglected or downgraded: quite the reverse. When situated in the broader theoretical framework, the 'normal science' questions of educational theory are themselves brought into sharper focus. When we understand practice, policy *and theory* as being, simultaneously, reflections of past social circumstance and aspiration and key components of future circumstance and aspiration, then the dialectic relationship between the world and our beliefs about it comes into sharp relief. It then is simply not enough to evaluate proposals for educational change against our existing theoretical perspective— asking, for example, how far the pursuit of those globally marketable skills sought by policy-makers may enhance or frustrate the development of rational autonomy, or querying whether the selective entry to schooling now back on the agenda compromises goals of individual emancipation—for to proceed *only* in this way is to leave immune from revision the very presuppositions whose past application to practice was the seed bed for today's values and circumstance.

Indeed, if we take those examples, we see that the pursuit of globally marketable skills reflects a conception of education as a publicly directed activity with (economistic) social progress in view, whilst the promotion of selection in schooling marries a notion of meritocratic individual emancipation through effort and self-help with a shrewd collective appeal to targeted return on social investment in a project of social progress. We also see, however, that both of these (in practice somewhat contradictory) commitments have their roots in elements of the same broad church of liberalism which also underpins a philosophical analysis of education where individual emancipation through rational autonomy is a central guiding principle. It is thus clear that what present themselves ostensibly as disputes about the proper conduct and organisation of education are at bottom disputes about defensible interpretations of liberalism. They cannot be adjudicated by straightforward invocation of liberal principles and precepts, for it is precisely these which are at issue.

The argument developed through this monograph will therefore tackle the problem the other way about. It will analyse these and related controversies as instantiations, in practice, in policy and in theory, of the contending elements of that broad church, in all its varying shades from the principled neutrality of atomistic individualism and substantive value agnosticism, through contractarian commitments to procedural arrangements for ensuring a framework of social justice, to perfectionist variants of liberalism which value freedom in part as a means to other independently worthwhile goods. In this way it will attempt to reconnect the problems of educational theory and practice with their intellectual context in order the more profitably to address them.

II

The education focus of this book is on those changes in education policy over the past two decades which combine to bring quasi-market conditions to the constitution and distribution of educational 'goods'. There is already a growing literature which defends or attacks such changes in terms of their implications for social equity, economic efficiency, educational quality, local democracy, etc. Adding to that literature is not my main purpose here. For the main thesis of my argument is not that this mechanism of distribution is a good or bad thing in terms of particular chosen criteria, but, more fatally, that its practice is inherently contradictory and its theoretical rationale is incoherent. If that thesis can be sustained, then fruitless arguments from consequences on competing parameters (where the basic criteria for evaluation range across social equity, economic efficiency, academic excellence, etc.) can be set aside.

The case I shall mount is not simply an attack on the social policies of the 'New Right' (now not so new), with education taken as one interesting manifestation of them. Nor is it simply an investigation in the education context into the neo-liberal rationale which underpins these policies, with its emphasis on a rights-based individualism and a neutralist state. Nor is the case to be mounted a general one against the extension of the 'free market' beyond the economic sphere (though it will have implications for those general practical considerations): my thesis is both more specific in its target and, I believe, more far-reaching in its implications. What I shall try to show is that the merits of the free market as a principle for the distribution of 'goods' in society cannot rest on an ideological justification which seeks to legitimate a universal, all-pervasive set of distributional arrangements, irrespective of contingent conditions in the society in question and regardless of the logical features of the goods at issue— be their value private or public, individual or social, intrinsic or exchange. That there are limits to the justifiability of the market is scarcely a new insight of course: these limits have long been a staple of political debate, with contending positions grounded in competing conceptions of distributive justice. The case which follows will attempt to reverse the logic of argumentation: rather than ground those limits in competing conceptions of justice, it will use boundaries to the market established independently of those commit- ments to evaluate the commitments themselves. The basic thesis will be that in any open society *the social practice we call education must represent the limiting case of the free market*. This will be argued on the logical grounds that liberalism (and ironically neo-liberalism the more so) as a social philosophy defined by *the priority given to preference satisfaction*, presupposes an arena of *preference formation* which is exempt from the vagaries of the 'hidden hand'.

In the development of this case, many of liberalism's central tenets will come under scrutiny, from the primacy of rational autonomy as a key value for individuals, to the ideal of a state free from any determinate idea of the good. A range of issues which are central both to educational theory and to political philosophy, such as the scope of value-neutrality, the liberty versus equality debate, the public/ private distinction, the status of competing rights, etc., will necessarily be revisited in the course of the inquiry. Since I support the view that "A notable feature of the most recent liberal theorising of all ideological persuasions has been its mixture of philosophical sophistication and social and political naiveté"[3], part of the object of the exercise is to bring these theoretical debates hard up against our institutional arrangements for the formation of the young and the renewal of the social world. One consequence of that, I shall argue, will be to show that neutralist liberalism (in both its morally scrupulous and its fundamentalist variants) is inadequate to guide either our political arrangements or our educational practice and policies. Just as the development of rational autonomy is of itself empty as the principal justifying aim of liberal education, and 'free' choice as it stands is vacuous as the principle for endorsing and sharing educational goods, so the state's abdication of responsibility for social evolution in favour of the blind forces of the market strips it of any substantive role. The commitment to neutrality (which the early liberals would have found hard to comprehend) confronts us with an impasse today out of which there seem only two ways forward. One of these presents us with the social fragmentation of

neo-liberalism: the other offers the nostalgic possibilities of communitarianism. A third possibility of course is always to try and stay
where we are, adopting a Rortyesque ironic posture towards our
predicament.[4]

The case which follows aims to show that none of these alternatives
is theoretically adequate or practically acceptable. In doing so it
should provide weight to a rather different regeneration of liberal
theory recently advanced within political philosophy, notably in the
work of Raz.[5] This approach explores an interpretation of liberalism
which regards modern neutralism as untenable in principle and
unrealisable in practice. This interpretation does not of course seek
like "paleo-liberalism" to resurrect the particular social thesis of the
early liberals, since discredited by history and circumstance.[6] It does,
however, call for some such thesis, as must any political theory with
pretensions to relevance to the real world. Part of that thesis would be
a theory of education and a theory of culture, which again cannot be
grounded in a neutrality which only *seems* to offer maximal freedom
for each to develop individually and all to share equally in social
development. That neutrality is at the root of the 'illusory freedoms'
of this book's title. We see it in educational practice in our attempts
to guide moral development without privileging particular values and
ways of life. We see it in educational policy when it is supposed that
individual preferences (say, in schooling choice) sum to aggregate
judgements of educational quality. We see it in educational theory in
the insistence that analysis has no prescriptive implications. And in
social and political life we live it to our cost. To quote only card-
carrying liberals, Macedo maintains that "Liberalism holds out the
promise, or the threat, of making all the world like California",[7] and
even more fatalistically Rorty claims that the price to be paid for
cherishing individual liberty is endorsement of a social world which
encourages people to be "bland, calculating, petty and unheroic".[8]

Were these states of affairs unavoidable accompaniments of
liberalism, there would be no morally significant educational
questions to fret about. What I have stubbornly referred to here as
'education' would indeed simply be a matter of acquiring marketable
skills, acceptable attitudes, a set of personal tastes and, if fortunate,
an advantageous position in the social structure. And the market
would indeed be as good a mechanism as any other (and more
democratic than some) for managing that production facility for skill
and taste. But this book will mount a case to show that we need
neither retreat from liberal commitments to the value of freedom, nor
accept the ironic stance (for ourselves) or alienation (for others)
which accompanies the principled refusal to concern ourselves with
ends. As another uneasy liberal notes: "If moral and political life
takes its distinctive character from . . . ends and purposes, how can

moral and political philosophy do other than address and attempt to resolve questions about ends and purposes?"⁹ We might also ask *a fortiori* how philosophy of education could evade these questions and yet retain its understanding of education as having a fundamentally moral purpose.

Sufficient has been said to alert the reader to my general intention to explore a richer notion of personal and social freedom. This in turn implies a 'thicker' concept of autonomy which takes account of the psycho-social context in which that valued capacity is both developed and exercised. It must be emphasised that this entails no rejection of liberalism as such, but only of some—and currently the most pervasive—of its variants. Although it is no overstatement to claim that "Liberalism . . . is the political theory of modernity,"¹⁰ that does not oblige us to lay all the ills of modernity at liberalism's door. Defenders of liberalism reasonably argue that many of our contemporary pathologies result from functionally independent features of modern life such as secularisation, mass society, rapidity of change, etc. To accept this, however, is to be the more aware that we now have even greater need of a political theory which respects liberty and the satisfaction of deliberated preferences but which can protect the cultural forms on which liberty and autonomy depend if they are not to lose their substance.

It also serves to remind us that, just as "A person's well-being depends to a large extent on success in socially defined and determined pursuits and activities",¹¹ so ". . . autonomy is only possible if various collective goods are available".¹² We do not compromise the ideal of autonomy "that people should make their own lives"¹³ when we insist that this has both personal and cultural prerequisites. The personal prerequisites to the development of autonomy—cognitive abilities, imaginative capacity, emotional development, settled character traits—together with the knowledge and skills needed for its effective exercise, combine to make up what a liberal education seeks to provide. The cultural prerequisites—satisfying occupations and professions, common cultural and leisure activities, a social framework for enduring relationships, a political community of trustworthy institutions and conventions—in turn require those personal capacities to sustain them. A liberal society's educational practices are therefore key guarantors of its social and political culture. If the hallmark of the latter is to be respect for the personal liberty to make satisfying choices from a range of worthwhile options for an autonomous life, then the purposes of the former must remain fundamentally moral. This leaves no place for an ideological privileging of open-ended neutrality towards competing conceptions of the good: it also entails that education is the one social practice where the blind forces of the market are not the expression of liberal freedom, but its nemesis.

Before I outline briefly the arguments which will be deployed to support these claims, something must be said about the third 'contested concept' in the book's title. Throughout this inquiry, I shall use the term 'education' to refer to those institutionalised practices by which society enables the rising generation to construct the future. I am concerned with these practices in all those contexts in which we publicly sanction the intentional or foreseeable passing on of knowledge, skill, beliefs, values, attitudes and dispositions. I am also concerned with policies for directing these institutional arrangements and for providing access to them, precisely because such policies have a direct impact on the intrinsic as well as the exchange value of educational goods. I shall not make the currently fashionable distinction between 'education' and 'schooling' (which seems to have become *de rigeur* among theorists at the same time as the old distinction between 'education' and 'training' has been elided in policy and public debate), and this not for reasons of imprecision. I shall stick to the term 'education' deliberately for several reasons.

One is linguistic, though not merely so. Different languages (even among our nearest European neighbours) reflect different cultural and historical usages for the descriptive terms education/ training/ schooling/ upbringing/ socialisation/ enculturation etc. Within any given society these classifications are modified over time. The waters are further muddied by the honorific use of 'education' normatively to confer status on favoured practices. My subject is all of these activities, in whatever forms they are provided or sanctioned by the state. There are therefore substantive reasons for the general use in this text of the term 'education' to refer collectively to those social practices which we publicly sanction and support in order to enable people to develop in ways intended to be to their own and society's benefit (this duality to be examined later). Since none of these practices can be carried on institutionally in a manner which does not reflect our values, and all of them carry implications for future personal and social value development; since all of them are saturated with value, in intent, process and effect, so our social provision for them can be generally referred to in what follows as 'education'.

III

This book is concerned with claims to freedom. It focuses on those new freedoms the public is supposed to gain by the extension of market conditions beyond the economic sphere, most specifically to the world of education. It does not write these off simply as alien challenges to the practice of liberal education, but recognises that they represent crass extensions of cherished liberal dogmas about the sovereignty of the individual, the overriding value of personal autonomy, the separation of the public and private spheres, the proper response to value pluralism, and the permissible role of the state. It sees these changes as part of the phenomenon which MacIntyre has aptly described as "the privatisation of good".[14] It also acknowledges, more controversially, that many of those same dogmas—in more benign form—are implicated in the practice and theory of that liberal tradition of education which these new 'freedoms' threaten to erode. That tradition's goals of individual emancipation through a de-moralised rational autonomy, its silence on the relation of individual to social benefit, and its scrupulous even-handedness with regard to judgements of value can be seen as well-intentioned manifestations of that same privatisation of good. The attractions of "the privatisation of good", in both its benign and its virulent forms, lie in its promises of freedom: from state interference, from obstacles to self-advancement (intellectual or social), from the unacceptable imposition of values or constraining of personal choice.

The case advanced here is that these freedoms are illusory, when offered (as democratically they must be) as promises which can equally be made good to all. When they are appealed to in order to legitimate either the process or the distribution of education, then the realities of our personal and social worlds reveal them to deliver less than they promise. Those realities, in the key context of educational practice and policy, not only reveal that particular notions of liberal freedom cannot be cashed out in practice whilst "equally respecting the like liberty of all"[15]: they also indicate how these might be regenerated as part of an ethical reinterpretation of liberalism. When we acknowledge certain intractable difficulties with the theory and practice of a democratic liberal education, and see these compounded by recent neo-liberal policies for controlling and distributing that social good, disquiet grows with those neutralist interpretations of liberalism which have been in the ascendant for more than half a century. Their revision is needed to provide a sounder basis for the traditional emancipatory aims of liberal education in a democratic society which seeks to provide such an education for all.

The opening chapter, therefore, sets the scene by locating educational practice and policy in the current of evolving social and political change and sketches that recent array of educational 'reforms' which, by the introduction of quasi-market conditions and motivations, have brought a radical change over two decades in the way in which education is both constituted and distributed. These changes are then set in their relevant contexts: of educational process, of social policy climate, of economic circumstance, of political ethos, and of the current of social understanding. Taken together, these contexts show the frustration of differing interests interacting with circumstance to result in a legitimation crisis for the values, practices and policies of the post-war consensus and its social settlement. It would be a mistake, however, to see relevant education policies as simply one instance of socio-political changes which over that period have affected all public services. A closer look at the kind of good that education is—unlike, say, health care, housing or even the judicial system—shows us why that good presents itself as a key locus for privatising the public sphere. Interestingly, it also reveals why education represents a necessary limit to the reach of the market—a contention with far-reaching repercussions.

The next chapter describes the rationale for deregulatory social change put before the public by its advocates and relates this rationale to long-standing claims for the virtues and shortcomings of markets in general. A brief survey of classical arguments for the market in the economic sphere (which for early liberals had an explicit moral purpose), together with the logical and empirical contradictions (some of them foreseen even then) which are inseparable from market exchanges, alerts us to the fact that when these are extended beyond commodity exchange, then the benefits and disadvantages of the market vary with differing kinds of good. Given some of the more obvious problems with market exchanges beyond the economic sphere, an explanation for the political appeal of consumer rights and control in educational matters is required. That explanation cannot simply make reference to polemic for the virtues of the market as such, or to the plausibility of dubious supporting claims about the failure of public education to live up to expectations, for an analysis in these terms only prompts further puzzles.

So at this point the enquiry becomes archaeological. A third chapter excavates the development of public education to show how, in a democracy, directed social change reinforces the values which drive it until a clash between private and public aspiration forces revision. Trends in education policy over fifty years in the UK are seen as a playing-out of the long tug-of-war between the public's personal and societal expectations of education, underpinned by a long-running contest between the (apparently competing) claims of liberty and equality. Since it is these unresolved tensions which give the notion of a market in education its plausible appeal, they must be opened to scrutiny by an analysis of the logical complexity of educational value on both the private and the public dimensions. That analysis underlines the folly of ignoring classic caveats about social prerequisites to the virtuous functioning of free markets and the error of decreeing in neo-liberal fashion that all goods— individual or social, optional ephemera or constituents of identity—

are potentially tradeable for any other goods, in a common currency of exchange. Education is the paradigm case which shows that to be untenable.

This is soon clear when we look closely at certain deregulatory measures, such as additional independence from external controls for schools, or the granting of consumer rights to parents to select amongst schooling options. These have been sold as bringing increased freedoms to both 'consumers' and 'producers', though it is acknowledged (not always with regret) that they entail a retreat from earlier commitments to equality. On analysis, however, they are shown to bring about an overall reduction not only in equality but also in socially available freedoms. For individual producers and consumers, they at best allow increased immediate choice whilst curtailing negotiation on appropriate options for choice: and for society as a whole they foreclose on broader socio-political freedoms. The hidden hand of the market cannot operate in this arena to produce that progress in social welfare and individual flourishing which for the early liberals was the rationale for market exchange.

The case study thus set out then brings the analysis to the heart of many of the key tenets of liberalism, around which revolve current debates in social and political philosophy. Since it is the neo-liberal revival of a (de-moralised) classical liberalism which justifies the extra-economic extension of the market, underlying philosophical commitments must be scrutinised. Individualism, whether ontological (as the bedrock for our understanding) or methodological (as a heuristic tool for understanding consequent theory and its instantiation in practice) seems unfit to capture the interdependence and mutuality of personal agency in the actual conditions of contemporary society. Analysis of the construction placed, not only by neo-liberalism but (if less starkly) by the neutralist liberalism it challenges, on the key contending values of liberty and equality suggests that too negative a concept of liberty fuels conflict with too thick a conception of equality, advanced to mitigate neutralism's effects. Battles arising from those contending values have been particularly evident in the context of education, despite the fact that a focus on education should make clear that liberty and equality are each prerequisites of the other, since equal respect for the satisfaction of preferences requires equal opportunity for their formation. A reinterpreted liberalism requires a more robust conception of freedom, with a complementary conception of equality, if liberal ideals of equity are to be more firmly grounded.

To develop those conceptions is to challenge liberalism's metaphysical premises about the self and its formation, with that challenge having philosophical and empirical elements. A sixth chapter therefore focuses on the liberal view of the person, which exhibits an untenable dichotomy between the individual and society and cannot accommodate an adequate account of how persons become free agents. If we ask how the individual's attributes, talents and tastes evolve and their preferences develop, it seems clear that what is internal and what is external to the self is in dynamic interaction— and that not merely for the unformed young. If persons are seen as continuously recreating their environment at the same time as they are recreated by it, then the sharp divide between the public and private spheres, with the state's only role in the latter being to police its boundaries, looks less secure. Personal autonomy seen as the *exercise* of liberty begins to look like a hollow prize, without due attention to the prerequisites to its development and the range of options across which it can be exercised. The permissible role of the state in the provision, regulation and distribution of social goods looks rather different when these goods are seen, not as *means to* liberty, but as its important *constituents*. Moreover, the neutralist liberal assumption that the benefit of all will somehow result from each independently seeking his own good in his own way, comes under increasing strain when the limiting case is met in respect of a society's provision for forming its future. When our educational practices change in response to our beliefs about what the enterprise is for, and those changed practices in turn create changed parameters for personal and societal development, an atomistic notion of the individual seems unsustainable.

The final chapter will bring the upshot of these analyses to bear on the overall thesis of this monograph: that in regard to perennial tensions between individual freedom and social justice in a liberal society, education is a particularly fruitful field of application for the re-evaluation of social theory, just as it is the key site for the evolution of social value and circumstance. And education as a practice requires an ethical interpretation of liberalism for its direction, if it is to foster autonomy as a social value. For education is paradigmatic of those goods which are not convertible to other goods without destroying those values and principles which make truly free exchanges possible and provide their justification. To ignore this is to settle for illusory freedoms whose point and constituents are neglected, and whose apparent exercise is all.

NOTES AND REFERENCES

1. That sea-change was initially most marked in the U.K., the U.S., Australia, New Zealand and Canada. Its ethos, in part through the influence of international economic agencies, spread to many areas of the former eastern bloc and the developing world. West European democracies, to varying extents, have not been immune.
2. Gray, J., *Beyond the New Right* (London, Routledge, 1993).
3. Bellamy, R., *Liberalism and Modern Society* (London, Polity Press, 1992), p. 217.

4. Rorty, R., *Contingency, Irony and Solidarity* (Cambridge, Cambridge University Press, 1989).
5. See Raz, J., *The Morality of Freedom* (Oxford, Clarendon Press, 1986).
6. See Jonathan, R. (1995a), Liberal philosophy of education: a paradigm under strain, *Journal of Philosophy of Education* 29. 1, pp. 93–107.
7. Macedo, S., *Liberal Virtues: Citizenship, Virtue and Community in Liberal Constitutionalism* (Oxford, Clarendon Press, 1990), p. 278.
8. Rorty, R., *Objectivity, Relativism and Truth* (Cambridge, Cambridge University Press, 1991), p. 19.
9 Flathman, R., *Toward a Liberalism* (Ithaca, Cornell University Press, 1989), pp. 217–8.
10. Gray, J., *Liberalism* (Milton Keynes, Open University Press, 1986), p. 82.
11. Raz, J., *op. cit.*, p. 309.
12. *Ibid.*, p. 247.
13. *Ibid.*, p. 369.
14. MacIntyre, A. (1990), The privatisation of good: an Inaugural Lecture, *Review of Politics,* 52. 3, pp. 344–61.
15. Rawls J., *A Theory of Justice* (Cambridge Mass., Harvard University Press, 1971), *passim.*

Chapter 1
Re-ordering Society: Re-forming Education

Many liberal democracies with a long-standing commitment to social welfare through planned public policy have recently undergone a marked change of political climate. This change of ethos is represented by the state's ostensible retreat from regulation across a whole range of social as well as economic sectors. From banking and finance through labour relations to the judicial and penal systems, no sector has escaped far-reaching revision. Those public services such as health-care, housing and education which previously were believed to require close state regulation as well as state responsibility for adequate levels of commonly available provision have not been exempt. More than this, they have presented special targets for deregulatory fervour. Among these, it is education which has attracted the most attention from government, from the earliest days of visible cracks in the post war settlement.

Indeed, throughout two decades of social change, education policy has been at the forefront of the political agenda. In this respect the attention given to education by administrations concerned to 'roll back the state' has been superficially surprising and quite unique. Whereas in relation to deregulating banking and finance, to privatising utilities or to selling off public housing stock, the retreat of the state requires primarily that controls be removed or responsibilities handed over, with education we have seen not only more legislation and policy initiatives in this period of the shrinking state than in the previous forty years of welfarism: we have arguably seen more state interference in the actual conduct of education than in any previous period. This should not surprise us. To lament the golden days when 'politics was kept out of education', as many of the public—and educators themselves—are heard to do, is fundamentally to misunderstand the nature of education as a social practice and to misinterpret the earlier settlement in which local control and professional interests were largely left to guide its conduct. It is also to take at face value the claims of the deregulators.

The rise of what was dubbed 'the New Right' in the UK in the early 1980s, as of similarly motivated neo-liberal, anti-welfarist regimes (or indeed those simply in retreat from the demands of public provision) was presented to the public as an overdue reduction in the controlling powers of the state and its satellite bureaucracies. These were claimed to have grown over-powerful during the post-war period of welfarism and to have eroded the rights and initiative of individuals, resulting in a culture of dependency and escalating expectations from public provision. This process, it was claimed, had to be halted for economic reasons: and for neo-liberals, it furthermore needed to be reversed on grounds of principle. Its reversal was therefore presented not as an abdication of responsibility on the part of the centre but as a democratising measure which would place citizens once again in control of important areas of their own lives and give institutions across all sectors more autonomy to direct their own affairs.

Underlying this was a series of empirical assumptions about the ability of institutions and individuals to function more effectively when freed from external controls. Whether for car manufacturing plants or housing associations, more efficient running was seen to require removal of the hand of the state. More importantly, this political position was motivated by considerations of principle. It was not just that things would go better strategically if people were given more responsibility for their own affairs, but also that they *ought* to be given this responsibility and its accompanying freedom, as a matter of duty and of right. It was therefore not only that institutions and individuals should be free of state control in how they chose to achieve their ends, but that those ends themselves were none of the state's business provided they did not obviously infringe the rights of others. Judgements about ends were the private concern of individuals, to be expressed with minimum interference either by individual exchanges in the market place or by share-holding within private companies and representation on the boards of hospital trusts or the governing bodies of locally managed schools. The role of the state was to legislate to remove earlier welfarist controls and make this desirable state of affairs possible. What was presented, then, was a vision of a politics to reduce politics; of legislation to deregulate; of policies to institutionalise freedom from control; of government whose task was to reduce government: in sum, of a state in retreat from the previous scope of state power.

It should be readily apparent that this vision of turkeys campaigning for Christmas has another aspect. What is obscured by this picture portraying a political philosophy in which the state remains agnostic about ends, retaining only a policing role to provide a framework in which each can seek his/her own ends, is that this does not add up to an agnostic political position. This political philosophy, like any other, has a strong vision of what constitutes a good society, and its realisation requires enabling legislation. More than that, it is a vision of the good society which is markedly altered from that which informed the earlier consensus: thus in certain spheres of life, more substantive measures than enabling legislation are required. We would therefore expect the practice of education to come in for radical revision, since any society's education provision is not just a potential *object* for social reform by the government of the day, like any other social practice or public service. It is also a powerful *agent* of (or barrier to) social change which none who aspire to root-and-branch social change can afford to leave to its own devices.

EDUCATION AND POLITICS IN A CHANGING SOCIAL ORDER

Just as at the end of the second world war in the UK the 1944 Education Act[1] was conceived not only as an important element of the welfare state, but also as an instrument for expressing the new social order's values and achieving its goals, so from the early 1980s a tide of legislation has sought not simply to free up education from earlier controls, but to change its culture and in so doing to facilitate and foster a changed social ethos. Social theorists and policy analysts who too often conceptualise education as if it were just another (particularly costly) public service have seen the two themes in New Right thinking as mutually supporting in theory but contradictory in practice. Thus King, observing what he saw as two contradictory tendencies—the push to deregulation and the pull to revision—explained their conjunction by the fact that each is theoretically strengthened by combining with the other: "Liberalism is the source of New Right political and economic objectives; conservatism provides a set of residual claims to cover the consequences of pursuing liberal policies".[2] This is only half the story. What can be understood by a proper focus on education is that these themes are of course far from contradictory in practice. There is nothing surprising about a programme of legislation *for education* which is a superficially contradictory mixture of measures: designed on the one hand to deregulate its management and distribution and on the other to overhaul and carefully specify its constitution. The prime legislative example of prescription and deregulation working hand in hand has been the *Education Reform Act* (1988) for England and Wales through which, whilst 'rolling back the state', the Minister acquired 415 new powers.[3]

As Ranson noted shortly after its publication; ". . . the 1988 Act will seek to emulate as well as replace its revered predecessor. For the intention of both pieces of legislation was and is not only to recreate the form of education government but to do so as the significant part of a broader reconstituting of the social and political order".[4] This should surprise no-one, when from the time of Plato and the *Republic* it has been well understood that social and political culture is both reflected in *and produced by* educational practices. When these are seen as out of alignment with changed social sympathies and changed political goals, then the practice of education becomes a primary focus of interest for the government of the day. Nostalgic pleas for politics to be kept out of education are simply a mistake made after a long period of stable consensus during which it became easy to lose sight of the necessarily reciprocal relation between education and social change. It is true of course that the 'reforms' which have swept through education provision share with other public services and social practices a place in the general current of social values and political ideology. Uniquely among those practices, however, education is a powerful source of that current as well as a partial determinant of its further course.

We shall see that this particular status and function of education among a democratic society's social practices has especially interesting implications when ostensibly the shift in the *zeitgeist* is towards not just a change of course, but one which thereafter is intended to allow a lighter hand on the tiller of the ship of state, with the auto-pilot powered by the forces of the market. Although the inherently political nature of education is a necessary truth— deriving from its function in forming future value and circum- stance—we see this empirically confirmed *both* when political change is towards a reformed substantive vision of the good life for society[5] *and* when it is towards greater laissez-faire as a matter of ideological principle. For in these latter conditions equally, any changes in social life designed to be far-reaching must be underpinned by a new educational culture. Ostensibly, part of the avowed rationale for the particular attention paid to education by recent administrations in the UK and elsewhere has been their hostility to what they see as an unacceptable 'social engineering' function for education in a reformist welfare state. It should be clear that this special attention is not in practice (and impossibly) a retreat from education's role in the formation of the future, but rather renewed attention to it under a different guise.

Two factors made it easy for many members of the public (and many educators too) to lose sight of the inescapable fact that education is central to future development not only for individuals but for the structure and ethos of their social world. The first has already been noted: after a long period of consensus settlement, deliberate social change through education seems like an unaccep- table perverting of ideally apolitical processes.[6] The second is more interesting. It relates in part to the kind of social change intended by the earlier welfarist settlement. That settlement was primarily concerned with questions of distributive justice. Then, the pre- existing distribution both of intrinsic goods like health and education, and of instrumental goods such as income and educational credentials, was seen to be unequal in ways which reflected neither merit nor need and therefore was unjust. The primary purpose of educational changes then proposed was to remove barriers to participation for less advantaged members of society, enabling all to seek an appropriate position in the social structure, freed from the handicapping conditions of their current position. Changes in access to education, to facilitate movement within that social structure, were the primary focus of reform. There was no attempt at political control of educational content, partly because its relation to social structure and value was unacknowledged by the interpretation of liberalism then in the ascendant, and also because, in accordance with this 'end of ideology' perspective, root-and-branch, centrally-directed changes in structure and ethos were seen as not the business of government in a liberal democracy. Any structural change to the constitution of society was to result incrementally from the twin workings of social mobility and the enhanced prosperity and rational autonomy which more fairly distributed educational experiences and consequent life-chances would bring.

Later, this vision and the part it has played in creating some of the conditions and motivations for today's 'radical' revisionism will be looked at more closely. What is of interest here is that we have become accustomed, consistent with a neutralist interpretation of liberalism, to seeing education as an agnostic process by which individuals shape their own futures and in so doing incidentally modify the future of their societies. Indeed this has become a truism of much liberal philosophy of education, as of professional discourse and institutional statements of purpose. There have been dissenting voices, especially among some educational sociologists and Marxist and neo-Marxist philosophers of education, but those concentrated chiefly on how existing structure frustrates the accepted aim. Only recently, with the influences of critical theory and a revived political philosophy, do we see disquiet with an essentially agnostic conception of education as the emancipation of rationally autonomous individuals. How we came to develop this ideal and where its difficulties lie will be considered as this enquiry develops. At this point it is enough to note that the watershed which the social order has reached in many liberal democracies[7] has resulted in part from the practical contradictions entrained by modernity's (often successful) attempts to realise its pervading political philosophy. Some of those contradictions, it will be argued, can be fruitfully examined in the educational context, following the intuitions of a growing number of political philosophers who now suggest that "The dispute over liberal neutrality would be more fruitful if both sides moved away from general questions of 'individualism' towards more specific questions about the relationship between state, society, and culture in liberal democracies".[8]

FROM CONSENSUS TO CONTESTATION IN A NEUTRALIST FRAMEWORK

It is uncontentious to note that the neutralist interpretation of liberalism has become the dominant political theory of western liberal democracies. From its earliest beginnings, liberalism has held the freedom of the individual to be sacrosanct, provided only that the exercise of individual freedom does not infringe the freedom of others. The value of individual freedom is predicated on a notion of persons as creatures who stand at a more or less reflective distance from their contingent circumstance. From the transcendental subjects posited by Kant, through the self-interested (but morally motivated) agents of early anglophone liberalism, mutually interacting to produce social progress, we arrive at the modern conception of a self which is prior to its ends. "Freed from the dictates of nature and the sanction of social roles, the human subject is installed as sovereign, cast as the author of the only moral meanings there are".[9] We become, as Rawls succinctly puts it, ". . . self-originating sources of valid claims".[10]

This metaphysic underpins a politics, and the hallmark of contemporary neutralist interpretations of liberalism is that the state remain neutral between differing conceptions of the good, "not in the sense that there is an agreed public measure of intrinsic value or satisfaction with respect to which all these conceptions come out equal, *but in the sense that they are not evaluated at all from a social standpoint*"[11] (italics added). Whilst this pervading philosophy does not imply the relativism that is sometimes imputed to it, it does require that the state (and the social practice of education) not privilege particular conceptions of the good, whether for individuals or for society as a whole. Of course this kind of neutrality "is consistent with the legitimate non-neutral consequences of cultural competition and individual responsibility",[12] indeed in government (as we see with the rationale for post-war welfare reforms) and in liberal education (as we see with the elevation of rational autonomy as overarching aim) the implicit assumption is that good ways of life and worthwhile individual lives are most likely to evolve from the self-denying ordinances both of the state and of the cultural institutions of the social order.

Given allegiance to a liberalism which ". . . in its contemporary versions, typically presents itself as immune from most controversies to which political theories have traditionally been vulnerable, especially on questions of human nature and the meaning of the good life",[13] it is not surprising that the post-war settlement reflected broad agreement about the basic constitution of society, with dissatisfaction focused on unjustifiable inequalities within it and dissent reserved for the legitimate extent and proper means of their remediation. Where structure was the focus of critique, this again was principally in terms of its propensity to reproduce inequality. Claims that this settlement and its legitimating politics represented 'the end of ideology' have now recently shown themselves to be *hubris*. Political philosophy has become revitalised as changes to the social order, produced in part by the successes as well as the failures of the earlier settlement's aspirations, place the legitimate role and function of the liberal state at the centre of practical politics as at the centre of theoretical debate. And the primary social terrain on which the battle was first engaged, and over which it has continued for fifteen years now to be fought, is that of education.

I do not mean to suggest, of course, that the period from post-war to the late 1970s had been without educational controversy: none need reminding of the long-running disputes about equality of access, about 'more means worse', or about the relative merits of traditional versus progressive methods of teaching. But it must be emphasised that these took place against a general consensus on broad educational aims, and that these in turn reflected a considerable degree of consensus on aims for the social order. Both social justice and economic development were to be served by educational practices and policies which were thought appropriately judged by (supposedly apolitical) educational criteria, and by the equitable fostering of the human capital on which society's open-ended (but progressive) evolution was thought to depend. We might have expected therefore that when a watershed was reached some fifteen to twenty years ago, and the nature of the social order (and hence of the role of the state and of key cultural institutions) came up for radical contestation, the extent of the challenge would not be appreciated immediately. Thus for many commentators and theorists the obvious response to a barrage of 'educational reform' directed at established practice and policy by neo-liberals would be to ask two familiar kinds of question about the consequences of these measures: on the one hand for the quality of educational experience, and on the other for their effects, through education, on equity. That response seemed the more appropriate as those were precisely the dimensions along which their proponents—also creatures of their time, (presenting a new agenda, whether innocently or disingenuously, in terms of the old)—defended them. Hence also much indignant talk about who had stolen whose clothes.

These debates, though important in themselves, deflected attention from the far more significant role of a tide of policy initiatives and legislation designed not to make internal modifications to a continuing social settlement (either with the intent as forty years before of decreasing unmerited disadvantage or indeed, as some suspected when the new tide was gathering strength, simply as a malign device to restore those primary inequalities), but intended rather to produce a quite new social order. For this was no modifying of the rules so that the same social game might be more fairly played, nor even merely so that it might be played more cost-effectively: it was a new set of rules for playing a different game. The role of the state, and hence the rights and responsibilities of the individual, were to be thoroughly revised as part of a re-constitution of the social order. This was no less than a repudiation of the particular form of neutralist liberalism briefly sketched above, where the state takes responsibility for ensuring the fair distribution of those 'goods' without which autonomy is hollow, and where the rationale for both state control and its boundaries is not merely liberty itself but its equal distribution.

This vision had indeed been coming under strain, with neo-Aristotelians exercised by its tendency to fragment moral and cultural value, communitarians concerned with its threats to social solidarity and cohesion, and 'perfectionist' liberals fearing that neutralism risked damaging the very values and institutions whose health they see as essential to the liberal project. The successful *practical* challenge, however, came from quite another quarter. For the neo-liberal movement is animated by the belief that short-comings in the pre-existing social order arise rather from a political settlement which is *not neutral enough*. On this view, the state should retreat from its earlier responsibilities for ensuring as equitable a distribution as possible of freedom's prerequisites, since this involves interference with the free play of individual effort, merit and preference. It should occupy itself initially with dissolving existing constraints, to facilitate a social order in which individuals would be both enabled *and obliged* to take over responsibilities they had previously delegated to the state to perform on their behalf. So the rise of neo-liberalism and its political expression in several liberal democracies in the late seventies and early eighties (perhaps with most triumphalism in the United Kingdom) represented a sharp break with the recent past. Accompanying 'reforms' were indeed truly 'radical' as their proponents dubbed them—in the descriptive sense of that epithet which denotes root-and-branch change (though not of course in the normative sense, endorsed by previous consensus, of incremental improvements in equity). As such, the re-forming of education was a necessary cornerstone for the re-forming of the social order in accordance with neo-liberal beliefs and principles.

The significance of this point is considerable. It reminds us forcibly of the inherently political nature of education. It alerts social policy analysts to the need to differentiate between education and other public services when seeking to understand deregulatory change. It enables analysts of education policy to see radical reforms (scare quotes will be omitted from here onwards) not as the curious conjunction of two contradictory tendencies, the one to *laissez-faire* and the other to increased prescription, but as one single process of purposive social change through policy and legislation. Most of all, however, the same point has a further consequence which gives rise to a significant paradox for born-again classical liberals.

EDUCATION AND PREFERENCES: A PARADOX?

All those features of education which make it not merely a suitable *object* of reform for those who wish to change society, but also a powerful *agent* of reform, *create a constraining paradox for those whose vision of a changed social order is ultra-neutral neo-liberalism.* In practical politics it requires, as noted above, a much reduced role for the state, if not quite the 'minimal state' of Nozick's ideal.[14] This entails a correspondingly changed set of rights and responsibilities for the individual. These in turn require changed aspirations and values among the public to prepare them to exercise these rights and carry those responsibilities. At least in the medium term, therefore, radical change towards a reduced role for the state requires it to play a more prescriptive part in ensuring those values and aspirations on which in a democracy both its legitimacy and the realisation of its ultra-neutrality depend. This has not been lost on practical politicians: as Prime Minister, Thatcher announced on election ". . . our aim is to renew the spirit and solidarity [sic] of the nation",[15] and again "Economics is the method. The object is to change the soul".[16] Economics, of course, cannot be the only method. Indeed, classical liberals like Adam Smith[17] whose precepts are selectively invoked to justify the handing over of duties from the state to the market were well aware that the state must guard and foster those dispositions and abilities on which the market depends. Little wonder then that an education system which neo-liberals saw as representing and reinforcing those very values and expectations they wished to overturn should be seen to require *two* kinds of urgent attention from government.

Thus the New Right in the UK set out to overhaul both the governance and distribution of education, and also its content and process so that these were no longer out of alignment with its values and inhospitable to the social changes it sought. So far, so unremarkable, provided only we acknowledge the necessary relation between education and the social order which 'the end of ideology' had tempted us to overlook. There is a special problem for neo-liberals in assuring this alignment, however, which presents itself only to a political programme for the democratic shrinkage of the state. With any other vision, both the substance of education and the mechanisms for its governance and distribution can reflect the values and circumstances it endorses. Against the background of these values, content and process can either (as in 'closed' societies) drive the social train down pre-designed tracks, or (as in 'open' societies) enable citizens to modify both rolling stock and track as they ride or drive the train. Liberal education, as it has been conceived until quite recently, seeks to promote the latter of these outcomes (with mixed success, to be examined later). With the neo-liberal vision however, in which society consists in a market in goods of all kinds, there is a special difficulty to which neo-liberals seem oblivious. The social practice of education cannot provide adequate underpinning for the social arrangements these reformers seek to promote if *both its substance and the mechanisms for its governance and distribution* are to reflect their ideological commitment to a free market in goods of all kinds.

The argument in outline, to be developed more fully later, goes as follows. Education is one of society's primary sites for the formation of preferences (and the only institutionalised one for a captive audience of the not-yet-fully-autonomous young). The rationale for curriculum prescription and increasing influence on process by government can only be that those exerting this control have both the duty and the capacity to make a substantive input to preference formation. The rationale for deregulation in the management and distribution of education can correspondingly only be that in respect of the exercising of preferences once these have been formed, it is not government but private citizens as consumers who have both the capacity and the right to make choices, resulting in whatever outcomes their aggregate choices produce. There would be no clash between these positions if the processes both of forming preferences and of exercising them were functionally separate, as indeed they are in respect of many social goods. For example, I exercise my preferences in respect, say, of health-care by choice of medical practitioner, institution, or given procedure: although my values and understandings with respect to health might incidentally be modified by the consultation or the intervention I select, the develop-ment of those values and understandings is not a primary purpose of medical attention.

Once again, however, education is the limiting case among social practices. There, changes in how this good is distributed produce fundamental changes both in its constitution and in our conception of it. As the exercise of consumer preference places a premium on process and content which seem to have obvious use and immediate relevance to the needs of the moment, so education's instrumental benefits become prioritised.[18] Scant attention is given to that change, despite the fact that, even among strong advocates of the market, it is understood that "The market . . . is not a self-sustaining order, but presupposes a network of intermediary institutions animated by a culture of liberty".[19] That such institutions as property, contract, a financial system and so on are required is uncontroversial. The existence of schooling and training are equally basic in a developed society: moreover, a tradition of learning and enquiry beyond what present contingencies seem to demand is clearly necessary to sustain even a market-driven society which aspires to continued development. Gray goes on to note that "The political legitimacy of the free market depends on these institutions being in good repair and, where necessary, on their being tended and nurtured by government".[20] (That is only, of course, to acknowledge that government should ensure the existence of necessary institutions, not their regulation.) Notwithstanding some recent writings which advocate the wholesale privatisation of education[21] (flying in the face not only of actual social constraints but also of the very neo-liberal principles they claim to represent) this could not be otherwise. As has been argued here, the political legitimacy—and the functioning—of any social order in a democracy requires the broad and approximate alignment of its educational practices. Since the outcomes of the hidden hand are, as an article of faith, quite open for neo-liberals (unlike their classical forbears[22]), education above all requires to be "tended and nurtured" by the state. And there, precisely, lies for them the rub. In respect of education, the overall neo-liberal project to re-form society cannot be reliably assured if this particular good is to be governed (and hence constituted) by the market *and if* choices in the market are truly free, giving rise to whatever outcomes arise, whether or not these maintain in good order those cultural institutions on which the market itself depends. Conversely, if choices are not truly free, deregulated governance of education loses its justification, and the project loses its rationale even on its own terms.

If this line of reasoning can be sustained when elaborated, it would provide a transcendental argument against the extension of the principles of free-market exchange into the governance and distribution of education, over and above any arguments against that in terms of damaging consequences for learning and for equity. Furthermore, if neo-liberal principles can be shown incompatible with the governance of that social practice without whose alignment no vision for the ordering of society can be realised, then the vision itself is called into question, not only on grounds of equity—which are debated without resolution when competing conceptions of justice are a stake—but on grounds of coherence. If this can be defended, it would have consequences going beyond a root-and-branch rebuttal of a neo-liberal approach to educational theory and practice. Since that approach exacerbates the perceived defects and damaging side-effects of the educational arrangements it finds wanting rather than resolving them, and since those challenged arrangements had a neutralist liberal justification, then remedy for the problems seen in that earlier rationale will have to be sought elsewhere than in an ultra-concentrated dose of the same medicine.

THE RE-FORMING OF EDUCATION

To take Britain (or more specifically England and Wales[23]) as a prime case study for the introduction of a free market philosophy into educational policy is instructive, since nowhere has this approach to re-forming the social order been applied with such triumphalism. Throughout four consecutive Conservative administrations, education there has had a much raised political and media profile which is now so taken for granted that it promises to survive any opposition election victory. A series of Education Acts (1979, 1980, 1981, 1984, 1986 (2), 1987, 1988 (2), 1989, 1993, 1994, 1995, 1996 (4)) have enshrined in legislation a comprehensive swathe of measures prefigured in a bewildering succession of policy proposals and White Papers, and together these add up to a wholesale re-forming of the practice of education at all levels.

No area with significance for the content, process, distribution, governance or funding of education has escaped attention. The relations between parents, schools, local education authorities and central government have been thoroughly redrawn as a result of school de-zoning and 'parental choice'; of encouragement for schools to 'opt out' of the control of (often left-wing) local government authorities to become directly funded from the centre; of the removal of further education from local authority control, giving institutions 'autonomy' under stringent central constraints; and finally through the capping of local government budgets and through political reorganisation to disband concentrations of local power over educational matters, as with the abolition of the Inner London Education Authority or, in an awkwardly reluctant Scotland, the dismembering of what the tabloid press referred to as the "people's republic" of Strathclyde. These loosened or redrawn relations evolve now in a different culture, brought about by changes to the role, constitution and membership of schools' governing bodies, and by wholesale changes to the systems of both local authority and schools' financial management.

Meanwhile, the entire curriculum and assessment system for compulsory schooling has been revised, with the introduction of a prescriptive National Curriculum and national benchmarks for achievement at the ages of seven, eleven and fourteen years as well as through revised public examinations at sixteen-plus. The mandatory publication of examination and test results provides information to parents and other interested parties as consumers, giving the information on 'product quality' which is needed to motivate market choice. 'Product diversity', another key feature of lively markets, has not been neglected either, with the establishment of grant-maintained (i.e. 'opted-out') schools, City Technology Colleges, 'assisted places' at independent schools, proposed 'magnet schools', and new powers for any school to select a (growing) proportion of its intake. These innovations combine to break down the comprehensive state secondary schools' previous near-monopoly on all but private provision, and put pressure on them to court their 'customers' (in content and process as well as presentation) or face decline.

'Curriculum delivery', as the business of teaching is now called, also attracts thorough scrutiny which in one sense can be called deregulated but in another is carefully managed. The former H. M. Inspectorate of schools, a career body recruited from the teaching profession with a policy advice role for government as well as an advisory and regulatory function for schools, has been disbanded in England and Wales, to be replaced by Ofsted (a name which seems to echo Ofgas, Oftel and Ofwat, the watchdog bodies with oversight of 'fair trading standards' in the former public utilities). Ofsted, referred to routinely as "the new independent inspectorate", can recruit from outside the profession, has required representation for employer-interests, evaluates performance against government standards, and has powers to recommend closure of schools or their removal from local control. Finally, the training of teachers, both pre- and in-service, is no longer a matter of a compact between professional bodies and the colleges and universities which provide it, but is now heavily influenced by government, with centrally directed control of curriculum change backed by centrally supported targeted funding.

And that welter of change relates only to compulsory schooling, which, together with vocational preparation, was the first urgent concern of New Right administrations. With the exception of the Technical and Vocational Education Initiative, and possibly of the launching of National Vocational Qualifications alongside reformed public examinations, vocational initiatives (such as the short-lived Youth Opportunities Programme and its replacement the Youth Training Scheme) are often seen more as emergency responses to labour market problems than as part of the 'marketising' of education. However, many government-inspired changes (such as pre-specified teaching outcomes, transferable skills, item-banking for teaching and assessment, and elements of remedial 'social education') were easier to introduce into these schemes than into the traditional preserves of the teaching establishment. Position papers prepared in the early 1980s by the then-powerful Manpower Services Commission for the government of the day gave assurances that these initiatives, once piloted, could then be introduced into the formal schooling system, and this has indeed taken place—with significant impact on the practices of liberal education and on the professional autonomy and standing of teachers.[24]

With wholesale change assured in the schooling system, the tertiary sector was also ripe for reform. In Britain the universities had enjoyed considerable autonomy over many decades, supported by a block grant from central funding and the mandatory provision of grants to students who gained entry on the basis of public examinations overseen by consortia of universities.[25] Much has changed. Though institutions are still formally autonomous, fifteen years of 'efficiency gains' in the higher education sector have reduced staffing and increased student numbers to the point where strategic planning for anything other than retrenchment is in jeopardy; 'teaching quality assessment' and 'total quality management' measure the measurable according to the dictates of the day; the assessment of research (with important core-funding consequences) encourages the tactical planning of research and publication; external consultancies are often perforce sought for benefits which are primarily financial; and the earlier ideal of the university as a community of scholars becomes hard to sustain when half of the staff are on short and insecure contracts and most of the students (even when registered as full-time) carry outside employment obligations to part-finance their study.

Universities still control curriculum and student entry, but the latter is a formal autonomy for all but those with highest prestige, with consequent threat to the former. In an effort to speed change in a sector seen as hidebound by tradition, legislation was enacted in the early 1990s which flooded the market with new universities: the former polytechnics and colleges, now liberated from local financial control and external academic regulation. This again was presented as a liberalising and anti-elitist measure, but the new-found autonomy of these institutions carries heavy penalties in many cases. Often unable—as a result of their different histories and past staffing criteria—to secure, in competition with longer-established universities, resources from the assessment of research proportionate to those diverted from the former 'block grant' to that stream of (now targeted) funds, they have little option but to cover their operating costs by adapting to the aspirant students available. Effectively, this hands over decisions regarding appropriate types of preparation and standards of entry to the ultimate source of the funds; and the current characteristics of the student entry drive institutional decisions on 'marketable' courses and the level and mode of their 'delivery'. Nor is this decrease in institutional clout confined to the newly-liberated elements of the sector. The very rapid increase in 'products' in the higher education market, as in any other, creates conditions of producer insecurity which reduce producer bargaining power in negotiation with the 'end-user'—the government of the day. Institutional autonomy is doubly constrained since any realignment or shrinkage in the market becomes a function of consumer choice. In this sector particularly, when many 'consumers' borrow to fund study, consumer choice inevitably reflects second-guessing of labour market opportunities rather than longer-term personal or academic considerations. These losses of institutional autonomy are presented as social gains, in which the feather-bedded denizens of the ivory tower are belatedly forced by the public to respond to the 'needs of society'. Little need be said here about the self-defeating short-termism of this mode of governance in a sector with dual functions: for higher education is charged with the production and development of knowledge and understanding as well as with its (conceptually inseparable) dissemination and critique.[26]

Just one sector remained immune throughout this whirlwind of change: that of pre-school education for the under-fives, provided unevenly by local authorities and the private sector. Then, in 1995, consultation took place on a centrally funded voucher scheme for pre-school education. This scheme was comprehensively opposed by both providers and consumers on educational and equity grounds, and rejected by professional bodies who saw it as a Trojan horse for the wider extension of vouchers. Nonetheless, voucher schemes are being 'piloted' in that sector as this account is written, with plans for their extension before pilots are completed.

Though schematic and far from comprehensive, that overview should suffice to indicate the range and extent of changes instituted in how education is provided, conducted and controlled in one society which for the time being has taken the neo-liberal path. I shall neither describe nor analyse in detail specific policy initiatives or legislative measures except where these illuminate issues of principle which arise from market distribution (thus the consumer rights of individual parents will be the focus of chapter four). There is already a considerable literature devoted to deregulatory or privatising measures in social policy in general,[27] and a great deal of writing on specific measures and policies which combine to both deregulate and reconstitute education. My purpose in this opening chapter is simply to report the extent and type of change in education policy which has accompanied (and underpinned) an intended re-ordering of society: subsequently, I shall examine how public endorsement for it was sought—and why, perhaps, it was given. Taken together, these measures represent the radical and deliberate re-forming of that social practice which is central to any project for the reconstitution of the social order. Prime Minister Major acknowledged the comprehensiveness and the broader purpose of this programme in a 1991 speech: "Disraeli declared that the fate of the country depended on education, and almost every subsequent Prime Minister has echoed that sentiment . . . Balfour's Education Act came in 1902, and Butler's Act in 1944. Now we are embarked on an even more radical series of reforms, which began in the 1980s and are continuing into the 1990s".[28] Indeed, the changes to which he referred had broader political aims than their forerunners, as we see both from the rationale offered to the public (not to mention internal position papers from government and quasi-government agencies as well as relevant 'think-tanks'), and from their actual and foreseeable effects.

CONCLUSION

We see then that in focusing on the contradiction and inconsistency of the Education Reform Act, or indeed of the whole tenor of educational reform since the ascendance of the New Right in Britain, many commentators have overlooked its full significance. By attending to the surface of disparate legislation, they have missed its ideological coherence and reciprocity in practice which together make of these particular educational reforms an unusually hegemonic project. Macro-provision and curriculum change, centrally imposed, structure the options among which consumers can choose, and the introduction of market mechanisms allows consumers to make 'rational' choices amongst these options. Such choices do not, as we shall later see, reflect the context-independent preferences of asocial individuals, for such individuals do not exist. They necessarily constitute a response to perceived social realities which include both the altered cultural ethos reflected in changed public provision and also the intensified climate of social competition which in turn is driven on synergistically by the market mechanisms themselves.

That being so, the introduction of market forces into the evolution of the state education system cannot be seen as a neutral procedure of 'rolling back the state' in order simply to devolve power to the people, with government seeking only to maximise individual freedom. For by delegating to individuals decisions which, in aggregate, have substantial social, cultural and political effects, legislators are not lessening the extent to which they direct policy, but radically changing its direction: and the power of the state is not shrinking, but is rather being directed towards substantive change in the social order. Indeed, freedoms to make rational individual choices, when centralised policy prestructures the options, and social realities (and position) largely determine which choices are rational, are not like freedoms to devise a game of one's own choosing, or one which reflects the goals, priorities and values of autonomous persons. They are much more like freedoms to compete in a prestructured game whose parameters correspond to the newly dominant ideology, but whose finer details (and outcomes) are to be blindly produced by 'the forces of the market' as players make rational, self-interested, non co-operative decisions. Though these outcomes may be produced blindly by individuals, they are far from unpredictable. Some of their aspects are foreseeable when existing social circumstance is taken with due seriousness: others can be understood in the light of warranted scepticism about key elements of the neutralist interpretation of liberalism.

More than a century has passed since T. H. Green insisted in response to a nineteenth-century Home Secretary's distaste for "grandmotherly government"[29] that: "Our modern legislation then with reference to labour, and education, and health, involving as it does manifold interference with freedom of contract, is justified on the ground that it is the business of the state . . . to maintain the conditions without which a free exercise of the human faculties is impossible".[30] In this chapter I have claimed, and will hereafter elaborate, that public education is the most crucial of these conditions (once physical needs are acceptably assured) and that its proper maintenance implies that the hidden hand of the market is no substitute for public deliberation and co-operative, democratic control. To make this case is necessary, most obviously in order to ensure the appropriate development of that social practice which both reflects social value and circumstance and creates them anew. It is also urgent, since the response of deregulators to the paradoxes their policies have entrained is not to be deterred but to advocate a further and faster retreat of the state. Gray is not untypical in urging that now "Reviving the project of limited government involves adopting policies which effect a massive withdrawal of the state from many areas of social life and which subject its remaining interventions to radical amendment".[31]

It is the more important to make the counter case as the paradoxes to be seen in attempts to serve liberty by establishing a free market in its constituents are instructive far beyond social and educational considerations. Sandel, disturbed by the modern gulf between social and political life and our theorising about them, notes of the contemporary neutralist interpretation of liberalism that ". . . despite its philosophical failure, this liberal vision is the one by which we live".[32] He goes on to urge that we re-examine theory, the better to understand manifest problems of practice: as this vision is "the theory most embodied in the practices and institutions most central to our public life . . . seeing how it goes wrong as philosophy may help us diagnose our present political condition".[33] Conversely, I believe, seeing how it goes wrong in practice may help us diagnose some of its philosophical shortcomings. Since there is no more appropriate place to enquire into its social manifestation than in the practice of public education, it is to that examination that we now turn.

NOTES AND REFERENCES

1. 1944 Education Act, England and Wales; 1945 Education Act, Scotland, HMSO.
2. King, D. S., *Politics, Markets and Citizenship* (Macmillan, London, 1987).
3. *The Education Reform Act (1988)*, HMSO. This was followed by the *Self-Governing Schools etc. Scotland Bill (1989)*, HMSO, which has less extensive powers due to the distinctive system of Scottish education.
4. Ranson, S., From 1944 to 1988: Education, citizenship and democracy, in: Flude, M. and Hammer, M. (Eds.), *The Education Reform Act 1988, its Origins and Implications* (Falmer Press, Basingstoke, 1990).
5. As today in South Africa with its *National Commission on Education*, or in 1989 in Hungary with the *New Education Act*.
6. Mistaken claims that politics should be kept out of education are particularly tempting in adversarial democracies where 'the political' and 'the party-political' become conflated.
7. That term is used throughout this analysis to refer broadly to those democracies whose political culture is underpinned by liberal ideals of the equal freedom of citizens. Terminological confusion can be caused by the fact that sociological subdivision of such democracies into three basic types of regime, corporate-statist, social democratic and liberal (of which Germany, Sweden and the U. S. respectively would be ideal types) allocates the epithet 'liberal' in a narrower sense to only one of the three types. However, although this typology usefully represents different clusterings of political and social characteristics, each of the three types are overlapping clusters of features of the same phenomenon: it is that phenomenon I am referring to as 'liberal democracy'.
8. Kymlicka, W. (1989), Liberal individualism and liberal neutrality, *Ethics* 99, p. 883.
9. Sandel, M. (1984), The procedural republic and the unencumbered self, *Political Theory*, 12, p. 88.
10. Rawls, J. (1980), Kantian constructivism in moral theory; the Dewey Lectures 1980, *Journal of Philosophy*, p. 543.
11. Rawls, J., Social unity and primary goods, in: Sen, A. and Williams, B. (eds.), *Utilitarianism and Beyond* (Cambridge University Press, Cambridge, 1982), p. 172; cf. Rawls, J., *A Theory of Justice* (Oxford, Oxford University Press, 1971), p. 94.
12. Kymlicka, W., Liberal individualism and neutrality, reprinted in: Avineri, S. and de-Shalit, A. (eds.), *Communitarianism and Individualism* (Oxford University Press, Oxford, 1992), p. 169.
13. Sandel, M., *Liberalism and the Limits of Justice* (Cambridge, Cambridge University Press, 1982), p. 10.
14. Nozick, R., *Anarchy, State and Utopia* (New York, Basic Books Inc., 1974).
15. Thatcher, M., 1979, speech to Conservative Party summer school.
16. Thatcher, M., speech quoted in *Sunday Times*, London, 7 May 1988.
17. Smith, A., *The Wealth of Nations*, also *The Theory of Moral Sentiments* (annotated edition, Callan E., London, 1904).

18. See Jonathan, R. (1990), The curriculum and the new vocationalism, *Journal of Curriculum Studies*, 22. 2, pp. 184–188.
19. Gray, J. (1993), *op. cit.*, p. 60.
20. *Ibid.*
21. e.g. Tooley, J., *Education Without the State* (Institute of Economic Affairs, London, 1995).
22. For the loss of classical liberalism's 'social thesis' see Bellamy, R., *op. cit.*, 1992.
23. The separate education system in Scotland has to some extent acted there as a buffer against many measures and as a dilutant to some legislation.
24. See Jonathan, R., The Youth Training Scheme: an educational initiative? in: Holt, M. (Ed.), *Skills and Vocationalism* (Milton Keynes, Open University Press, 1986).
25. This latter arrangement in Scotland was more in the hands of the teaching profession, which has had greater status and autonomy there, expressed in part through the General Teaching Council for Scotland.
26. See Jonathan, R., Education and the 'needs of society', in: Hartnett, A. and Naish, M. (eds.), *Education and Society Today* (London, Falmer Press, 1986).
27. See, for example, Dowding, K. H., *Rational Choice and Political Power* (Sussex, Edward Elgar, 1991); King (1987) *op. cit.*; Plant, R., *Equality, Markets and the New Right* (London, Fabian Tract 494, 1984); Self, P., *Government by the Market* (London, Macmillan, 1993), etc.
28. Prime Minister Major, speech to the Centre for Policy Studies, Cafe Royal, London, 3 July 1991.
29. Sir William Vernon-Harcourt.
30. Green, T. H., *Liberal Legislation and Freedom of Contract*, in: *Works of T. H. Green* (London, Longmans, 1888), pp. 370–377.
31. Gray, J. (1993), *op. cit.*
32. Sandel, M. (1984), *op. cit.*, p. 81.
33. *Ibid.*

Chapter 2
Reform: Rhetoric, Rationale and Representation

The hallmark of the educational reforms sketched in the last chapter is the combination of increased state intervention in the content and range of provision, together with increased deregulation in governance and access to stimulate market activity. The avowed rationale for deregulation is that the competitive ethos created by market conditions will shake up a service hidebound by tradition, wrest control from the vested interests of professionals and bureaucrats, and promote more rapid response to the needs of society, understood primarily as an economic entity requiring particular skills and dispositions. The first part of this chapter will set out that rationale, by reporting, elaborating and assessing the claims of government policy-makers. A second section will step back and review the general merits claimed for a market distribution of goods, together with long-standing caveats concerning conditions of 'market failure'. Given these well-known caveats, and having seen on what basis neo-liberal reform of education was sold to the public, the burning question then becomes one of understanding the popular appeal of a two-pronged reconstitution of public education which deregulated access at the same time as it prescriptively revised content and process.

Though ideologically central, the claimed virtues of the market as such were not, at least at the start of the reform period, the most dominant among the arguments advanced for change. Indeed, on its own, the neo-liberal rationale might have been insufficiently persuasive to justify a shift away from that systematic local control and provision, intended for social as well as individual benefit, which had prevailed throughout the decades of post-war consensus. It is therefore not surprising that ideological polemic has been buttressed throughout the reform period by claims about the prior state of education and its role in economic and moral decline, and predictions about the salutary effects of proposed change. The plausibility of these claims will require closer examination in this analysis, since it is an uncomfortable reality that the re-forming of education as a key element of the re-constitution of the social order was not something imposed by a totalitarian regime on a thoroughly resistant polity. Rather, it was endorsed, democratically, by a substantial proportion of the public as a response, in part, to their personal dissatisfactions with the social and educational outcomes of the previous social settlement.

By raising in the final section queries about the plausibility of scapegoating education for social decline and individual frustration (and pursuing these queries further in the chapter which follows), my intention will not be to adjudicate the charges and counter-charges levelled at each other by educational and political lobbies with respect to educational practice prior to recent reforms. Since questions of whether education is adequately 'delivering the goods' are (despite populist debate) only to a limited extent empirical—unless the 'goods' at issue are rudimentary or purely instrumental skills and attributes— my purpose here will rather be to understand why, in the case of education, a neo-liberal appeal to individual interests finds the fertile ground that it lacks when the public considers the distribution and planning of, say, health care. And the point of that enquiry is not to indulge in speculation about the dynamics of democratic political change. Rather, it is to flag on the one hand the uniquely complex nature of educational value—the kind of 'good' that education is— and to raise questions on the other about the logical coherence of the social project of liberal education for all: questions which later in this analysis will serve to highlight pervasive problems in neutralist liberalism. First, though, we must set in their social and political context the changes in educational policy and practice which chapter one merely reported. This chapter, therefore, looks first at the rationale offered retrospectively to the public for a market-inspired reconstruction of public education; then sets this in the context of arguments for the value of markets and their extension; then notes how change was sold at the outset, asking what it is about education which makes the appeal of the free market seem strongest precisely where it is least appropriate.

PRIVATISING THE PUBLIC SPHERE: RATIONALE AND RHETORIC[1]

Depending on one's theoretical perspective, there are several ways in which one could analyse the recent large-scale changes in educational policy in the UK and elsewhere. From the neo-liberal perspective, a new ethos of competition and accountability shakes up a fossilised system which fails to reward effort and depresses standards to the detriment of all. From a Marxist perspective, in contrast, one might see reforms as symptoms of a triumphalist late capitalism, turning the screw in the reproduction process, to produce a more rigid stratification of role and a deskilling of some members of the workforce combined with a reskilling of others, to serve a high-technology, low-wage economy and an enterprise culture of unequal opportunity. From a continental, critical theory perspective, one might see them as symptoms of the progressive colonisation of the life world by the system (or a significant shift within the purposive sub-system), with a key social activity which was once traditional and taken on trust being opened up to technical and managerial examination and organisation, partly as a result of a legitimation crisis in schooling and partly due to a breakdown in the wider social consensus. From an anglophone critical liberal perspective (which I shall develop as my argument proceeds), one might see them as the latest social symptoms of a mistaken emphasis on the atomistic, asocial individual combined with an inadequate, rationalistic conception of understanding, and of a public backlash against an over-optimistic belief in the capacity of liberal education to emancipate individuals across society independently of social structure.

At this stage in the analysis, however, an open perspective may be the most useful, allowing the proponents of recent reform to speak for themselves, and connecting their rationale and rhetoric to actual policy change. It is easy to do this, since—most unusually for a governing party in a liberal democracy—the recent third successive Conservative administration in the UK embarked on an extensive, formal propaganda exercise, distributing to all households (at public expense) a series of glossy publications which celebrated the "policy achievements" of the previous decade, flagged changes still to come, and elucidated the rationale and claimed public benefits of radical change in social practice and ethos. Those publications consisted in a series of "charters", of which the covering document was *The Citizen's Charter*[2] published after a decade of right-wing populist government to celebrate the recently-established concept of the citizen as consumer of private and public goods in a market-oriented enterprise society. That document made explicit the changed ethos for the provision of all public services, setting out specific rights for consumers and placing specific demands on professionals. Separate charters for health, housing, the social security system, the judicial system and for schooling detailed how that new vision of social relations was being realised in each public service.[3]

That overt ideological declaration highlighted the fact that it had been the education system which, over the previous decade, had provided the test bed for the new market-model social ethos. For although formally *The Citizen's Charter* was the flagship document, in fact it was *The Parent's Charter*[4] (focusing principally on schooling) which contained the core elements of the rationale, just as the education system was where its practical working-out was furthest advanced. Indeed, it seems highly likely that the whole charter exercise, announced then in parliament by the Prime Minister as the government's ". . . big idea for the 1990s", was inspired by public and media response to *educational* change, since for a decade the deregulation of schooling access had been informally dubbed—by enthusiasts and critics alike—a "parents' charter".[5] With hindsight, what some had noted a decade earlier became clear for all to see during the subsequent propaganda exercise: the educational 'reforms' which had then begun had had less to do with improving the public education system in terms of overall quality than with establishing a revised concept of personal emancipation and empowerment which brought the ethics and problems of the market-place into all areas of social life and ostensibly placed all social outcomes, and most notably those arising from education (on which so many others are predicated), in the individual's own hands.

The overall promise of the charters was that those deregulatory strategies, recently adopted by many societies which had previously seen education as a social project, furnish "the best spur to quality improvement" in this and other 'public services', by offering "choice wherever possible between competing providers" in order to give consumers "value for money within the tax bill the nation can afford".[6] The recurring themes of all these documents, as of the social policy changes they celebrate and entrench, are threefold: firstly, that all 'goods', whether they be private or social in nature, are most effectively distributed by the mechanism which works best for consumer-goods—a free market in which consumers reward preferred providers with their patronage; secondly, that giving individuals choice rights to public or social goods like education will not only improve quality, but will distribute the goods in question more equitably, since individuals thus become responsible for their own fate; and thirdly, that extending these consumer rights to the users of public services is a democratising measure, which encourages active participatory citizenship and lessens the power of faceless bureaucrats and professional vested-interests. There is much to be said about these central themes in relation to a decade of educational change, but what should be noted here is that they affect all public services, and most significantly the education system, in two ways. They bring about change directly, by altering the mechanism by which the good in question is distributed, and they entrain more far-reaching change indirectly, by altering the public's perceptions and expectations of that good.

Each separate apologia—and the one for schooling is typical—celebrates changes achieved, and announces those still to come. The *Parent's Charter* accordingly justifies education policy change in terms of the values of individual rights and consumer choice, and of professional accountability and competition, and then flags, on the same grounds, specific future commitments like performance-related pay. It is repeatedly claimed that through the measures enacted, the 'users of public services' (that is citizens, in a 'consumer democracy') are newly-empowered by greater information, wider choice, and redress where they find a service unsatisfactory. For example, when schools must publicise their examination results and rates of truancy, they can be ranked into league tables so that parents are enabled to choose "the best school" for a child, with redress taking the form of a "right of exit" from options which fail to meet expectations. The supporting rationale is that when resources follow consumers this applies both carrot and stick to providers and at last holds the public sector properly to account. Quality is to be improved by two processes: by unpopular schools gradually shrinking and shedding their under-performing staff, and by the forces of the market encouraging those types of provision which are in line with consumer demand. Where there are problems with schooling (as with any public service), these are ascribed to the failure of relevant professionals: policy-makers are absolved at a stroke from the consequences of reduced levels of resourcing and changed mechanisms for distribution. That absolution of policy-makers from responsibility for the results of policy, together with the implicit denial that social structure powerfully shapes individual opportunity, serves in turn (as chapter four will show) to legitimate a market model of social provision and to promote a consistent set of political values.

In chapter one I briefly indicated radical changes throughout the education system which on the one hand introduced the kind of diversity of 'product' which is needed for a market to operate and on the other altered arrangements for access to provision in a manner designed to stimulate market activity on the part of 'consumers' and market-led response on the part of 'providers'. This is not the place to describe how, having been piloted in education, the same types of change were subsequently introduced into, say, the health service, with public hospitals, like schools, invited to opt out of local control and become self-governing trusts; doctors, like teachers, invited to control their own budgets (though not to set them); and consumers of health-care, like those of education, given the right to compete with each other across a range of service providers for the best option they might secure for themselves. What must be stressed, however, is that it was the education system which provided the beach-head for this radical shift in social practice and ethos. It is also important to emphasise that measures adopted to bring about that shift are *cumulative in their effects*. The education context demonstrates particularly clearly that a process which may at first be slow to get under way soon picks up speed as its introduction alters the climate in which both 'consumers' and 'providers' deliberate and act. For example, though parents were initially slow to exercise choice, the process develops its own momentum, and as league tables of school performance in terms of crude measures like test scores and truancy rates are given prominence in the media, and as the 'good' schools get 'better' and the 'bad' schools get 'worse' with the outflow and inflow of pupils and resources, so more and more parents become prompted to take up their choice rights. For in this competitive situation there is no neutral option: to stand still when others move is to suffer a relative change of position and to become relatively disadvantaged.

The direct effects on the school system of putting into practice the consumer rights-based rationale of the Charters need scarcely be elaborated. Formally, schools and teachers are made accountable to their users by providing information about the standards of service they give, so that consumers can seek redress by taking their custom elsewhere. These output measures, which ignore structural factors (from the socio-economic background of learners to the characteristics of nearby alternative provision), lend impetus to the real accountability stick. This lies in the operation of consumer choice rights, which in schools with an unfavourable social-economic base serve only to demoralise teachers and penalise pupils. In a market, moreover, teachers in the 'worse' schools work under the additional adverse conditions of a shrinking resource base caused by parental flight to more favoured options. Of course, all consumers have the right of exit, but they cannot all exercise it, or the logical outcome would see schools at the top of the league growing indefinitely, and the others empty. It is claimed that those others, threatened with falling resources, will be forced to improve by competition, and where poor performance is the fault of teachers that might occur. But where problems stem from the alienation and marginalisation of relevant consumers, then teachers with career aspirations come under pressure to seek better options themselves, thereby exacerbating disparities still further.

Whilst it is arguable that during thirty years post-war of political consensus about the general conduct of education, professional vested-interests and local bureaucracies may have developed a culture which was insufficiently open to democratic accountability,[7] it seems clear that the use of market forces to constrain professional power brings with it serious side-effects. Most notably, it threatens to commodify the transmission of knowledge, culture and value (as if these were private goods or had mainly instrumental purpose) as well as to stultify a long trend towards a more equitable distribution of social advantage. Few would dispute that professionals must be accountable where they are responsible, but they cannot be held responsible for what lies outside their control, precisely because they cannot remedy it. To gloss over this is to deflect responsibility from the level of decision-making where control truly lies, and to turn accountable professionals into scapegoated technicians. More importantly for the general climate of social relations, it is also to characterise those who perform least well in the educational competition for exchange value as social failures, whose position is seen to result from a combination of their own inadequacy and the failure of their parents and teachers to lobby or act effectively on their behalf.

The reality, of course, is rather different from the *Citizen's Charter* vision of a failing public service whipped into shape by consumer demand. Whilst there may have been some accountability gains—and a welcome renewed public interest in what goes on in educational institutions—the operation of the market does not entrain the virtuous spiral lauded by its proponents, whereby poor practice goes to the wall and enlightened consumers, all equally empowered by the same rights, apply appropriate pressures to lax or self-serving providers. What actually happens, unfortunately, is that the flip side of the mechanism comes into play and oversubscribed providers start choosing their consumers. For when the goods in a market are social, consumers as well as providers are in competition with each other—*and competition, justified as a means of driving out poor providers, effectively marginalises poor consumers*. In a private market, the losing consumers are those who are economically worst-placed. Where provision is wholly or largely public, it is those lacking cultural capital who come at the back of the queue (this foreseeable logical consequence has incidentally been empirically exacerbated by new rights for 'comprehensive' schools to select a growing proportion of their intake). To introduce market conditions is therefore to abdicate responsibility both for the public project of social reform and the equitable distribution of individual opportunity and also for the democratic oversight of that practice which is most central to society's renewal.

It is worth noting that with a market in schooling (and other key social goods) in place, those political values which underpinned a decade of policy change are further reinforced by the operation of the relevant markets themselves. The policy justification as publicly presented is plain and deceptively simple. Public services like schooling are paid for by the public for the good of the public. The public is made up of individuals, each with equal rights to seek their own welfare, and each responsible if they fail to do so. A 'caring society' will come to the aid of those who cannot cope in this new environment, but only with a safety-net sufficient to ensure societal stability; gone is the social aim of evenly-distributed common provision (claimed to depress individual effort and dissipate resources): that earlier aspiration is set aside without the need for any unpopular central manipulation of resource allocation, since all resulting unevenness in distribution seems attributable only to market forces. With four election victories for such a programme (and mileage for political opposition to it gradually eroded), there is no denying its popular appeal, and this is easy to understand. For the language of rights, choice, control and individual responsibility appeals to public intuitions about the conditions for *formal distributive justice*. However, that same rhetoric leads the public to overlook the fact that these are also the very conditions for *substantive injustice in distribution* when the goods in question are social and the context of distribution is competitive.

In reviewing the three themes of neo-liberal rhetoric which informed the charter exercise, there is no need to labour the first at this point: that all goods can be treated as equivalent for the purposes of distribution, whether they be public or private, individual or social. It is clear that the nature of non-private goods is altered for all when these are competed for in the market place, and equally clear that the winners in any such competition are most likely to be those in the most advantageous starting positions. That the problem is compounded in the case of a good like education whose value is both individual and social, both intrinsic and instrumental, merits detailed later analysis (to be developed in chapter three). On the second theme, that consumer choice will improve quality and distribute equitably, we have seen that there is necessarily a double-edged sword in play. Resourcing follows consumers, who are attracted by quality output, so that 'quality' (measurably defined) is rewarded. But where 'quality' depends on an interaction between providers and consumers, the most sought-after providers are prompted to exercise choice between their potential consumers—with schools in demand choosing pupils likely to maintain or improve their league rating (even without powers formally to select, which, when added, increase and institutionalise market diversity), and teachers whose career aspirations outrun their (progressively more costly) social commitments turning to posts in more privileged schools. Equity is apparently served by giving choice rights to all, to be exercised individually, as if choice affected only the chooser. But when each person's choice affects the nature and range of choices available to others, *formal free choice for all necessarily entails curtailed possibilities for some*. This, of course, is precisely why social and public goods were publicly provided and socially distributed in the first place.

However, the most significant theme running through these policies and their justification is the consumer view of citizenship, generated less by direct polemic than *by the social conditions which increased deregulation and competition—most particularly in relation to education*—*create*. This view of social engagement casts aside the former understanding of democratic citizenship as a sharing in collective decision-making to negotiate "the appropriate distribution of the benefits and burdens of social co-operation" so as to agree "a proper balance between competing claims".[8] With a market in social goods, the proper balance is whatever the hidden hand produces, with the extent of any individual's enfranchisement thus depending to a considerable degree on market acumen and (cultural or economic) capital. Although citizen-consumers competing for a quality experience, say of education, can scramble for the best of what is on offer, what they cannot do, acting as individuals in the market, is to raise the overall standard of provision within which they exercise their new found rights of choice—unless we believe, in the face of both logic and experience, in the fictitious virtuous spiral noted above. In addition, the ablest competitors in the market do not have the same incentive as before to lobby for general quality improvements or to support increased overall levels of resourcing. The overall size of the social cake is necessarily of less concern to individuals when it is their own choices or market activity, rather than global features of provision, which determine the size and quality of the slices they obtain for themselves. With social concerns fragmented in this way, then if individual citizens really do deliberate and act like the 'rational utility-maximisers' of neo-liberal theory, they might be expected to settle for public provision which was relatively poorly-resourced in global terms, provided that they each believed that in their own case they might gain access to its more advantageous elements.

Moreover there is an even more important consequence of this individualistic notion of citizenship, which affects all citizens whatever their individual preferences and whatever their level of social privilege. The one choice that a market in social goods cannot deliver is the more fundamental political choice of whether to distribute such goods this way at all. Choosing between options, when this replaces deliberation over appropriate distribution *criteria*, fixes the rules of the social game and sets in motion a spiral of social competition such that each is riding a tiger off which none can afford to climb but from which some must fall. And when citizens are thus given formal rights to compete 'equally' within these rules, in a revised social game which very many of them have not chosen, that is not just an inevitable pendulum swing of adversarial democracy. Rather, it is a real loss of democratic freedom, for in this set of rules the odds are not just stacked from the start: they also become progressively heavier as the game proceeds. This is because individual 'free' choices are doubly factored into context. They are not just *shaped by* a context of political values and social conditions: those same choices then go on to *create* changed social conditions and changed political values.

Education again provides the best example to show how the hidden hand of the market acts to twist our evaluative arms. In schooling, each choice right exercised by each parent is (among other things) a perfectly proper attempt to secure the best relative advantage for a child, which the chooser rightly intends. But it also constitutes a ratchet to the spiral of social competition, which the very same chooser might well deplore. This dilemma cannot be avoided by a neutral stance, for there is none: to stand still when others move forward is to fall back. Consumers of schooling thus gain rights to affect their children's welfare by additional means of influencing their place in the social future, but this is at the expense of the lost opportunity to shape that social future through co-operative democratic deliberation, since there is no abstaining from a set of revised rules for play which push the social future in a determinate direction. This is a crucial loss, for the world each will inhabit is logically more basic to their well-being than is their own place in it. The citizen as educational consumer thus becomes prisoner of a dilemma where choices, whether from enlightened self interest or from prudential concern for dependants, have twin and inseparable effects. Whilst bringing desired benefits of an immediate kind to some individuals, they also sum unavoidably to changed social conditions which many *even of the same individuals*, all things being equal, would have been anxious to avoid. This process will receive closer attention in chapter four.

Throughout the documents that I have referred to here, in order to allow one neo-liberal political programme to speak for itself, it can be seen that the language of policy and legislation, headlining "choice" "rights", "self-management", "decentralisation", "devolution", "local participation in decision making" etc.,[9] capitalises on the rhetoric of the left whilst shifting policy significantly to the right, presenting sweeping centrally-directed social change as an exercise in 'rolling back the state' and giving power to the people. Once the appeal to individual rights and freedoms has established a beach-head, market mechanisms have a momentum of their own which constantly ratchets the social competition, impelling individuals to look to their own welfare and placing an increasing premium on self-interest and an increasing cost on social solidarity and altruism.[10] It would be difficult to find a more vivid illustration of the two-way relationship between the constitution of education and that of the wider social order than we see in the neo-liberal reforms of education and society in the UK since 1980, and in the rationale and rhetoric which have surrounded their presentation to the public and its summation in the published "charters" of relevant consumer rights.

THE VIRTUES OF THE MARKET

At this point it may be useful to recall briefly the general theoretical rationale for free market exchange and distribution, together with some of its long-acknowledged accompanying problems even in the economic sphere: problems which become progressively compounded with the increasing complexity of the 'goods' for distribution. This will be helpful since the re-forming of education as described is justified by two theoretically separate but in practice mutually reinforcing sets of claims: on the one hand concerning the virtues of markets as such, and on the other the vices of state interference, particularly in social affairs as significant for personal development and prospects as is education. Since the claimed failures of education in educational terms were seen and presented by neo-liberal reformers as direct or indirect consequences of an over-intrusive state, best ameliorated by the state's deregulatory retreat, then we should first recall the alleged inherent virtues and acknowledged shortcomings of markets, before examining the plausibility and appeal of claims for the failures of education which those virtues are invoked to address.

The juxtaposition of those two theoretically separate but in practice mutually reinforcing sets of claims—the virtues of market distribution and the vices of an overweening state apparatus—is of course far from new. From the time when Locke defended the state as a mechanism for avoiding the "war of all against all" (as the "state of nature" was characterised), in order to allow each to go about his/her legitimate business unhindered by the predations of others, a matching set of defences for the individual was required to ensure that the cure for anarchy was not worse than the disease: to set limits to the permissible interference of the state in the affairs of the individual. From that time to this, liberalism, in its varying forms, has seemed the most adequate bulwark to protect the individual's liberties and rights against the illegitimate incursions of a state apparatus into the private sphere: and the demand on the *liberal* state is that it offer a procedural framework for regulating the (competing) rights and (conflicting) aspirations to liberty of its members.

Liberalism, of course, like any other social philosophy, necessarily developed and continues still to evolve in a context of contingent historical conditions, with certain economic and social structures, and particular beliefs about the nature of man and about individual and social development and their interaction. As Bellamy notes: "The examination of the fate of liberal ideas within a variety of intellectual and historical contexts reveals the historically contingent nature of many of liberalism's key propositions."[11] Early liberalism, being essentially a perfectionist social theory which addressed the evolution of society under particular social and economic conditions, and evolving as it did during a period of massive expansion in trade and manufacture, developed a vision of social freedom for the individual which had free market exchange at its heart. This paradigm of unconstrained social action, it was claimed, not only allowed individuals freely to express (and bargain to obtain) their preferences: it also promoted the social good, since, whilst acting severally in their own interest, individuals secured a beneficial result which, in the much-quoted words of Adam Smith, was "no part of their intention".

That beneficial result was most obvious in straightforward economic exchanges. Adam Smith's butchers and bakers, competing in the market, would flourish in proportion as they offered goods of the desired type, of the best quality, at a fair price: free competition between them would ensure that purveyors of inappropriate or shoddy goods—or of short change—would go to the wall. The market would thus maximally satisfy the wants of the public, whilst providing a discipline for production and trade whose result was that the skilled and honest would flourish. And all of this without state interference in free transactions between freely contracting individual agents. The legitimate role of the liberal state was in maintaining the conditions which would optimise free exchange. For the early liberals, of course, this was not simply an economic theory for the efficient maximisation of consumer preferences and the stimulation of economic growth. The divine hand which in Locke lies behind an essentially virtuous process is in Smith and Mill replaced by social forces, so that expansionary economic conditions and loosened political structures provide a framework for *political, social and moral progress*.[12] The economic conditions of industrialisation and the rise of capitalism both permit and require market relations between freely contracting individuals, since such relations, in their ideal form, place a premium on certain virtues and dispositions and encourage their growth in individuals and their gradual spread though society.

The philosophical core of nineteenth-century liberalism was thus that open-ended expansion of individual and social liberty which still constitutes liberalism today. However, the endorsement of free exchange was emphatically not then a morally neutral position, designed to produce whatever social states of affairs best represented the aggregate choices of individuals about whose ends (and the means to them) liberal thinkers were agnostic. On the contrary, the justification for providing political and social structures which would optimise liberty through free exchange was explicitly moral. Market relations were seen to require, encourage, develop and reward certain personal qualities such as independence, responsibility, far-sightedness and commitment to self-improvement, and to penalise, discourage and place at a discount their converse. Perfectly-competitive market relations were to create a moral meritocracy by rewarding these qualities of character, and representative government would enable moral meritocrats to pull up their fellow members of society behind them, in a synergistic process of moral and social progress.

From the earliest days of liberalism, however, it was fully understood that 'ideal markets' were precisely that: that the state, in its role as safeguard of individual liberty, had a dual part to play: firstly in maintaining those social structures and practices on which free markets depend, and secondly in minimising the opportunities for what economists call 'externalities' (free-riding, prisoners' dilemmas, etc. and subsequent 'Pareto-inefficiency'[13]) to develop. Thus Mill endorsed a delicate balance between *laissez-faire* and regulation. The overall duty of government was to maintain conditions which would inculcate character, specifically maximising the capacity for and conditions of autonomy. Free exchange had three virtues: its preference-satisfying efficiency, its tendency under 'ideal' conditions to promote individual morality, and its democratic power. Where free market exchange did not bring these outcomes, Mill supported state intervention on the grounds that "trade is a social act" and is therefore "other-regarding". Without appropriate regulation, failures of the market and its virtues would multiply, negating the moral purpose of free exchange and leaving the state in dereliction of its duty to protect individual freedom.

The nub of debate, then and still, is what constitutes the scope and limits of appropriate regulation. Through the nineteenth century, theoretical debate developed between liberals in Britain and continental Europe with British liberals emphasising changes in morality consequent on market capitalism and increasing democracy (seen to provide the engine for further changes in the social order), whilst many continental thinkers saw organic evolution of the social order as the driving force for moral and psychological change.[14] This debate was not abstractly ideological, but hung on the disputed validity of elements of British liberalism's social thesis, made up as it was of psychological beliefs about human motivation and the formation of character, sociological beliefs about the relation of individuals to each other in the polity and of political to economic processes, and economic beliefs about the long-term workings of the free market, the relations of capital to labour, and the role and effects of the profit motive. On the tenability and interdependence of these beliefs also hung intra-liberal disputes about what constituted free-contracting between market agents, about what actions and consequences in the market were 'other-regarding' and how, and most crucially about what might be the necessary social preconditions to the exercise of liberty. Perhaps the most well-known practical issue illustrating these intra-liberal debates was the *furore* which surrounded the passing of the Factory Acts[15] to regulate employment conditions, setting a limiting framework for agreements individuals might be willing to enter into with an employer. Like contemporary controversy in Britain over the moral (and economic) undesirability of employment legislation (exactly mirroring the nineteenth-century debate in theoretical terms), the crux of dispute over the Factory Acts legislation was whether a contract between an employer who—as a matter of contingent fact—had an adequate pool of available labour from which to select, and a prospective employee whose choice was between taking or leaving whatever return for his/her labour was on offer, could be deemed to be freely entered into by both parties, each maximising their preferences.

Key disputes, then as now, were thus not between two factions, the one valuing liberty and the other prepared to sacrifice it for some other value (equality, social justice, etc.) but between parties who were in theoretical disagreement (with profound practical implications) about how liberty itself should be understood. This question will be returned to when liberalism's social thesis is explored in chapter five: the point of recalling here the role of market exchange in early liberal theory is to emphasise that its value was always conceived as instrumental to a moral and political purpose. This was no prioritisation of economic over moral ends: rather liberalism was born as a vision of society prioritising individual freedom which sought to harness emerging economic conditions to moral ends. Thus de Toqueville in *Democracy in America* saw the market economy as both the expression and the seed-bed of the democratic process, with order and institutions arising from contract and agreement, whilst Mill in *On Liberty* saw a free market in ideas and beliefs as the royal road to truth through a process of quasi-Darwinian epistemological natural selection, and liberals in general saw free exchange in the market as the foundation of individual liberty for all and, by extension, of democracy.

The converse has been claimed of neo-liberalism by some of its opponents, who see this resurrection of early liberal prioritisation of market arrangements, stripped of the caveats concerning market failure of which Adam Smith already warned, and cut loose from nineteenth-century scruples about social preconditions for the exercise of individual freedom (which led Mill to end his life as a socialist), as the elevation of economic considerations over all others. Indeed nineteenth-century liberal niceties about the relation of the individual to the social are conspicuous by their absence in the pronouncements not only of politicians of New Right persuasion (such as Prime Minister Thatcher with her oft-quoted "There is no such thing as society. There are only individual men and women . . . ."[16]) but also in some philosophical writing[17] and in the exhortations of 'opinion-formers' in right-wing 'think-tanks'. The claim that neo-liberalism represents the eclipse of politics by economics may seem superficially surprising when apologists are typically keen to adopt the mantle and invoke the authority of the early liberals, but that invocation is seriously misleading.

The brand of neo-liberalism currently most politically prominent, which has underpinned the recent reconstitution of the social order in Britain, can be fairly represented by quoting at some length from a keynote lecture entitled "The Morality of the Market" given by one of its well-known public apologists there. Lord Harris began: "My argument stands like a tripod on the three legs of politics, economics and ethics. First, if we prefer individual freedom to coercion, we have no choice but to accept the competitive market economy as providing the fullest scope for its political expression. Secondly, the market system also provides the most efficient solution to the economic problem of making the best use of resources in the creation of wealth. Thirdly, and overwhelmingly important, the competitive market provides the most moral order available to man as we know him— and as we know ourselves".[18] In the course of that lecture, Hume, Smith, Mill *et al.* are selectively invoked to give warrant to a dismal view of "the Devil's streak"[19] in human nature such that "The challenge . . . is to help leaven society by voluntarily striving to shift the balance in personal conduct away from avarice, self-love, vanity, and towards friendship, generosity and more sensitive concern for others".[20] Both this noble aim and the proper restraint of the state apparatus can be achieved by "the miracle that without central direction—but within a framework of market incentives and penalties—a spontaneous order emerges that brings supply and demand of myriad goods and services into approximate balance".[21] Thus, "Competition is like the alchemist's stone which transmutes selfish, leaden motives into a beneficial, if not golden, outcome. So long as government maintains the legal and institutional framework of a competitive economy, producers can advance their sectional interest only by serving and satisfying a sufficient number of customers".[22]

It is allowed, nonetheless, that that is not the end of the duties of government, whose role also extends to providing those public goods, such as "national defence, law enforcement, a stable monetary system, street lighting etc."[23] which the market cannot supply. But education, healthcare, housing, income distribution etc. are matters best left to the market which "is the most lavish distributor of good things".[24] Once government moves into social provision, the spectre of state coercion is raised: "We should not make the poverty or incompetence of a dwindling minority the pretext for denying the growing majority the boon of free choice. The constant danger is that well-intentioned paternalism chains us altogether and marches us further along the collectivist road to authoritarian coercion".[25] These quotations are sufficient to indicate some elements of the eighteenth- and nineteenth-century premises which, in a more strongly ideological form, lurk beneath revived, contemporary "paleo-" liberalism. A supply-side approach to growth, a trickle-down theory of public prosperity, an 'original sin' conception of moral motivation and its appropriate restraints, a view of individuals as unrelated to their fellows except through the bonds of free contract for mutual self-interest, and the bogey of state domination combine together to serve a conception of liberty in which there is truly ". . . no such thing as society . . .". This conception invokes the Millian precept that the only freedom worthy of the name is that of pursuing one's own good in one's own way, but neglects both Mill's own awareness of unresolved questions about the interdependence of agency in the social world and all that has been learned in the intervening period about the empirical workings of 'free' exchange to produce market failure of various sorts. Most crucially of all, it divides "good things" (and indeed the whole complex business of life) unproblematically into the clearly public and the unquestionably private, with the aggregate choices of sovereign consumers ensuring optimum provision and fairest distribution of whatever is deemed to fall in the latter category. That matters are very much more complex than that will be elaborated as the case here proceeds.

Now despite insistence by apologists that they are in part conducting a moral crusade by economic means, commentators have noted that government by the market—that is to say the introduction of market mechanisms into the provision and distribution of *social* goods as described in the last section—represents an economic model of politics which takes economic transactions as basic and extrapolates to social and moral life. In this model 'public choice' serves as the theoretical rationale which legitimates both market outcomes and the extension of the market into the social sphere, importing into political policy a methodology appropriate at best to unproblematic economic transactions. As Mueller notes: "The subject matter of public choice is the same as that of political science. . . . The methodology of public choice is that of economics, however. The basic behavioural postulate of public choice, as for economics, is that man is an egoistic, rational utility-maximiser".[26] The goal of public choice theory is to make bureaucracies directly accountable to the public they serve, but its basic economistic premise contrues that public as simply an aggregate of atomistic individuals. This would imply that there is no distinction between public interest and private interests in individuals' decision strategies, making individual preference the ultimate criterion for public policy—a position clearly false in respect of many social goods, most notably education, as we shall see in chapter three. It also presupposes that markets in goods of all kinds tend towards conditions of perfect competition—a belief contra-indicated by both evidence and logic.

Commentators have been quick to note empirical changes in the actual conditions of markets, from the much-invoked original paradigm of small traders motivated by self-interest ensuring the prosperity of society by choice, competition and high quality goods in the battle for consumers, to the present-day realities of global economics and cultural change through mass-media advertising: Self writes, "The giant multi-national is light years away from Smith's butchers and bakers and in a position to subordinate political power to economic power rather than vice versa".[27] More importantly, there is also a long tradition of debate about the actual workings of the 'invisible hand', largely ignored in neo-liberal ideology. As one writer sums this up: ". . . the nice invisible hand results come only when certain idealised conditions are met: that everything that matters in life comes from the private consumption of goods; and that information is perfect, commodities infinitely divisible, and economic agents perfectly rational".[28] And what is worse: "Even if the fairy tales of perfect competition could be realised, there would be no practicable way of arranging initial endowments so as to achieve equitable distribution as exchanges proceeded".[29]

Leaving aside questions of equity for the moment, the literature abounds in analyses of the necessary conditions of inevitable 'market failure' which will not be detailed here.[30] One example will suffice to illustrate that, given the interdependence of agency for social creatures, individual rational self-interest cannot sum to optimal outcomes for agents *even when exchanges are of that most clearly economic commodity: cash.* If we take, say, the interests of investors in pension funds, these are best served by growth in the economy. That in turn is best served by stable investment. However, each time investors trade equities—as they must to maximise their holdings— they frustrate the overall economic project on which their gains *collectively* depend. Activity which is agent-rational thus sums to collective folly. This is just one obvious current example of the classic 'prisoners' dilemma' in which "rational, self-interested non-co-operative behaviour may lead to stable inefficiencies".[31] Much of the standard literature is concerned to detail how economic *laissez-faire* produces these latter: "When markets fail, however (which in the real world they do without exception), and conditions of perfect competition do not obtain, the self-interested, utility-maximising behaviour of each individual leads to a Pareto-*inefficient* outcome— that is, one in which at least some individuals could be made better off without worsening the condition of others".[32] Coleman follows this observation by noting that, beginning from the Hobbesian "state of nature"—which in effect can be characterised as a failed market—both moral and political solutions are required to achieve "the mutually beneficial gains available only when individuals constrain their utility-maximising behaviour".[33] Problems in arriving at Pareto-efficient outcomes are radically compounded when the goods concerned are social in constitution as well as in context, as has long been recognised.

Moreover, once moral considerations re-enter the picture, Pareto-efficiency on the economic, public choice model—even were it achievable[34]—offers a very attenuated goal. As Sen points out in revealing the dismal consequences of allowing economics to drive politics: "A social state is described as Pareto optimal if and only if no-one's utility can be raised without reducing the utility of someone else. This is a very limited kind of success, and in itself may not guarantee much. A state can be Pareto optimal with some people in extreme misery and others rolling in luxury, so long as the miserable cannot be made better off without cutting off the luxury of the rich".[35] This is because at the social level, the market failures flagged above pay no attention to distributional considerations. Thus what is most conspicuously forgotten by today's free marketeers is that public provision and regulation grew up in the first place in response both to market failure and to the cumulative inequalities produced in the real world by less-than-free exchange. As Heald writes of the economic sphere: ". . . these freedoms to use or dispose, which are extensive and very real under capitalism, generate a matching set of unfreedoms, whereby non-owners are precluded from either using or disposing".[36]

Now already in Aristotle we find elegant arguments against allowing economics to drive politics, particularly in the service of freedom. Politics must remain "the master art", using "the rest of the sciences" and certainly economics to *its* ends since "the life of money-making is one undertaken under compulsion, and wealth is evidently not the good we seek: for it is merely useful and for the sake of something else".[37] We have seen that this "something else" which in classical liberalism free exchange was to serve was the liberty of the individual, with for Mill (and others less explicitly) each counting as one and none as more than one. Hence the nineteenth-century debates, in theory and in public policy, about the social prerequisites to liberty. Just as financial regulation grew up in the intervening period to combat economic conditions of market failure, so social provision and regulation grew up to redress the inequities—and the frustration of liberty for some—which resulted from both the cumulative tendencies of capitalism and the social nature of liberty's prerequisites. As Plant argues, "the libertarian's defence of liberty is disingenuous because it neglects the resources and opportunities which make this defence of equal liberty of equal value to all citizens".[38] To enable individuals to pursue their own good in their own way requires "the marshalling of economic and social resources".[39]

And that marshalling of social resources, long seen as necessary to the achievement of liberal ideals, is not merely a call for *economic* redistribution in the name of greater social equality. The basis for opposition to a neo-liberal approach to politics and public morality is not simply that this offends against egalitarian claims, discounted in advance by its central thesis that "rewards in the market system cannot be equal across all individuals if that society is to prosper: and in the long run, all will eventually benefit in some way from the prosperity and progress initiated by the market system".[40] It is rather that this approach to the ordering of society fails to engage with important social realities. For people do not differ merely in their preferences and their resources for obtaining them. They also differ in abilities, understanding, experience and cultural capital, all of which structure preferences, making some possible and others not. Dworkin points out that under a market distribution of "good things" this fact of life frustrates the aims of liberalism itself: ". . . these inequalities will have great, often catastrophic, effects on the distribution that a market economy will provide. But, unlike differences in preferences, the differences these inequalities make are indefensible according to the liberal conception of equality".[41] Dworkin is here arguing for forms of compensation, but his insight (as I shall argue more fully later) can take us further than that. Whilst such arguments have telling force as pleas that fair-minded lovers of liberty should additionally care about equality and be prepared to trade some of the former for the latter, they can also draw attention not only to inadequacies in the conception of liberty which informs much neo-liberal thinking but also to the need to review modern liberal neutralism in its various interpretations. At this point, however, my concern is with the starkest interpretation available, deployed for example by Nozick. It seems clear that despite Nozick's claims to the contrary (as in the famous Wilt Chamberlain example[42]), redistributive taxation, minimum wages—and indeed Factory Acts—are not sacrifices of liberty, but part of its necessary institutional framework. As is well argued by Gibbard, "They are part of a pattern of restrictions on liberty, the pattern constituted by a system of property rights. They are not added restrictions on liberty, over and above the restrictions on liberty involved in a system of pure exchange. They are restrictions on our legal powers to alter the restrictions on liberty that constitute a system of property rights".[43] That subtle point simply reminds us that markets, in whatever goods, are *social* artefacts. Further problems with the neo-liberal conception of liberty (and less obviously with the neutralist conception it aims to supersede), which arise notably in respect of social goods and most particularly education, will be deferred to chapter five.

Not all neo-liberals, however, are insensitive to social realities. The contemporary thinker who most consciously attempts to combine a social with a philosophical thesis for neo-liberalism is Hayek, and it is his arguments which particularly require to be countered by any opponent of a market distribution of non-private goods who wishes to avoid being accused of attacking theoretically straw (though politically ascendant) persons. Unlike for example Nozick, Hayek does not make the pervasive mistake of treating all goods, of whatever kind, however produced and exchanged, as if they were like the change in one's pocket. Dubbing socialism as the "atrocious idea that political power ought to determine the material position of the different individuals and groups",[44] he sees the great merit of classical liberalism as the restraining of (arbitrary) state or interest-group power, with modern demands for social justice threatening to resurrect this. Nonetheless, sensitive to the institutional prerequisites to a market society, he supports ". . . a wide field for the non-coercive activities of government",[45] including "taking the initiative" in the provision of education. He would still, however, support the deregulatory measures towards consumer choice and control of that good, as detailed in the first section here, on two kinds of grounds. One is the familiar horror of state power and self-aggrandising professional interests and bureaucracies; the other is more interesting. For Hayek sees the market as a paradigm of 'social epistemology' which does not merely reflect democratic preferences accurately, but also embodies social understandings which are too complex, variable and mutable to be vested in or deferred to bureaucracies or professional experts. Since social practices involve forms of reasoning which are tacit, practical and collective, their optimal conduct issues from the aggregate of the several market decisions of each. It will be my contention that such claims, though of considerable force as arguments against a centrally-planned economy,[46] or, as in Polanyi, against the central planning of science,[47] are not extensible to the deregulation of education. I shall defend that counter-claim as my argument unfolds, not only on grounds of social justice (appeal to which Hayek—not alone—sees as a disreputable cloak for envy), but also on the grounds both that inevitable 'market failure' ensues with respect to this good and that the good in question suffers a significant change in constitution with consequent loss of public value.

The point of pursuing this question is not, of course, to come down in one or other of a series of dogmatic camps about the virtues of markets as such. Arguments abound asserting that markets are: efficient but often unjust (generating goods optimally but distributing them unfairly); that they are just but inefficient (rewarding contributions to want-satisfaction, but wastefully); that they are both just and efficient (as propounded in the Charters discussed above); or that they are necessarily unjust and inefficient (producing cumulative inequality and failing to respond to needs).[48] To adopt any of those positions as a global judgement of markets as such is to make the mistake noted by Bellamy when he points out that ". . . one of the chief perils of abstract argument resides in a lack of engagement with the social and political problems confronting the theory you seek to propose"—a common procedure "fatal to contemporary political philosophy . . .".[49] What is at issue here is how the nature of a given good and the differing resources of individuals in its market affects both the efficiency and the justice of its distribution. That there can be no ideologically grounded verdict either for or against markets as such will be particularly evident as the case of educational goods is developed, since, as well as being especially problematic on those two general issues—of their kinds of value and its beneficiaries—such goods also profoundly affect the subsequent resources of individuals in a series of other markets, and also the nature of subsequent goods for trade. The implications of this are far-reaching. That there can be no such generalisable verdict for the virtues of market arrangements in social life would not only be fatal to neo-liberalism: it should also have significant implications for contemporary debates about defensible re-interpretations of a liberalism which seeks to respect the like liberties of all.

A SUITABLE CASE FOR TREATMENT: PERSUASION AND PLAUSIBILITY

The ideological rationale reported in the first section of this chapter was not of course spelled out at the start of the period of radical change. The electorate was therefore in no position to survey proposed reforms as a possible instantiation of the counter-factual practical elaboration of the market's limiting case. Though *particular* early policies, such as the de-zoning of schools, were presented from the outset in terms of rights and freedoms, the justification for the general overhaul of education made overriding reference to the failure of past practice, deemed to have met neither the social nor the individual goals espoused for public education. In this, indeed, the New Right in the UK was simply taking further the dissatisfaction with the 'pay-off' for educational expenditure which had already been placed on the political agenda by the previous Labour administration there.[50] That both major political parties in an adversarial system should have identified education as a suitable case for treatment (though at the time with different diagnoses, implying differing future prescription), and that the electorate should find this persuasive (though often for conflicting reasons), ought to give us pause. It would be over-hasty, however, to conclude that this necessarily points to pervasive failure of the system in educational terms: to inappropriate content, misguided pedagogy, lax standards and/or poor teachers. All of these charges have indeed been levelled at the system throughout the reform period, and an analysis such as this is not the place to adjudicate them. What is appropriate here is to examine, not the actual practices, but the *logical features* of the project of mass liberal education. When these are unpacked, we see not only how reserves of disappointment are created among the public, but also why, paradoxically, the individualistic approach of the neo-liberals has particular appeal, both to past winners and to past losers.

Given their allegiance to the virtues of the market, it is clear why neo-liberals seeking social change might *wish* to target education initially on both political and economic grounds. Some account is needed, however, of why this of all social practices provided the most promising first focus for radical, privatising reform. Since a primary formal function of education is the passing on of a society's understanding of worthwhile knowledge and belief, that practice would not *prima facie* seem an obvious candidate for the newly established status of (publicly provided) private good. So what kind of shortcomings with the previous settlement have lent plausibility and democratic legitimacy to recent radical reforms?[51] We may need to delve quite deeply to understand the particular success of neo-liberalism in harnessing latent public disappointment with education and thus establishing what would at first sight seem a surprising beach-head for the privatising of the public sphere. Political rhetoric notwithstanding, the explanation cannot be put down to a previously unacknowledged, pervasive failure of public education in for example the UK, unless we suppose that such failure was similarly exhibited in very different education systems across all those societies—from New Zealand to Hungary—which came under the sway of these ideas within a short historical period. Nor can it be ascribed to public credulity in the face of constant assertions of failure. After all, education, unlike say, the judicial system or the health service, is necessarily the one public service of which every member of a developed society has first-hand experience (even though in most cases that experience is very dated, since demographic change means that fewer of the voting public than ever before have current direct connection with educational practice). Nor does it seem plausible to suggest that, prior to the ascendance of the New Right, a substantial proportion of the public were deeply dissatisfied with the public provision of education, but remained strangely silent.

In any event, this shift in political ethos, reflected in and compounded by concomitant demands for educational change, has not been a local phenomenon. Political commentators rightly note that the rise of neo-liberalism was prompted in many industrialised societies as a political response to three sorts of conditions. The 1970s saw fiscal pressures on government in affluent societies, resulting from demographic change, rising expectations and world recession. This came at a time when the social reform project of the post-war era was coming under strain, and the tenability of Keynesian economics in an increasingly global economy was under question. Commentators again often ascribe the initial political focus on reform of education as a consequence on the one hand of that being a particularly costly social service and on the other of its outcomes having direct links to collective economic performance. And an economistic rationale for the urgency of reforming education (through more 'relevant' content and better-targeted social investment) was buttressed, in the UK as elsewhere, by the strange economic determinism of New Right politicians, with their insistence that "There is no alternative"[52] to measures proposed.

Despite that rhetoric, it is quite clear that specific reforms of social practices cannot be *determined* by economic conditions, even if these could be accurately analysed and fully understood. So we must look beyond contingent economic conditions and actual educational practices in order to understand what it is about the democratic conduct of public education which makes it fertile ground for the political exploitation of latent discontent. To be sure, when in Britain reappraisal focused initially on the education service, its claimed shortcomings served as a convenient scapegoat for the (politically damaging) problems of escalating unemployment and rising crime among some sections of the young; both of these being phenomena which arouse civic as well as parental anxiety. Of course, failure of education *as a system* cannot sufficiently account for these social phenomena, though failure for some at school might plausibly play a significant part in which individuals are most likely to be touched by them. Nonetheless, though there was scepticism among many of the public over specific charges levelled against the system, it remains undeniable that attacks on education tapped a reservoir of popular unease (with electoral receptivity to change which it would be complacent to write off as simple ignorance, reaction or prejudice). That unease is not altogether surprising since, despite reformist measures over three decades, the post-war education project of individual emancipation for each and simultaneous social progress for all had failed to deliver to many what they had hoped for from it.

To acknowledge that, however, is not to make common cause with those who urged deregulation to bring the carrots and sticks of consumer pressure to bear on a lax, introverted and self-serving system delivering a failing public service. Even without adjudicating on those conveniently imprecise charges, it would be over-hasty to assume that failures of public education—if such there be—are due to inadequacies in *implementing* its goals, let alone to lay those inadequacies at the door of loosely specified culprits. For that leaves unexamined a series of questions, not only about the execution of the project, but also about its conception. Latent public disappointment there clearly was after thirty years of investment and effort aimed at realising a system of liberal education for all which met both private aspirations and social goals. But before apportioning blame to those who failed to deliver all that the project promised, or attributing fault or inadequacy to those who failed to reap its benefits, we should question whether its diverse aims were all capable of simultaneous fulfilment by similar means. For one of the most startling facts about the erosion of loyalty among a significant proportion of the public has been that disaffection was not confined to those who might be described as having most clearly lost out. Indeed, there was a broader base of dissatisfaction with a project which was seen to have been *unable to fulfil the mutually contradictory expectations even of its greatest direct beneficiaries.* For one reading of attitudes to the individualistic, consumerist 'reforms' of mass liberal education in the UK since 1980 might suggest that the disappointment of collective aspirations—the slowness and unevenness of progress to a society both more equitable and more prosperous through educational reform—led the public to endorse an abandoning of collective aspiration and to replace this with an individualist scramble for adequate slices of a finite cake. A key question for analysis, therefore, is whether the project of liberal education for all, as it has been conceived over the past half-century or more, can at the same time deliver the social benefits we expect from it collectively (prosperity, international economic competitiveness, a good rate of return on social investment in terms not just of the economic but also of social stability and cohesion and public civility and culture), and also make equally available to all those private benefits (of both intrinsic and exchange value) which in a democracy all are promised.

To enumerate that (indicative) list of aims is already to suggest that the demands made of public education would be empirically difficult to meet, with shortcomings in some aspects, arising from any given set of policies and practices, more than likely to occur. Indeed, educational controversy within the so-called period of consensus prior to neo-liberal reform was frequently driven by the perceptions of differing interest groups that *their* most cherished aims within the total set were being sacrificed to the priorities of others. Thus the authors of the 'Black Papers' argued from the 1960s that the pursuit of individual excellence was at risk from the demands of social cohesion,[53] whilst a left-wing government in the 1970s urged that the prerequisites to collective prosperity were being neglected in the name of personal emancipation, hence the "Great Debate". All of that is unremarkable, being part and parcel of the compromises, trade-offs and shifting priorities of policy and debate during periods of broad consensus on complex social aims. As such, it is insufficient to explain an eventual legitimation crisis for those shared aims, and a more generalised loss of confidence in that social project most crucial to their realisation. To understand this, we need to look beyond empirical difficulties in delivering public education's designated 'goods', and focus on the logical problems which for so long those empirical difficulties served to disguise.

It is significant in this respect that when in Britain a watershed in the social settlement was reached towards the close of the 1970s, although the political complaints made about education were based on its claimed failure to have lived up to *social* expectations—to deliver increased GNP and adequate social control—these complaints found little echo among the general public. Indeed public interest became engaged, and popular dissatisfaction was successfully awakened, when an incoming neo-liberal regime emphasised the *rights of the individual* to make good their personal claims on the public system. Market-inspired reform was thus sold to the public by harnessing frustration with the public project's *individual* outcomes. Though indeed neo-liberal proposals were bolstered by claims that public education had failed to deliver *social* prosperity, harmony and progress (and arguably were motivated in government by those perceptions to a considerable extent), both the polemic of the time and the official rationale presented a decade later in the Charters demonstrate clearly that the neo-liberal appeal did not depend on those charges for populist persuasion and popular acquiescence. The particular appeal of libertarian reform in relation to education made direct reference to *individual* concerns and resonated with either the experience—or the fear—of the individual disadvantage which may result from an inferior personal holding of educational goods. *Neo-liberalism's appeal to the public, therefore, was paradoxically strongest where it was logically most problematic.*

With reform policies presented then as libertarian measures to extend individual freedoms to compete for many more kinds of goods, including educational experiences, policy proposals are taken off the old agenda of mundane debate about likely effects on, say, the education system as a whole and on the general good which a publicly provided and regulated system was designed in part to promote. Perhaps more importantly in respect of education, they deflect attention from the need to consider a new agenda which might take more seriously the logical as well as the empirical obstacles to the simultaneous realisation of public liberal education's often conflicting aims. Debate itself, on whatever agenda, is placed at a discount whilst the rhetoric of rights functions as a 'trumping' move,[54] decreasing the weight of dissenting views or alternative analyses, and reinforcing the culture of individualism which neo-liberalism espouses and seeks to encourage. Indeed, so appealing did these arguments become in the UK that no opposing political party included encroachment on these recently-granted rights as part of their platform for the revision of neo-liberal measures, should they come to power. When, in the educational context, individualistic appeals are not to naked self-interest but to responsibilities to dependants, they seem particularly persuasive. When that context itself is inherently competitive, they appear compelling, and also thereby gain political legitimacy for their extension to other arenas of public life.

It should perhaps be added here that to stress the popular appeal of individualistic reforms is not to impute cynicism or Macchiavellian acumen to policy-makers. It seems reasonable to suppose that neo-liberal reformers of education, though exercised by the system's claimed failure to deliver its goals for society as a whole, continue to believe, like reformers in the previous settlement, that these are best approached through a redistribution of individual opportunities. In this, they share some of the ontological assumptions (though not the social values) of the neutralist liberal consensus they seek to supplant—assumptions which will be looked at in later chapters. In both approaches to the ordering of society, the good of each and the good of all are to be simultaneously served by a redistribution of educational opportunities. What distinguishes the two perspectives is the direction and grounds for redistribution. For although the benefits which public education has always been expected to bring to society as a whole in terms of order and prosperity have long been subordinated in policy and debate to its benefits to the individual, this has not been from political unconcern for societal goals, far from it, but rather as a consequence of the pervasive assumption that individual benefit, if rightly arranged, would bring society's well-being in its wake. A review of the broad outlines of educational policy during the earlier consensus period (in which a vision of social progress through enhanced educational opportunity underpinned thirty years of reconstruction and expansion post-war) may help to explain why neo-liberalism in social matters is most seductive where it is least appropriate. That paradox can help ground a critique of some of the philosophical assumptions on which it rests. The most significant of these for the purpose in hand is an atomistic conception of the individual which places liberty and equality in competition with each other, with neo-liberalism polemically (but falsely) announcing "advantage, liberty".

CONCLUSION

The wave of neo-liberal 'reforms' of education reported and examined in these first two chapters were not imposed on the public by an illegitimate regime. They were voted for democratically (though never by a straight majority of the electorate), and not just by those whom the project of liberal education for all had clearly disappointed but also by many of that project's evident beneficiaries. The key question which arises is whether we are entitled either to believe that this disillusion arose simply because the pace of social and educational reform was too slow and resources inadequate, as educators suggest, or to conclude conversely that it resulted from failings by educators, as politicians insist. In either of these cases we would be faced with a practical problem, requiring a response from policy and practice. What these claims and counter-claims overlook, however, is that the problem may be deeper and more intractable than either of those diagnoses suggest. For we may be faced here with a problem of theory, which perpetuates pendulum swings of policy and practice. It may rather be that the perceived failure of social progress (in both prosperity and its equitable distribution) through the enhanced rational autonomy that a liberal education aims to foster lies only in part and incidentally in mistakes of implementation—on whoever's part. That third possible explanation would imply that there have been flaws in our *conception* of the project of liberal education for all—a project which, we shall see, set out to achieve its goals of social progress *by purely individual means*. With some of education's social goals (notably those which seem in the short-term to serve the needs of the economy) now eclipsing its emancipatory aims except in the case of individuals who are socially well-placed, and with many of those who are least well-placed giving democratic support to policies likely to rebound to their further disadvantage (riding the tiger of competition), possible flaws in the liberal conception of that project need now to be entertained.

Given the diverse claims for the virtues of markets and their extension from economic to social exchanges, it is not surprising that in relation to education, the moral and practical appeal of the market unites conflicting dissatisfactions across the political spectrum and draws allegiance from diverse interest groups with differing priorities among education's aims. To some it promises the preservation of academic excellence in the face of a democratising dilution of standards; to others it promises the eclipse of irrelevant mandarin content by the operation of consumer choice and control driven by economic 'realities'; to yet others it seems to offer greater control over access to social promotion through the enhanced exchange value which has so far eluded them. Clearly, not all of these contradictory promises can be delivered by the same political mechanism. Unless we wish to attribute pervasive bad faith to policy-makers, and pervasive foolishness to a significant proportion of the public (which in a democracy, however imperfect, bears some responsibility for the direction which policy takes over a period of several political administrations) then attention to the deeper foundations of the public project of liberal education for all is required. This may be an appropriate time to consider how we might reconstruct education as a project of *societal* emancipation, and jettison the convenient assumption that this will arise as a happy by-product of the emancipation of individuals, provided only that we emancipate enough of them.

The theoretical analysis required can be seen as one element in contemporary attempts to escape from some of the contradictions of a neutralist liberalism which tends, when guiding social practices, to place in jeopardy those goods and values on whose maintenance the realisation of its ideals depend. Nowhere is this more evident than in our repeated attempts to deliver increasing and equally distributed social freedoms to all through the individual emancipation of each. At the level of practical politics and social policy, the response to the impasse has been, not to reconsider our taken-for-granted assumptions about the priority of the individual, nor to query the inevitability of a dichotomous clash between the claims of individual liberty and of social equality, but to settle for prioritising an even more starkly individualistic conception of liberty and for radically individualising the whole social enterprise. The resulting reconstitution of public education is as reported here. Whilst at the level of practice, society throws in the towel, a move beyond 'normal science' (or consideration, within the prevailing paradigm, of questions prompted by its premises) seems required at the level of educational theory. It is no longer enough to analyse and evaluate how the practical project now stands, nor to ask how its conduct measures up to reiterated aims. For a whole array of assumptions—ontological and metaphysical as well as empirical—are called into question by a survey of our current predicament.

NOTES AND REFERENCES

1. An earlier version of this section forms part of Jonathan, R. (1993), Onderwijsvandering in het Verenigd Kononkrijk in de jaren tachtig: Over het imperialisme van de instrumentele rationaliteit, *Pedagogische Tijdschrift* 18, 1, pp. 33–43.

2. *The Citizen's Charter*, London, HMSO. Command 1599, 1991.

3. *The Parent's Charter; The Patient's Charter; The Justice Charter, The Tenant's Charter; The Customer Charter* (issued by the Benefits Agency), etc.

4. *The Parent's Charter*, London, Department of Education and Science, 1991. *The Parent's Charter*, Edinburgh, The Scottish Office, 1991

5. N.B. when the popular slogan was adopted as a formal banner for policy, the apostrophe was significantly shifted.

6. *Ibid.*, p. 4.

7. See Prime Minister Callaghan's speech at Ruskin College in 1976 to inaugurate the "Great Debate" on education, with its references to "the secret garden of the curriculum". Note also public silence over the next two decades on old debates (as in Durkheim) over which social practices are fitting subjects for democratic accountability and which are better served by a measure of professional autonomy.

8. Rawls, J. (1971), *op. cit.*, p. 4.

9. 1988 *Education Reform Act, op. cit.*, *passim*; all charters, *passim*.

10. See Jonathan, R. (1995b), Education and moral development: the role of reason and circumstance, *Journal of Philosophy of Education*, 29.3, pp. 333–354.

11. Bellamy, R. (1992), *op. cit.*, p. 4.

12. See Dunn, J., From applied theology to social analysis: the break between John Locke and the Scottish Enlightenment, in: Hont, I. and Ignatieff, M. (Eds.), *Wealth and Virtue: the shaping of political economy in the Scottish enlightenment* (Cambridge University Press, 1983).

13. A Pareto-efficient outcome being one in which none can be made better-off without some becoming worse-off. Pareto-efficiency is thus posited as a measure of total welfare, irrespective of its distribution. It might seem piquant that a *collective* concept serves as prime evaluative benchmark for the outcomes of highly individualistic political policies. There again, it might be argued that only a peculiarly individualistic perspective could conceive of total welfare as being unrelated to its distribution.

14. See social Darwinist thesis in Durkheim, E., *De la Division du Travail Social*.

15. of 1833 (and 1874, 1878).

16. Prime Minister Thatcher, interview reported in *Woman's Own*, October, 1987.

17. e.g. Nozick, R. (1974), *op. cit.*

18. Lord Harris, The morality of the market, keynote conference presentation published in *The New Right and Christian Values*, Occasional Paper 5, Centre for Theology and Public Issues, University of Edinburgh, Edinburgh, 1985, p. 2.

19. *Ibid.*, p. 3

20. *Ibid.*, p. 4.

21. *Ibid.*, p. 6.

22. *Ibid.*

23. *Ibid.*, p. 7.

24. *Ibid.*

25. *Ibid.*, p. 8.

26. Mueller, M., *Public Choice* (Cambridge, Cambridge University Press, 1989), p. 1–2.

27. Self, P., *Government by the Market? The Politics of Public Choice* (Basingstoke, Macmillan, 1993), p. 199.

28. Gibbard, A. (1985), What's morally special about free exchange? *Social Philosophy and Policy* , 2.2, p. 26.

29. *Ibid.*, p. 27.

30. For a classic analysis, see: Knight, F., *The Ethics of Competition and Other Essays* (London, Allen & Unwin, 1935).
Also: Braybrooke, D., "Preferences opposed to the market" and papers by others in *Market Failure, Social Philosophy and Policy*, Vol. 2.1. Autumn 1984; Buchanan, J., "Asymmetrical reciprocity in market exchange: implications for economics in transition"

and papers by others in *Liberalism and the Economic Order, Social Philosophy and Policy* , 10. 2, 1993; Sen, A., *On Ethics and Economics* (Oxford, Blackwell, 1987).

31. Coleman, J. L., *Markets, Morals and the Law* (Cambridge, Cambridge University Press, 1988), p. 253.
32. *Ibid.*, p. 312.
33. *Ibid.*, p. 313.
34. For a review of fallacies involving the Pareto principle, see Sager, L. G. (1980), Pareto superiority, consent and justice, *Hofstra Law Review* vol. 8 pp. 913–938.
35. Sen, A. (1987), *op. cit.*, p. 31.
36. Heald, D., *Public Expenditure* (Oxford, Martin Robertson, 1983), p. 8.
37. Aristotle, *Nicomachean Ethics* 1.1 1–5, trans. Ross (1980) pp. 1–7.
38. Plant, R., *Equality, Markets and the New Right* (London, Fabian Tract No. 494, 1984), p. 8.
39. *Ibid.*
40. Heald, D. (1983), *op. cit.*, p. 9.
41. Dworkin, R., *A Matter of Principle* (Oxford, Oxford University Press, 1985), p. 195.
42. Nozick, R. (1974), *op. cit.*, p. 160.
43. Gibbard, A. (1985), *op. cit.*, p. 25.
44. Hayek, F. A., *Law, Legislation and Liberty, Vol. 2, The Mirage of Social Justice* (London, Routledge and Kegan Paul, 1982), p. 98.
45. Hayek, F. A., *The Constitution of Liberty* (London, Routledge and Kegan Paul, 1960), p. 257.
46. See much work of the 'Austrian school' of economics, also Lavoie, D., *Rivalry and Central Planning: the Socialist Calculation Debate Reconsidered* (Cambridge, Cambridge University Press, 1985).
47. Polanyi, M., *The Logic of Liberty* (Chicago, University of Chicago Press, 1951).
48. I owe that typology of global verdicts on markets to Campbell, T. D., Markets and justice, *Justice and the Market, Occasional Paper 21* (Centre for Theology and Public Issues, University of Edinburgh, Edinburgh, 1991).
49. Bellamy, R. (1992), *op. cit.*, p. 218.
50. cf. "The Great Education Debate" announced by Prime Minister Callaghan as a key political feature of 1976.
51. What constitutes 'democratic legitimacy' is of course the subject of considerable debate. This is well illustrated by these issues as at no time did a majority of the electorate cast their votes for the party driving relevant reforms. However, the party concerned was constitutionally elected, securing for its first three administrations a steadily increased parliamentary majority, though at no time did that reflect the endorsement of more than a minority of the electorate.
52. Prime Minister Thatcher, constantly throughout her terms of office.
53. Cox , C. B. and Dyson, A. E. (eds.), *The Black Papers on Education 1–3* (London, Davis-Poynter, 1970); also *The Fight for Education: Black Paper 1975* (London, Dent, 1975); also *Black Paper 1977* (London, Temple-Smith, 1977).
54. See Dworkin, R., *Taking Rights Seriously* (London, Duckworth, 1977).

Chapter 3
Educational 'Goods': Value and Benefit

With education now among the 'goods' to be understood, distributed and consumed as if they were private goods like books, personal computers or visits to the cinema, we might look to the past for clues to public acceptance of this process of inappropriate commodification and socially unworkable privatisation. The political engine for change was clearly supplied in part by the unease, growing since the 1970s (initially under a left-wing administration), that education's preoccupation with personal development was beginning to eclipse its duties to society. It seems arguable, however, that popular acquiescence in the general neo-liberal retreat from the public planning for common experience which had characterised the post-war settlement is also to be understood as the latest consequence of failure to square the circle of individual aspiration and of equity in a competitive social context. It is those latter conflicting goals which successive educational policies have sought to align for half a century now, with failure to square that circle from the individual's perspective masking the further conflict between private and public benefit.

The unavoidable difficulty of these matters arises from the special complexity of educational value. For this is a good with value for each and value for all, where benefit on the private dimension has both intrinsic and exchange value, and benefit on the public dimension has both inherent and instrumental value. We saw in chapter one why in principle political attention might focus on education when the intention was radical social change. It was noted in chapter two that appeal was made to the virtues of the market as the best mechanism for counteracting an over-intrusive state and its welfare provision which was claimed to have depressed effort and initiative to the damage of society as a whole, and in the process to have overridden the rights and freedoms of individuals. When we analyse the complexity of education as a good, and recall the long attempt to realise its conflicting benefits, we begin to see why in practice it was also politically astute initially to direct the neo-liberal challenge towards this particular social practice.

For the project of public liberal education is a paradigm case of incipient conflicts between the good of each and the good of all, which have long been—and are still—represented in public and educational debate as the practical consequences of a battle between the contending claims of liberty and of equality. With that battle recently turned into a rout, and matters for the time being decisively settled ostensibly in favour of liberty, it has become urgent to examine the complex kinds of value which inhere in and issue from public education, and to analyse how these construct the interplay between the good of each and the good of all. There are four immediate purposes to this inquiry: to understand the face-plausibility of the recent scapegoating of education for a range of social ills; to distinguish logical from empirical obstacles to the frustration of liberal education's aims; to emphasise how these are exacerbated rather than solved by the introduction of market conditions into the constitution and distribution of education; and lastly to flag for later analysis questions about the conceptions of liberty and equality which inform not only the neo-liberal agenda but also the neutralist liberalism it seeks to eclipse. These neglected issues, rather than debate at cross-purposes about the failure—or frustrated success—of the system of public education, will be a major focus of this chapter. If there is any profit to be had from the neo-liberal determination to distribute educational goods by quasi-market mechanisms, it lies in the fact that these questions can now no longer be ignored.

PUBLIC PROJECT : PRIVATE ASPIRATIONS

From the start of the post-war re-ordering of society, with education in the vanguard of social change, these issues have lurked unattended below shifts in educational theory and policy and changes in pedagogical fashion. When we look back at trends in education policy in the UK from the 1944 to the 1988 Acts we become aware of an intractable clash between the public's personal and societal expectations of education—a clash which also obscures latent difficulties in the post-war settlement's overarching aim of social reform through individual emancipation. On closer inspection it is clear that this project—which envisaged progress not only towards greater social prosperity but towards the more equitable distribution of its benefits—depended on an implicit faith that the equal emancipation of all through equitable access to a commonly provided, individually appropriate educational experience would bring those social benefits in its wake. The unacknowledged reality that education in a modern, knowledge-based society is inescapably a positional good from many aspects, and that the good of all and the good of each interact (and often conflict) in particularly complex ways with respect to education's benefits, may well have helped to ensure that this project carried within it the seeds of periodic public discontent.

To set the scene for three decades of policies which attempted to square the public/private circle, it is useful to spell out the truism that liberal education aims at both individual and social development. The aims endorsed by society *for individuals* centre on their cognitive emancipation "from the present and particular"[1] through increased knowledge and understanding. At the same time each individual also seeks for her/himself (through the exchange value of that knowledge) a favourable particular position if not in 'the present' at least in the immediate future as presently envisaged. The aims endorsed by society *for society* are on the one hand the realisation of the collective goals of social equity and harmony and on the other the efficient development of a pool of human capital for effective competition in a global economy. To suppose these twin objectives compatible is to believe they can be achieved by means consistent with the separate maximal development of the differing talents and potential of diverse individuals.[2] It is not difficult to see that there are latent contradictions within these aspirations on both the individual and the social dimensions. And if this were not bad enough, further incompatibilities arise between them, since each citizen in a democracy expects the public education system to deliver the full set of (conflicting) public benefits to society as a whole at the same time as it supplies her/him with the private opportunity to rise above collective demands and to stand outside their constraints.

At the time when the project of liberal education for all was inaugurated in the UK at the end of the second world war, these contradictions were invisible, for two main reasons. In the world of theory, neutralist liberalism was at its height with political belief in the 'end of ideology' in respect of 'liberal' (non-communist and non-fascist) societies, and with the eclipse of substantive moral and political philosophy by the ostensibly aseptic procedures of linguistic analysis and conceptual clarification. This eclipse took scrutiny of the conceptions of liberty and equality in play during that period, and of the relation between individual and social well-being, off the agenda of debate. Meanwhile, in the world of social practices, the pervasive inequalities of wealth and opportunity which had characterised the social world pre-war were the primary targets for reform as the public sought to create the kind of society which could offer to all the freedoms which all had made sacrifices to defend. A series of reforms in health care, unemployment insurance, state pension provision, etc. were democratically instituted, collectively comprising a welfare state designed to wipe out the scourges of "ignorance, idleness, disease and want". Pre-eminent among these reforms was free access for all to a meritocratic system of public education.

Reform of education, legislated for in the 1944 and 1945 Acts, was pre-eminent not just because this was considered a central social practice from which past inequities should be removed as one part of a broad reconstitution of the social order, but also because education was seen to be a key means to broader social transformation. Moreover, it was also seen to hold the key to social advancement for individuals. Since in a class-stratified pre-war society, social position in terms of wealth and opportunity had clearly been correlated with access to and experience of liberal education, it is not surprising that a causal relation between equitable access to educational provision and more egalitarian social relations was widely assumed. It thus seemed reasonable to suppose that to detach that access and experience from social origin, and attach it instead to merit and effort, would lead to a more morally defensible distribution of wealth and opportunity. Furthermore, democratic confidence in the potential of a public whose talents had till then often been frustrated by lack of opportunity led to the belief that access for all to educational opportunity would result in a distribution of rewards which was not only morally defensible in terms of merit but also considerably more egalitarian than hitherto.

In this way the *social aims* of the project, on the dimensions both of equity and of prosperity, were to be achieved as a straightforward consequence of the realisation of its *promises to individuals*. A more equitable (and egalitarian) society would be more harmonious, and the full exploitation of the pool of underused human capital, through the appropriate development of the individual talents and potential of all, would bring the enhanced collective prosperity on which the broader project of a social welfare state depended. Since it was thus assumed that societal needs would take care of themselves, provided only that individual opportunities were appropriately provided, the 1944 and 1945 Acts represented the start of half a century of attempts to fulfil the reproductive and emancipatory functions of public education co-extensively. Looking back at the first three decades of this period we see successive high hopes followed by swift disappointment as, one by one, the empirical and theoretical assumptions which underpinned attempts to benefit all through greater opportunity for each were called into question by experience. Time and again, the response was to look for better methods of implementing goals which themselves remained largely unchallenged.

Initial post-war reforms of education were inspired both by social egalitarianism and by the need for economic reconstruction, with these two purposes to be fulfilled by the equitable development of human capital, happily coinciding with the emancipation of each/all through education. A tripartite system of secondary education (grammar, technical and secondary modern schools) was instituted in England and Wales in the 1944 Act,[3] with places in these schools allocated on the basis of cohort-screening by tests of English, arithmetic and 'general ability' at the age of eleven. Opportunity for all to experience education suited to their aptitude was for the first time extended to the end of secondary schooling irrespective of family financial circumstance (no fees being payable for tuition or books, and subsidised transport, meals and clothing available for the needy). These schooling arrangements were backed up by the provision of State Scholarships for university study, competed for nationally on the basis of public examinations. This package of reforms was seen at the time as providing equitable access for all to the experiences and opportunities which till then had been the preserve of the socio-economically well-placed.

Though the 'tri-partite system' now evokes nostalgia from the New Right for its selection, streaming and 'academic standards' and obloquy from the old left on similar grounds, the intent of these arrangements was unashamedly egalitarian at the time. Indeed their effects would arguably have been equitable (though not thereby egalitarian) had the beliefs on which they were based been true. That is to say, had it been the case, as then believed, that testing at eleven plus could reliably identify innate aptitude and potential, that differing types of provision could maximise differing types of talent, and that these differing types of provision—and aptitude—would receive parity of social esteem, then there would have been no inequity in these educational arrangements. With hindsight, of course, we know that all of the assumptions made were false. The identification of potential through IQ testing was both theoretically and empirically flawed,[4] and parity of esteem between differing types of school proved a chimera, with non-grammar schools attempting over time to approximate as closely as they could to their higher status counterparts, compounding the entrenched belief that only certain types of aptitude and education were of real value.

Thus within a decade this initial attempt to square the circles of social progress and individual emancipation (with each and/or all as ambiguous beneficiaries) brought disappointment to many. The meritocratic tri-partite system of secondary education came under attack for perpetuating class divisions and reproducing rather than transforming social structure, and by the end of its second decade was seen as a bastion of elitism and inegalitarianism. The cohort-screening at age eleven was judged to allocate both educational and social failure to the majority of children before they even left their primary schools, with success in the competition correlating worryingly closely with social origin and cultural capital. There *were* undeniable benefits to individuals, with the meritocratic intent of reforms working effectively for some. However, hard evidence shows that the lower down the social scale one looked, the less likely were the chances of social promotion through this educational route for given individuals. When this writer (who started school in the year of the 1944 Act) obtained a State Scholarship for university study in the late 1950s, the odds against doing so for a female from the Registrar General's lowest social class were estimated statistically as one thousand times greater than for a professional class male. As the fairness or otherwise in practice of the meritocratic competition was debated, its problems in principle were largely ignored.

These were obscured, not for the last time, both by the practical failures of educational arrangements to live up to their ideals, as noted above, and also by their (limited) successes. The fact that *in individual cases* the goals of equity and prosperity were simulta-neously achieved for some led public and policy-makers to continue the long search for more effective means of extending these benefits to all. For when the aims of the project remain unquestioned, and fault is ascribed to failure in the process of implementation, there are only two directions for the allocation of blame. Either there are shortcomings in the educational process, or there are inherent inadequacies in its intended beneficiaries. (It is of course possible to compound this diagnosis by ascribing blame in both directions, as did many members of the cabinet which a generation later first introduced market mechanisms into the UK education service. For many of those reformers were among the earliest beneficiaries of post-war meritocratic arrangements and apparently still believed that since they had succeeded 'by their own efforts', all could do the same.)

So when the failure of meritocracy to benefit more than a small proportion of individuals became the focus of attention in the late 1950s and early 1960s, this was seen as a problem requiring a solely educational solution. Scant attention was given to the limits of what such a project could have achieved even if all the empirical obstacles could have been overcome. A thought experiment would have shown that *even if* talent and potential could have been reliably identified and provided for, and *even if* parity of esteem had been accorded, this would not of itself have brought about the egalitarian changes which had earned the meritocratic project its democratic support at its inception. For unless that parity of esteem in educational terms had also been matched by parity of social status and reward, the removal of social class and financial barriers to appropriate educational experience would not of itself have brought significant structural change to the social order. Whilst a successful educational meritocracy might allocate social position according to criteria which would arguably be somewhat less arbitrary than accident of birth, no such meritocracy, even were it achievable, could deliver to all the enhanced social opportunities which all were promised. To make this point is not to echo the counsel of despair of reproduction theorists who claim that schooling can do no other than reproduce existing social divisions and stratifications. It is simply to note that since *one* function (though not the only function) of schooling is to allocate social position through education's exchange value (which is not its only value) and hence to provide *part* of the legitimation for a given social structure, so education of itself cannot radically alter social structure directly. At best it modifies who comes to sit where within the hierarchy of status and reward, thus modifying the nature and range of stratification slowly and indirectly. To express the same point logically rather than sociologically: one aspect of the complexity of educational goods is that its exchange value for individuals is necessarily positional.

Practical disappointment with the meritocratic project did generate considerable theoretical debate during the 1960s, but this was largely a dialogue of the deaf between on the one hand sociologists of education and Marxist and neo-Marxist philosophers of education who subscribed to reproduction theory, and on the other neutralist liberal philosophers of education who denied the inevitability of social reproduction and continued to endorse an open social future through the emancipation of individuals. For the former, who were concerned primarily with schooling's exchange value, education was at best a side-show with reforms diverting public attention from the need for social overhaul, and at worst a sop to enable each to believe that they might be the lucky winners in an unfair distribution of social rewards. For the latter, the chief concern remained liberal education's intrinsic value, since this was believed anyway to bring incremental social change through the cognitive emancipation of individuals and consequent more even allocation of social reward, provided only that access, content and process were appropriately designed. Both wings of this dispute focused on education's benefit to the individual, with its value construed in wholly individualist terms. Controversy turned accordingly to common, comprehensive provision versus meritocratic selection, to content selection driven by social versus epistemological considerations, and to child- or learner-centred pedagogy versus control of process in accordance with teacher expertise and epistemological authority.

As the 1960s progressed, the gradual replacement of the tri-partite system through the abolition of the eleven-plus selection procedure in all but a few Local Authorities and the establishment of common provision in secondary comprehensive schools, accompanied by pedagogical reform of the primary sector and large-scale expansion of the tertiary sector, together promised to address the popular disappointment which had followed the well-intentioned post-war policies of reform. Dissent, which raised the spectre of decline in academic standards (and/or the end of a 'fast-track' for the very able, highly-motivated underprivileged) remained grounded in dispute primarily about the means to education's goals. Gradually, a new educational dispensation, which it was hoped would deliver at last on earlier promises of egalitarian change through individual benefit, received democratic endorsement. Again, within a decade, dissatisfaction began to grow with yet another set of educational arrangements which had again been oversold as the means to enable 'all' to succeed. With common access to comprehensive schools in place, sociologists of knowledge now blamed 'schooling failure' on inappropriate and class-biased curricula, policy-makers extended public examinations to a larger proportion of the age-cohort and raised the minimum leaving age to improve motivation and participation rates respectively, and practitioners looked for more effective teaching styles and modes of classroom organisation. Still unaddressed was the logical point that although in principle all could succeed in *educational* terms under better schooling arrangements which removed social barriers to the intrinsic value outcomes of learning experiences offered (and indeed, despite subsequent polemic, general levels of achievement rose significantly), no arrangements, however ideal, could bring for all the pay-off in social advancement that all expected from the exchange value of educational outcomes. Nor indeed was there any attention, in practice or in theory, to the implicit assumption that the benefit of all would follow from (or be comprised by) the elusive benefit of each.

The focus of debate remained on searching for means to achieve the individual aims endorsed for the project (with its benefits to society assumed to follow in their wake), to the neglect of the prior question of which among our personal and social goals could coherently be simultaneously achieved by educational means. Debate (worthwhile and important in itself) continued to focus on the conduct of education for maximal individual growth and development, with policy-makers and the educational establishment taking stances on the basis of differing priorities, and discussion of means muddied by unacknowledged conflicts between ends. This still continues. When the intrinsic value of education is at issue, conflicts between egalitarian aims and individual demands for freedom to develop and achieve differentially underlie disputes about the public provision of appropriate content and process. When the exchange value of education is in focus, conflicts between social equality ideals and the demands of social efficiency through schooling and training (best served by priority for the holders of readily convertible cultural capital) lie beneath disputes about access and common provision.

And throughout we hold in tension the personal expectations individuals have of education with the perceived needs of society which those same individuals also expect the education system to serve. The project thus generates individual frustration for many, compounded at a different level by growing collective unease that past investment in public education has not produced the inevitable increases in national prosperity and social harmony which had been confidently anticipated as the longer-term consequence of equitable access thirty years before.

Thus when in the mid-1970s economic recession brought political disquiet with the level of return on past investment in public education, and when this was compounded by popular disillusion with public services in general in a shrinking economy at the end of the decade, the time was ripe for a scapegoating of education. And the time was particularly ripe for an attack on past policy and provision which challenged the preserves of professionals in the name of the rights of individuals. For once again, in an increasingly uncertain social situation, individuals were seeking someone or something to blame for their economic anxieties and disappointed hopes of social advancement. Just as disillusion with post-war meritocratic reforms in education, which had promised that any person with sufficient ability and motivation could get to the top, had set in with the belated public realisation that 'any' does not mean 'all', except in the ambiguous sense that 'any' person can gain a place in the national football team, so the honeymoon of common provision for all was coming to an end. For as meritocratic reforms had been replaced during the 1960s by the gradual adoption of comprehensive secondary schooling, this had again been oversold to the public as a mechanism for *really* giving room for all at the top. When this expansionary vision and its egalitarian aspirations in turn came into question, public disillusion was ripe for political manipulation. And the need to address twin conundra in our expectations of education continued to be ignored as professionals defended a system under attack and politicians piloted a radical shift in social ethos within that social practice which is most crucial to the production of both structure and value. For this shift, as we shall see, compounds all earlier confusions by strengthening the power of education as a force for social reproduction at the same time as it further exacerbates the competition for its private benefits.

CONFLICTING EXPECTATIONS: PUBLIC BENEFIT AND PRIVATE REWARD

Two sources of contradiction, then, lie at the heart of the public project of liberal education for all as it has been envisaged over the past half-century. One of them was aired more than a decade ago by Hollis in his paper "Education as a positional good"[5], and will be pursued in the next section. The second, internally related to the first, concerns the mutually contradictory expectations which each of us entertains for the social and individual outcomes of public education. During policy debates in the 1970s about return on investment in education these conflicts remained ignored. Shortly after, popular acceptance was sought and gained by a subsequent New Right administration blaming rapidly rising youth unemployment and associated social unrest on claimed failures in past educational policy and practice—and promising to remedy these by giving parents as consumers the right to compete with each other for the more desirable options within uneven provision delivering unequal outcomes. The plausibility of those claims, and the popular appeal of the deregulatory measures designed to address them, is grounded, I shall argue, in these two souces of contradiction.

If we wish to understand how slow and partial success can suddenly be represented as failure when the self-interest of the fortunate combines with the frustration of the less fortunate to lead a society to turn its back on a long process of social reform, one quite crucial but largely unrecognised point must be made. This concerns the special nature of education as the one social project on which each of us in a democracy *necessarily* makes twin and incompatible demands. When we look closely at these conflicting demands, it is clear that so long as we continue to see public education as simply a matter of extending to all, those aims and procedures which were originally endorsed by and for a minority elite, the project is bound to disappoint some of our contradictory expectations. For each member of society stands in a dual relation to education, being at the same time providers who fund this social practice and both direct and indirect recipients of its benefits. As providers and indirect recipients each expects collective benefits, in both social and economic terms, whereas as direct participants each seeks personal emancipation through intrinsic value and individual advantage through exchange value. So this public project is expected at the same time to deliver social benefits to all of us collectively and individual benefits to each of us separately. Collectively, we expect it to deliver economic growth and social stability, with whatever divisions of labour (and concomitant disparities in aspiration) are conducive to those ends. But individually, we each want from it personal emancipation and relative socio-economic advantage. Given that these demands are embedded in a social context where technological development and global economics require a wide spectrum of skill and knowledge with an associated range of status and reward, we clearly have a stark problem when each of us seeks, through participation in education, a position at the more favourable end of that spectrum or range.

Since this conundrum of conflicting expectations arises as a consequence of full democracy and equal citizenship, it creeps up invisibly in societies which have developed democratic rights and educational reforms incrementally over long periods of time, as in the UK. Given its invisibility under those conditions, individual disappointment with social position, and democratic disappointment with public culture and conduct—and GNP—tends to be politically interpretable as a dissatisfaction with the prevailing conduct of education, amenable to improved pedagogy, more appropriate curriculum and/or changes in access. All of these things are important, of course, and all require continuous re-evaluation. Nonetheless, attention solely to these intra-educational factors enables us to evade an uncomfortable reality: in a social structure which has little choice but to be internally competitive as well as collaborative (in order to be externally competitive under conditions of globalisation), the clash between private aspiration and public expectation from education is an unwelcome side-effect of democratic citizenship in modernity. (If ignored, it can only become exacerbated in a globalised world in which many of the social as well as the individual outcomes of education also become positional, as the next section will show.)

We can see the problem in sharp focus by looking back, say to the nineteenth century in the UK, to a time when the twin functions of education under liberalism—both social reproduction and the emancipation of individuals who would take forward an open future—were separately deemed appropriate (by those in power) to different groups within society. In looking back we see that the collective benefits which we look for now *as providers and indirect beneficiaries of education* are little different from the benefits once sought by paternalistic providers who a century ago funded public education for others than themselves. Those providers expected increased labour-market fitness and productivity in the general population and the development of a pool of human capital only insofar as that was consistent with social stability and control. As providers through universal taxation, we now all require much the same collective outcomes. *As direct participants in liberal education* on the other hand, we each also seek the individual advantage and personal emancipation which minority providers of public education once sought from their separate private arrangements for themselves and their own children. Today, in our contemporary role as providing participants, we all, severally, seek an advantageous position in the evolving economic situation and an active social role in defining and modifying the parameters of stability and control. It is clear therefore that under modern, democratic conditions, where the group of providers becomes coextensive with the (now theoretically homogeneous) group of beneficiaries, *the collective benefits we expect from the extension to all of a liberalising education are not compatible with the aggregate fulfilment of our individual aspirations as participants in a project we collectively underwrite.*

To sum up this conundrum, we each look to the public provision of education for two kinds of pay-off: the smooth social and economic functioning of a diversified society, and, for ourselves, self-development, emancipation and social advancement. The more of us that receive the second kind of pay-off, the less manageable the former becomes. And conversely, the more we try to engineer socio-economic efficiency, the more we ensure not only that some must lose out in the individual emancipation stakes, but that current inequalities will strongly influence just who those some will be. This is the impasse in which many societies with formally equitable educational access currently find themselves. To put the matter starkly, it could be argued that the long liberal education reform project began to run into trouble, not because past reformist measures had failed, but because they had begun sufficiently to succeed in delivering education's emancipatory aims that they were no longer efficiently meeting parts of its package of social goals. And in delivering emancipatory aims to many, they continued to raise the hopes and deepen the disappointment of those left behind in the social project. Hence the subsequent neo-liberal emphasis on 'schooling' and 'training' the public, together with deregulatory policies to deliver emancipatory outcomes to those most likely to succeed (or least willing to acquiesce in failure) in a heightened social competition.

That something might well eventually give in that clash of demands is clear to see. Where frustration has prompted the public to demand or endorse an education policy response, there have seemed for fifty years now to be only two possibilities. The first has been to continue seeking social change through individual emancipation, with changes to educational arrangements which progressively attenuated, delayed or disguised the inescapable logical point that in a competitive social structure the exchange value of educational attainments is a positional good. This approach to the problem results at best in meritocracy and at worst in the reproduction of structural inequalities. Planned policies for open access to common provision in schooling produce the least worst outcomes here, but still outcomes which lead to the individual disaffection of many as well as to general disappointment with promised public benefit. Public education thus remains vulnerable to disaffection when it fails to deliver outcomes beyond its purview. In part, this can explain popular acquiescence in the wave of 'reforms' brought by the second and more recent response to conflicting goals. This latest response has been to exploit latent disenchantment by thoroughly individualising the whole enterprise, letting the forces of the market replace planned policy, thus giving individuals the belief that their advancement is in their own power: *a reassurance which may be valid for any, but cannot be true for all.*

This amounts to a new evasion of the old contradictions and a partial return to a previously rejected resolution of the tension between education's public and private benefits, in which some fulfil the demands of social reproduction whilst any can compete for emancipation. Increased individual competition for provision of diverse type and quality brings to an end many decades of attempts to offer a common educational experience to all, but in the new dispensation, the inevitable relative failure of some—which assigns them to social roles which all require to be performed, but preferably by others—is not the fault of policy, requiring additional resourcing or improved process for schooling. What each must seek in this re-ordering of society are additional means (extended deregulation, further rights of choice and control, greater 'product' information) to ensure that society's less desirable—but nonetheless necessary—roles and positions do not fall to them.

What we have here seems to be a classic conflation of the good of each with the good of all. Priority for the former, with the latter either downgraded or assumed simply to follow (as a consequence of trickle-down theories of economics, of culture and of welfare), is openly espoused by neo-liberals. Priority for the latter, to the perceived neglect or detriment of individual good, is clearly unacceptable to any who endorse a liberal theory of the state. Liberalism, and liberal public education, have long held the two in uneasy tension. That tension (exacerbated under modern, democratic conditions) rests on early liberal assumptions about the relationship between the individual and the social, in which the workings of a continuous process of moral meritocracy were expected to entrain the steady expansion of social freedom (with its material prerequisites) and its equitable distribution. That this balancing act can no longer be performed must therefore alert us to deeper problems at the heart of modern liberalism itself. First, further attention is needed to the public and private benefits of that emancipatory practice on which the maintenance of a liberal polity depends.

THE VALUE OF EDUCATIONAL 'GOODS'

With most goods in the social market treated as equivalent for purposes of distribution, whether they be public or private, individual or social, differing anomalies arise with varying 'goods', and these are perhaps most complex in the case of education. Advocates of the market make exception for what are acknowledged to be 'public goods', with a standard indicative list comprising national defence, law-enforcement, a stable monetary system, street-lighting. Where (as in Hayek) there is concern for a necessary component of culture in public life, the state is also entitled to ensure that there is provision of museums, libraries, schools, etc. As long as provision exists, however, it is not the business of the state to police or mediate access. Thus it is deemed a public good that there should be both education and schooling, sufficient to ensure national prosperity and a continued cultural heritage: it is not so deemed that its private value—intrinsic or exchange—should be evenly spread. Indeed, to do so would be to devalue and depress individual effort, to frustrate the social aims of efficient return on public investment, and to neglect the need for a diversified range of aspiration and attitude consistent with society's diverse roles and demands. In this, neo-liberals part company from their classical forebears who were concerned with the extension of liberty to all, rather than simply with its optimum exercise by each. (They do so as a consequence of their beliefs about the relation between the social order and the distribution of knowledge, understanding and skill within it, to which I shall return towards the end of my analysis.)

Now a public good is thought of as something of benefit to all which cannot be subdivided into individual shares and can thus only be effectively provided by all, for all. In the case of national defence and other standard examples, this is clear: these goods are funded through universal taxation and provided by the state on behalf of all to obviate the possibility of 'free-riding' by individual citizens. If contribution to the costs of such goods were voluntary, all would have an incentive, as rational utility-maximisers, to abstain provided they could assume that a sufficient number of others would not do so. It is legitimate to insist that all contribute, since all potentially stand equally to benefit. By these standard criteria, it is evident that on the dimension of benefit to society (prosperity, a prerequisite range of knowledge and skill, a certain level of culture and civility, a necessary level of social harmony and co-operation) education is a public good. But it is equally evident that on the dimension of benefit to the individual, education appears to be a private good from which all do not—and in many respects cannot—stand to benefit equally. This point will need to be returned to later, but the initial consequence is that in an inescapably social world, 'goods' are too complex to be neatly divided into two categories, with those which are deemed unproblematically 'public' to be commonly provided and enjoyed under regulated conditions, and all the others to be deemed 'private' and best distributed and competed for through the market. (That the over-simple dichotomy between the public and the private most obviously breaks down in the case of education which so clearly falls into both notional categories goes some way towards explaining the apparently schizoid neo-liberal approach to educational reform, whereby content and process merits closer state supervision whilst distribution merits deregulation. This double-aspect approach relies, as I have noted, on the belief either that the constitution of education is unaffected by its manner of distribution or indeed that it is most likely to be enhanced by a market distribution.)

That for the purposes of its distribution nonetheless, education is treated as if it fell squarely in the category of private goods, should not be seen as merely a malign device by the New Right to wind back the advances in equity gained in part by educational reform over the previous decades. For this new direction for policy bases its claims to legitimacy on an old problem of theory. It was noted in chapter two that many early liberals were uneasy about the boundary between the public and the private spheres, acknowledging that in a finite world many goods which all require for their well-being are not of the sort where each can legitimately enjoy what each has merited, whilst leaving in the words of Locke "enough and as good" for others. And in the intervening period, theories of the market have long wrestled with the problem of public goods, which present problems of over-supply (and bureaucratic extensions of power) in periods of expansion, and of under-supply in periods of retrenchment, whether for economic or political reasons (hence Galbraith's "private affluence and public squalor").

Meanwhile, for half a century now, as we saw in the previous section, whilst for policy-makers and citizens as taxpayers education has been seen as a public good from which *collective* return on investment was expected, educational theorists and professionals, and citizens as participants in education, have envisaged it as a private good, for personal development and private advancement. For sociologists of education, emphasis was on the latter; for philosophers of education, primarily on the former. Thus Oakeshott, Peters and many following them emphasised the intrinsic value of education to the individual, on the grounds that knowledge and understanding seemed like just the kinds of things where addition to one person's holding does not diminish (and may well increase) what is left available to others.[6] Bowles and Gintis, Young, Harris *et al.*, on the other hand, focused on its exchange value for individuals, dismissing talk of "learning for its own sake" as a luxury of the privileged at best, or at worst complicity in long-standing structural inequalities.[7] As so often in dialogues of the deaf, what those two camps shared was more significant (in virtue of its invisibility) than what divided them. Shared was the underlying assumption that a focus on education's goals for the individual—however these were prioritised—would in some unspecified way (provided only that process and/or access were appropriately ordered) also advance the common good. Thus the neo-liberal stance, that education is a private good, best distributed by the market, shares in many ways the rhetoric of past theory as well as the perspective of participants in this social practice over a very long period.

What has been under-emphasised in theorising about education, as in public debate, is that this practice is irredeemably social. Despite recent formal acknowledgement of this point, its significance for the public project of mass liberal education has yet to be fully explored. If we are to gain a better understanding of how the good of each and the good of all relate to each other, and escape from the theoretical paradoxes and practical problems which arise when we assume without warrant that the latter flows from the former by happy accident, there may be no better context in which to examine this long-standing problem at the heart of liberalism—in all its forms— than the public project of education with its specially complex forms of value. To begin, two kinds of question must be addressed. It is first necessary to enquire what kinds of value all collectively and each individually expect from that practice, and additionally to examine which of these benefits is a necessarily scarce resource, or more fatally still is positional in character. For where a good is necessarily scarce, it logically cannot be enjoyed by all, but must be competed for.[8] And wherever a benefit is positional, it is not merely that the good of each logically cannot sum to the good of all by some mysterious natural process, but rather that the good of some entails, or is dependant on, the lesser benefit of others. Where 'goods' are either positional or necessarily scarce, the good of all can only be pursued if care is explicitly taken to ensure that benefits are not cumulative, and if some distributional principle is adopted to ensure that such benefits, as special social advantages, also benefit those who have not personally received them.[9]

Looking firstly at the public dimension, what then are the benefits society seeks from its funding of schools, colleges, universities, training programmes, etc.? That there is an economic function for all of this is undeniable, and it could not be otherwise. Without a reasonably healthy economy, the public provision of education could not itself be funded, let alone what have come to be normal expectations in public, social and private life. If the apparatus of public education turned out a generation incapable—through defects in knowledge, skill, attitude or behaviour—of maintaining and developing a healthy economy, the system would surely be failing to provide a reasonable return on investment. Neo-liberal demands for reform have indeed been accompanied by much talk of "the needs of society" and of the education system's failure to serve them. Publicly, it has been argued that the content of education needed revision to move away from a mandarin experience few wanted and collectively society could not afford towards more 'relevant' knowledge and skills: off-stage, in neo-liberal think-tanks and policy position-papers it was argued that liberal education for all raised expectations unrealistically and cultivated attitudes which for many were inappropriate to their likely social situation.[10]

This discrepancy between rhetoric and rationale in discussion of society's needs points to the fact that there is a strong positional element in the educational means to securing the economic good of all in a complex, technologically developed society. Though there is indeed a collective requirement for internationally competitive economic performance (to provide the means of funding differing aspirations), this does not translate into a need for public education to produce mostly rocket scientists, captains of industry or brain surgeons. Even were one to accept the economistic agenda, and to suppose that a primary function of education is to fuel the process of wealth creation, it must be the case that when social roles are functionally related but differentially rewarded (and differentially desirable irrespective of material or status benefits), if educational preparation is to match a range of functions, then the educational experience of some will be more personally emancipatory than that of others. And conversely, if it is not so matched, then the educational experience of some will coincide more closely with their later expectations and experience than will that of others.

To make that point is simply to note that ostensibly unproblematic talk of the needs of society obscures the fact that the more a society is functionally differentiated, the less do the *interests of each* coincide when we focus on the means to securing even what all agree to constitute the good of all. A similar problem arises with respect to the *attitudes of each*. Again, at the start of this latest reform period, the education system was castigated for failing to inculcate appropriate values: for fostering insufficient interest in enterprise, industry and commerce, and for neglecting to pass on those attitudes of loyalty and acceptance without which the "moral glue" of society (in Hollis's apt phrase[11]) risks becoming dissolved. Again, it is clearly the case that any society, however open and liberal, requires the basic allegiance of its members. However, the more differentiated the society is in terms of status and reward, the greater is the variation in congruence between a given individual's allegiance to the status quo (or an incrementally modified version of that) and her/his material interests. There thus seems also to be a positional element in education's necessary role in constructing personal and social values.

In those values which make direct reference to the economy, this can be clearly seen by recent policy responses in the UK to claimed attitudinal deficits in the young. Whilst tertiary institutions receive additional funding for "Enterprise Initiatives", and upper secondary schools are encouraged to enter pupils into business partnerships, so, correspondingly, 'social education' programmes for low achievers and training schemes for those who leave school at sixteen emphasise malleability, acceptance of authority, and preparation for social compliance.[12] Meanwhile, a positional element can be discerned even in those broader values and attitudes which do not relate directly to economic function. For whilst at high levels of generality we seek to pass on similar dispositions to all—towards independence of thought and action, personal responsibility, persistence and determination, respect for truth, courage in the face of injustice, etc.—the range of future social roles available ensures that each draws differing instrumental value from such dispositions when they are expressed in concrete social circumstance (some social positions requiring, for example, self-direction, some penalising its expression).

A third acknowledged public benefit of education is the maintenance of a cultural heritage, and a general level of culture and civility in the polity. It is perhaps in respect of this function that there is greatest open dispute across the spectrum of educational opinion. Among educational traditionalists, what constitutes the cultural heritage in question is fairly clear: what is open to dispute is the educational requirements for its maintenance. Thus whilst some conservatives argue that it is pointless and wasteful to cast pearls before swine—that what matters is that the torch is carried forward, burning brightest when in the hands of suitable initiates,[13] so others devise lists of texts and cultural items thought indispensable to all.[14] Meanwhile, mainstream liberal education theory exhibits varying degrees of caution about what constitutes culture, but is clear that it should be both open to contestation and made available to all. For many others, that caution is not enough, with culture seen as radically various and relative either to ethnic, class or gender perspective, or indeed to personal taste. From these latter positions it may either be maintained that the cultural content of education should be radically revised, or that any such content would necessarily be an unjustifiable privileging of one set or amalgam of values. Now with the first of all these stances (cultural heritage requires the relevant education of some), positionality is overt from any perspective, since the heritage concerned is admittedly not that of all, and its maintenance has a high opportunity-cost borne by all. With the second (that it requires the similar relevant education of all) and the third (that, subject to negotiation on content, the same is true), positionality would be claimed from radically pluralist, culturally relative or subjectivist perspectives, on similar grounds. And from any of those latter perspectives, the passing on of a *common* heritage is not a good of any sort. Thus the maintenance of a cultural heritage as a public benefit of education is hotly contested (whatever the tenability of varying challenges): without agreement on what that common heritage might be, either it is no public good at all, or it too is to some degree positional in character.

The fourth public benefit hoped for throughout a century of incremental reform, and adopted as an explicit aim of policy from the 1940s to the 1970s, was the gradual dissolution of inherited class hierarchy and the establishment of a more egalitarian social world. Now were it achievable, social equality (if agreed to be a good) would be neither scarce in principle nor positional in character, by definition. However, although this was treated as an aim empirically difficult to achieve, as repeated revisions to policy described in the first section of this chapter indicate, logical obstacles to its realisation would necessarily have prevented its realisation by primarily educational means. This once hoped-for benefit cannot be delivered by education to more than a limited extent simply because, whatever contention there may be about the latent positionality of the three public benefits already listed, there is a fifth still to consider which is uncontroversially and overtly positional. To be precise on the matter of social equality through educational means: supposing the successful removal of all empirical obstacles, inherited class hierarchy could in principle be drastically diminished, and with supporting social change, eliminated. (Conversely, of course, it can be re-inforced by educational policy.) *Social equality*, however, rather than *the inheritance of social advantage or disadvantage*, is another matter, being logically unrealisable by educational means, as consideration of a final public benefit will show.

That fifth benefit to society as a whole is basic to the enterprise of public education, but less widely advertised than the first four here. Hollis draws attention to general coyness about this—an ambivalence which arises because this is where the good of all and the good of each clearly do not sit comfortably together. He points out: "Employers pay taxes partly so that there are schools to pre-select labour for them. Schools earn their bread and butter therefore by differentiating and ranking their students. Students demand of schools to be equipped for success in the division of labour. This symbiosis is somewhat discreet and, when talked about, is usually dressed in an absolutist language of quality, specialisation and opportunity. But it is undeniably at work".[15] The veil drawn over this "symbiosis" is no sinister conspiracy of silence: to down-play it is basic to teacher morale, to learner motivation and indeed to the success of the educational enterprise in educational terms. For the silent exhortation of educators in home or school can only be 'If you work hard, you will do well'. It would be unpersuasive and not at all uplifting to add the corollary ' . . . only of course if others do less well'. For this fifth public benefit of education—the sorting of the next generation for diverse social roles—is inescapably positional, and no promotion of co-operation rather than competition between pupils during the learning process, nor any replacement of norm-referenced testing by criterion referencing of tests (however desirable for other reasons), can eliminate that function of education, though it can delay or disguise it. It is, moreover, independent of the efforts of teachers and learners as categories of individuals, and of the overall level of 'educational standards', for "the better the comprehensive schools do in raising the number of well-qualified applicants for the nation's jobs, the less their efforts will count when it comes to placing them",[16] or as Hirsch notes, "if everyone stands on tiptoe, no-one sees better".[17] (It might be objected here that this is an over-simplification which takes too little account of economic and technological development: though there is no space to do so here, that objection can be rebutted on the grounds that the inevitable positionality of education's instrumental economic benefits is not infinitely exportable in a globalising and finite world.)

This fifth public benefit brings us to the private dimension: to the benefits that each seeks from education on his/her own behalf. These have both intrinsic and instrumental value, with value-in-exchange associated uncontroversially at least with the latter. And the exchange value of knowledge and skill (as of what is broadly termed 'cultural capital'), as well as more obviously of formal credentials, is clearly positional in character. For as Hollis noted, educational attainments are in some respects like numbered lithographs, having additional worth to those who gain them precisely because not everybody gains them".[18] Clearly, even if in an ideal world all poor teachers could be eliminated, all social effects discounted, and resources indefinitely increased, not all children could go to schools which produced mostly high flyers. For to fly high under those circumstances, some would have to fly higher still. To the individual then, education's value-in-exchange is necessarily positional, whatever our educational or social arrangements, though the social consequences of that logical point depend upon the arrangements for economic and social life which we endorse.

To all of the above it may be objected that the benefits enumerated so far leave out what liberal education's theorists and practitioners hold to be its primary purpose: the development of rationally and morally autonomous individuals through the fostering of cognitive ability, interests and character. These are the private intrinsic benefits of education, of which exchange value for the individual is simply a side-effect and from which various public benefits for society in general incidentally follow. This primary educational good cannot surely be positional, or even subject to scarcity, since my learning causes no-one's ignorance, my talents harm no-one and may well benefit others, and my autonomy, morally exercised, cannot inhibit the development or exercise of a like autonomy in others. And indeed this seems plausible, all things being equal, at the level of abstract argument. In the real world, however, where time and resources are finite, where we become increasingly mutually inter-dependent as social and material complexities multiply, and where the tastes and preferences of each must be negotiated with those of others, all things are almost never equal.

At this point it must be remembered that we are considering the goods which individuals may gain from *the social practice of public education*. We are not considering the nurturing of a single mind and soul, in private, by private means fairly gained, for private flourishing in a solipsistic world. Given that proviso, education's intrinsic goods, though personal, are not purely private, since they all have a social dimension and social parameters. What counts as my learning depends not merely on what I know, but also on what others know; my learning has an opportunity-cost which affects what others come to know; and the value of my learning to me depends to varying degrees on social and material conditions developed and inhabited by others. Similarly, what counts as a talent in me depends on the skills, abilities and valuations of others; the development of any talent has an opportunity-cost borne by others as well as the talented; and my exercise and enjoyment of my talent, as well as its development, depends to varying degrees on the skills, abilities and valuations of others who share, admire, facilitate or merely tolerate its exercise. Finally, we could only suppose that my autonomy, responsibly exercised, does not restrict the similar autonomy of others if we believed that the talents and preferences of each will harmonise and sum to a collective reality which equally permits their expression, or if we supposed instead that the talents and preferences of some are inherently restricted. The former of these possibilities was the pious hope of nineteenth-century liberalism: the latter is the implicit counsel of despair of neo-liberalism. Both of these positions can be shown to be theoretically untenable,[19] revealing a problem at the heart of liberalism in all of its forms hereto. This question will be returned to in later chapters: for now it is enough to note that even these most apparently individual benefits of education have inescapably social parameters.

To sum up, when we examine what kind of a good education is, we see that all of its hoped-for benefits, whether to the individual or to society as a whole, have an inevitable social dimension. None of its benefits are wholly private, since all result from the use of finite resources—of time, energy, commitment and cash—and finitude implies scarcity in principle. Scarcity, in turn, implies competition, with consequences for both equality and liberty, as Green pointed out a century ago: "In the stream of unrelenting competition . . . the weaker has not a chance" for when "the good is being sought in things which admit of being competed for . . . the good things to which the pursuits of society are directed turn out to be no good things for them".[20] With social goods, where supply is not unlimited and demand increases as expectations rise—as in healthcare or housing—competition brings both winners and losers, with the level of penalty for losing depending on overall levels of resourcing, beyond the control of either users or providers. Nonetheless, the obstacles to an equitable distribution of such goods as those are empirical and thus amenable to removal in principle. To temper the inequitable consequences of competition feared by Green, such goods require distributional principles which prevent the social accumulation of advantage and disadvantage. It was policies aimed at mitigating that accumulation process which were gradually put in place in the historical period between the classical liberal endorsement of the free market and the recent neo-liberal vaunting of its universal virtues.

With goods which are not only social but also positional, as I have shown education to be in many of its aspects, the situation is even more problematic, for the obstacles to an equitable distribution of these goods have a further dimension. Logical positionality ensures that pursuit of an *equal* distribution is a chimera. To note that, however, is not to abandon the claims of equity but rather to point out that the policies a society endorses for constituting and distributing such goods have an asymmetrical relation to equality. Though they cannot—as once believed—deliver social equality, they have an added potential for reproducing or increasing social *inequality*. With positional social goods, therefore, to abandon regulated distribution in favour of the forces of the market is not simply to abandon *the pursuit of equality* (which might or might not be considered inequitable), but to endorse *the ratcheting of inequality* which is clearly inequitable and demonstrably incompatible with liberalism's pursuit of the like liberty of all. This will receive fuller analysis in chapter five.

Positionality, then, becomes starker when the social world grows more competitive and increasingly differentiated in terms of material reward and status. It becomes starker still as advantages of differing kinds become cumulative. Such conditions are not merely visible outcomes of neo-liberal policies, but among that position's explicit aims. And positionality itself becomes cumulative (and less related to effort and merit) when a market distribution of education diversifies for example schooling provision and encourages parents as proxies to compete for more favourable options on behalf of learners whose capacities are yet to be developed. That distribution mechanism tends to reproduce and intensify structural inequalities (through the inter-generational transmission of advantage) even more forcefully than the ostensibly meritocratic arrangements which had previously been (rightly) found wanting on grounds of equity as well as (confusedly) on grounds of 'flat' equality. From the point of view of neo-liberal policy-makers, the foreseeable reversal of earlier equity aims is not to be regretted, since these (conflated with demands for 'flat' equality) are claimed to have depressed individual effort and educational standards. It is just one of many contradictions in their position that the accumulation of positional advantage serves rather to distance reward from the individual merit they claim to value and prioritise. However, from that same point of view, the new approach has the (dubious) advantage—through diversified provision under conditions of heightened competition—of restoring social reproduction as a central function for public education.

To emphasise the fact that education, at least, is a good both social and positional is to stress that since 'we are all members of one another' or 'no man is an island', then in at least some areas of social life ". . . benefit to each depends on benefit to all, whereas benefit to all does not guarantee benefit to each".[21] This clearly demonstrates that the long-standing attempt to distinguish between public and private goods, establishing exhaustive categories for what falls within and outwith legitimate distribution by the market—a distinction which has long troubled liberal thinkers—does not stand up to scrutiny. Still less does the neo-liberal return to a hard-line version of this distinction, with its article of faith that all goods, except those which are indivisible and can neither be privately provided or enjoyed, are best shared-out and regulated by the forces of the market. (Some might wish to claim degrees of positionality for other social goods than education. I am not concerned to explore that question here: merely to present education as the market's limiting case.) The claim of the free-marketeers is that the market is the fairest distribution mechanism for all goods except those they allow to be 'public' in the sense of indivisible. If it can be shown that this universal claim falls in respect of at least one social good, whose benefits are clearly both public and private, individual and social, its pretensions to universality are defeated. And the consequence for liberals of any hue becomes that the appropriate distributional principle for any good must be justified in terms of that good's complex and various benefits and their propensity to affect the like liberties of all.

A consideration of educational value thus highlights a long-standing difficulty in liberal theory, namely its understanding of the relationship between the individual and society. Closely connected with this is a second fault-line which lies along the relation between the good of each and the good of all. This in turn reveals serious problems with modern liberal concepts of both equality and liberty, which seem to be perennially in conflict, in spite of the fact that the former is constitutive of the latter. At the heart of contemporary concerns with re-interpretations of liberalism is the uncomfortable fact that "No-one has yet devised a system of rules to serve the general welfare which leaves no room for protest on behalf of individual freedom".[22] There are two things to be said about this. Firstly, though our current theoretical understanding gives rise to tensions we have not been able to resolve, some attempts to deal with this difficulty are clearly worse than others. Just as there are "systems of rules" which regulate so intrusively that individual freedom is seriously threatened, so there are also "systems of rules"—and a market distribution of educational goods is a paradigm case—which so prioritise individual freedom that social well-being goes to the wall. It may be that the current best practical option is simply to look for the least bad solution, which is certainly neither of these. That unsatisfactory state of affairs for practice, however, signals a second task for theory, alerting us to long-standing difficulties in our understanding of the relations between freedom, equality and equity which liberal theory struggles to resolve. For we should not imagine that *neo*-liberalism presents us with entirely new problems in social theory and pitfalls for social practice: *it merely presents more starkly in theory, and more crassly in practice, paradoxes which have long lain at the heart of neutralist liberalism.*

CONCLUSION

We cannot conclude this consideration of educational value, therefore, without flagging deep-seated difficulties in the relation between liberty, equality and equity, to which chapter five will return. Again, the educational context is an appropriate arena for this, since disputes over half a century about appropriate policies for public education (what constitutes appropriate content and pedagogy; does wider access conflict with the maintenance of standards so that "more means worse"; how do we prioritise individual and social goals; etc.?) can be seen on one level as the playing out of a long tug-of-war between the apparently competing claims of equality and of liberty. The particular conceptions of liberty and equality in play over that period require scrutiny, as they underpin the tension between individual rights and social aspirations which has not been amenable to resolution in the education context. Indeed, a focus on policy, practice and perception in public education over a fifty year period provides a key illustration of how intended social change reinforces the ideological commitments which underpin it until a clash between individual and societal aspiration (and the lessons of circumstance) forces revision. In this chapter the UK has been used as the case study illustration: the issues revealed, I believe, are extensible to relevantly similar liberal democracies. That point has now been reached in many areas of social life, across many societies: hence, in part, the recent revival of political and social philosophy.

An analysis of the education context has a particular contribution to make to this, as it makes clear that liberty and equality, whether as social values or as individual claims, are neither conceptually nor practically discrete. The tension between societal flourishing and individual rights and aspirations which has bedevilled both practical arrangements for public education and theoretical debate surrounding these arrangements can be seen to rest on a false dichotomy in which an overly 'thick' conception of equality is challenged by the competing claims of too 'thin' a conception of liberty. These apparently competing claims have caused us to believe that education's repeated failure to deliver to everyone the promises it makes to all of us arises from shortcomings with the *implementation* of the public project's aims. The latest, neo-liberal, approach does not create a new problem: it exacerbates an existing one. When exacerbated, by procedures which add further relative advantage to the already relatively advantaged, the problem is thrown into sharp relief.

The theoretical inconsistencies in the neo-liberal approach to solving a long-standing series of conflicts of interest and purpose are clear to see, since to emphasise the foreseeable inequity of that approach is not just to reassert the claims of equality, but also those of freedom. There is clearly an internal contradiction at the heart of a political programme whose principal justification is the overriding value of individual freedom when individuals are brought into exacerbated competition with each other, not just for private goods, nor additionally for social goods, but even for positional social goods like education *which are not the objects of freedom but its very constituents.* Under those circumstances, then when some *must* lose, *it is not just equity that is ill-served by giving reign to the market, but freedom itself.* This internal contradiction is only masked in public perception by our pervasive habit of judging our social arrangements primarily by their potential for individual benefit, as if the benefit of all could be unproblematically construed as the sum of the benefit to each. That pervasive habit is the unashamed hallmark of recent public policy and its justification. It also, however, lurks beneath much older policies and practices for liberal education, bedevilling its procedures and frustrating its conflicting aims. In this, that social practice (like its justifying theory) reflects the assumptions of twentieth-century liberalism with all their unresolved tensions at the same time as it seeks to realise liberal ideals.

When in the UK and other relevantly similar liberal democracies a watershed was reached in the 1970s, with recession fuelling a latent legitimation crisis for the role of the state in the provision and regulation of social goods, there were three possible ways of responding to unrealised expectations and public unease. The first was to claim, as politicians then did, that the perceived failure of public education to fulfil the aspirations of each individual in terms of both intrinsic and exchange value, and simultaneously to deliver the providing public's social expectations from this costly social service, was the fault of the people and institutions who comprised the service. The second was to counter this attack, as educators then did, by claiming that education was basically on the right track, but that more time and more resources were required for the original set of goals to be achieved in a publicly provided and regulated system. These two opposing responses made up the debate of the 1980s on education, which, along with labour relations, occupied the top of the political agenda for more than a decade. A third response would have been to shift the focus from successive difficulties in meeting conflicting public expectations to a reconsideration of those expectations themselves and the assumptions which underpin them. This reconsideration (a task for theory rather than practical politics) becomes urgent with the advent of neo-liberal policies which ratchet the social competition and offer a parody of an earlier (and democratically rejected) meritocracy, with fewer social safeguards. Scrutiny of those assumptions will therefore be the focus of chapter five, but first we must consider a further justification for prioritising the liberty of the individual; namely the appeal to individual rights which claims to make a liberal accommodation of equality redundant.

NOTES AND REFERENCES

1. Bailey, C., *Beyond the Present and Particular. A Theory of Liberal Education* (London, Routledge and Kegan Paul, 1984).
2. For the case against this supposition see, Jonathan, R. (1995a), *op. cit.*
3. And in Scotland the bi-partite system of Junior and Senior Secondary Schools after the 1945 Act.
4. See Jonathan, R., *Giftedness and Education*, 1986, report for the Scottish Office Education Department: research review and analysis of attempts over 40 years to identify and provide

for general potential and specific talents. pp. 1–110; also Simon, B., *Intelligence, Psychology and Education* (London, Lawrence and Wishart Ltd., 1971).

5. Hollis, M. (1982), Education as a positional good, *Journal of Philosophy of Education*, 16. 2, pp. 235–244.

6. Oakeshott, M., Education: the engagement and its frustration, in: Dearden, R. F., Hirst, P., Peters, R. S. (Eds.), *Education and the Development of Reason* (London, Routledge and Kegan Paul, 1972). Peters, R. S., The justification of education, in: Peters, R. S. (Ed.), *The Philosophy of Education* (Oxford, Oxford University Press, 1973).

7. Bowles, S. and Gintis, H., *Schooling in Capitalist America* (London, Routledge and Kegan Paul, 1976). Young, M. F. D. (Ed.), *Knowledge and Control* (London, Collier-Macmillan, 1971). Harris, K., *Education and Knowledge* (London, Routledge and Kegan Paul, 1979).

8. See Hirsch, F., *The Social Limits to Growth* (London, Routledge and Kegan Paul, 1971).

9. This is not necessarily to endorse Rawls' "difference principle", but simply to note that some defensible, anti-cumulative distributional principle is required.

10. I have cited some of these sources in several papers elsewhere, e.g. Jonathan, R., The manpower service model of education, *Cambridge Journal of Education*. Vol. 13, no. 2, 1983, pp. 3–10.; Jonathan, R. (1986b), *op. cit.*

11. Hollis, M. (1989), Atomic energy and moral glue, *Journal of Philosophy of Education*, 23. 2 pp. 185–193.

12. For supporting analysis of this see Jonathan, R. (1986c), Education for democratic participation, *Education and Community* (Edinburgh, Centre for Theology and Public Issues), and Jonathan, R. (1986b) *op. cit.*

13. See O'Connor, D. (1982), Two concepts of education, *Journal of Philosophy of Education*, 16.2, pp. 137–146, reply by Jonathan, R., *ibid.*, pp. 147–154.

14. As the conservative camp in the "battle of the books" in the US: see e.g. Hirsch, E. D. *Cultural Literacy: What Every American Needs to Know* (Boston, 1987); Bloom, H., *The Western Canon: The Books and School of the Ages* (New York, Harcourt Brace, 1995).

15. Hollis, M. (1982), *op. cit.* p. 236.

16. *Ibid.*

17. Hirsch, F. (1971), *op. cit.*, p. 5.

18. Hollis, M. (1982), *op. cit.*, p. 236.

19. I have developed the relevant argument in Jonathan, R. (1995 a), *op. cit.*: see further O'Neill, O. (1979), The most extensive liberty, *Proceedings of the Aristotelian Society*, 80.

20. Green, T. H. (1883), *Prolegomena to Ethics,* Bradley, A. C. (Ed.) (1924), (Oxford, Oxford University Press), para 245.

21. Hollis, M. (1982), *op. cit.*, p. 241.

22. *Ibid.*

Chapter 4
Rights and Choices: Illusory Freedoms[1]

When the benefits of public education are clearly social and in important respects positional, they would seem precisely the kind of goods which are unsuited to market distribution. Though there might be dispute about how many of those diverse benefits are indeed positional (with that aspect of value necessarily downplayed in the educational process both from respect for disinterested learning and for purposes of motivation) there can be no doubt that the exchange value of education (itself a powerful element in motivation) has this feature for each individual. And the positional nature of educational goods is their more dominant value for individuals in proportion as social position is insecure or threatened. Hence the popular appeal of openly acknowledging, in a period of economic and social insecurity, that the social project of public education is also the arena for competing private interests. We have seen that, with a legitimation crisis, dissatisfaction did not give rise, as in previous decades, to a social response and planned re-ordering of the system, but prompted instead a short-circuiting of such general deliberations about the conduct and purposes of education on the collective dimension, and simply alerted each member of the public to look out for themselves, giving each the responsibility for ensuring that where inferior holdings of education's positional goods were at issue, these did not fall to them.

Now from the individual's point of view, inferior holdings—or the fear of them—look plausibly like a matter for redress through the granting of individual rights to greater personal choice and control. And indeed in the polemic for neo-liberal reform (as in debate throughout the period of change) we have seen that when claims that education has failed *the public* are contested, the moral high ground is invoked and justification shifts from empirical claims about education or the economy which might be disputed, to moral claims which are presented as above debate. Redirections of social policy are thus presented as a championing of *the individual consumer* in terms of his/her rights firstly to select provision for themselves and secondly to influence that provision's development, with choices acting as quasi-votes, for or against what is on offer. Rights-based appeals to individual anxiety or frustration place at a discount debate about the truth or otherwise of the charges levelled against education in educational terms, and, more importantly, they once again inhibit serious and overdue consideration of relations between the good (and associated rights) of each and the good (and consequent rights) of all.

However, since it has been the appeal to individual freedoms to maximise private benefit which has gained popular endorsement for the re-forming of education (and the reconstitution of many important areas of social life), and since talk of individual rights and choices is introduced into debate as a trumping move at every point, the legitimacy of that appeal must be dealt with here. This chapter will first examine the role of "rights talk"[2] in relevant debates, asking for whom (and in respect of what) such rights are believed to be justified. Consumer rights in education must then be located within the spectrum of orders of rights which, despite popular rhetoric, differ in their moral force. The next concern is who is to count as the consumer of educational goods and who can best stand as their proxies, as well as what problems arise, for each and for all, in giving proxy rights directly to individual parents. A final section will then analyse what freedoms are increased and for whom by these new consumer rights, what corresponding freedoms are reduced and for whom, and which social freedoms are thereby forgone by all. In examining these matters, the triple focus of the previous chapter—the complexity of educational value, the relation between individual and social benefit, and the apparently competing claims of liberty and equality—will be brought into sharper focus.

THE POWER OF 'RIGHTS TALK'

As Dworkin noted, talk of rights often functions in contemporary debate to trump contending claims and cut short pragmatic considerations about the likely consequences of individuals' actions for the welfare of others. This prompts two questions. We must obviously examine the status of the trump cards to be played: and we must additionally ask whether the game into which these are introduced is one where trumping is a useful procedure, making winning or losing less of a forgone conclusion, and raising the level of the game for all players. When the game for consideration is social, and the trumps at issue are individual, it is clear at the outset that the analogy is strained. Not only must all players be accorded trumps of equivalent power, but this is a rather peculiar game in which players have no choice but to take part and the outcomes of the game also affect those who are not currently at the table. So individual rights clearly cannot function routinely as trumps in the social world: we must therefore first examine how they come to be deployed in polemic as if they could.

In popular debate, the question is caricatured as if this were simply a head-on collision between two contending and oversimplified theories of justice, with libertarians finding it abhorrent that the satisfactions of individuals should be sacrificed to the purported well-being of a collectivity, and egalitarians finding it unacceptable that well-placed individuals should have additional opportunities to further their advantage. The basis of the libertarian presentation is that each should have control over his/her own affairs, and of the egalitarian that, in an unequal world, opportunities for capital accumulation of whatever sort are just not the individual's own affair. Questions about educational rights in general, and in particular about the rights of individuals to select among options for their own (or their children's) experience and to influence how provision evolves, fall squarely into the middle of this dispute. With the justificatory issues presented like this, and with education so important for personal development and subsequent life-chances (both of which depend to varying degrees on individual effort), it is not surprising that for the moment libertarian claims seem to have won the day, with political parties of the centre-left subscribing also to consumer rights of choice and influence in this particular social practice.

To be sure, the granting of these rights was also defended in pragmatic terms, as in the Charters quoted earlier, on the grounds that consumer-power applies carrots and sticks to providers, improving provision and aligning it more closely with the needs of the real world. Were those claims uncontroversial, the appeal to rights would be redundant. They are, however, radically controversial and dependent on beliefs which are either highly contestable or demonstrably false. What counts as a 'better' education is a perennial subject of dispute when intrinsic value is at issue, and when exchange value is in question 'better' for some means worse for others. The 'needs of the real world' are similarly contestable, as is the role of education in meeting them, whatever they may be. The second line of empirical defence for market-style reforms is economic rather than educational, with the release of merit and talent through competition claimed to enable some to be more economically effective, with eventual benefit to those who are less well-placed. This defence of actual or proposed inequalities, challenged for two centuries now on empirical grounds by economists and on moral grounds by philosophers, is as low in populist appeal as it is theoretically suspect. (It is also frankly odd, since although present deregulation is acknowledged to redistribute to the disadvantage of the already disadvantaged, continued deregulation is claimed eventually to rebound in their favour. If this assumes the operation of the classical 'hidden hand', we might ask why that hand does not seem to be operating now; if, on the other hand, it assumes different future redistributive social policies, we might ask what will make such policies appropriate then, if they are not appropriate now.)

When reformers' pragmatic claims are highly contestable, their economic arguments suspect or incoherent, and their gloss on social equity unpersuasive, it is clear that the apparently knock-down moral appeal to individual rights, freedoms and opportunities is crucial to legitimating the extension of the market. After all, whilst it is not very compelling to urge people to accept a place in the economic cellar for an unspecified time, whilst a better structure—to which they may one day be admitted—is developed above their heads, it is much more persuasive to suggest to voters that if they or their children are not among the social winners, this is in large part due to experience of a monolithic education system over which they have had too little control. Furthermore, such measures are presented as extending to the clients of state education some of the freedoms already enjoyed by those who have had the option of purchasing independent provision. Thus, when the wisdom or the ethics of turning over 'product development' and distribution in education to the current preferences of active consumers is disputed, the rights of the individual to exercise choice and influence over a key constituent of their own future well-being serves as a justificatory trump card which seems unanswerable. Not only are the old claims of egalitarians routed and the perennial concerns of equity discounted; there is also no room for discussion of how this particular use of human capital affects the polity as a whole in both social and economic terms over the longer term. And so from an unsatisfactory solution to the tension between education's private and public benefits in which it was assumed that the latter flowed automatically from the former, we move to an even less satisfactory solution, in which the latter are simply conflated with or subsumed under the former.

The trump card produced appears at first sight to be straightforward and conclusive, for who would challenge people's rights to exercise a concerned interest in whatever affects their own (or even more so, their children's) welfare? And who would not welcome legislation to enable citizens to exercise those rights effectively? To challenge reform is surely to prefer uniformity to diversity, central direction to participation, and the good of a nebulous collective to the liberties of individuals. Indeed, those who are both educational providers or theorists and also, as parents, consumers of education, experience opposing intuitions in their differing roles. That apparent inconsistency, however, need reflect neither confusion nor hypocrisy, but rather the unaddressed problem at the heart of rights-talk in social matters, which mirrors the conundrum of public and private expectations of education explored in the last chapter. When the whole vocabulary of rights-talk is individualistic, whilst the business of education is unavoidably social, the dominance of a rights-based approach to its distribution and development serves further to compound existing confusions.

The seventeenth- and eighteenth-century concern with individual rights was central to delineating the extent and limits of the state. Correspondingly, the individual freedoms at the core of liberalism are those immunities which no just system of government may infringe. Where liberal freedom extends beyond these immunities, it is subject to the constraints imposed by potential "harm to others", which in turn raises thorny questions of what actions are "self-regarding" or "other-regarding". The contemporary tendency to talk of individual rights-and-freedoms is thus problematic at the outset, since rights claims are presented as non-negotiable, whereas only certain liberal freedoms have been seen as non-negotiable, with others, whilst claimed *prima facie* legitimate, being subject to negotiation with competing individuals under given contingent conditions. When particular conceptions of rights move beyond core immunities, they are predicated on views about human nature and hence about what constitutes a worthwhile life and a good society, as well as on implicit empirical assumptions. We would therefore expect such conceptions to be neither fixed nor uncontroversial. In liberal societies today, there is general agreement that whatever is basic to the life of rational and self-conscious social beings—whatever is required for autonomy—should not be interfered with. Slavery, arbitrary imprisonment and the deliberate curtailment of thought and its expression are held up as paradigm cases of the unacceptable infringement of individual rights. Beyond this central core of protected immunities, however, controversy soon develops. As the social world becomes more complex and possible forms of individual flourishing multiply, more and more aspects of life become open to rights claims, and as these also multiply, they tend to come into conflict with each other, so that fulfilling the rights claims of one individual or group may threaten or infringe the similar claims of other individuals or groups.

It is for this reason that within ethical, political and legal debate there has long been controversy about the usefulness of talk of rights to arbitrate in disputes in the moral and social spheres, with many maintaining that 'rights-talk' constantly throws us back onto the horns of just those dilemmas—between liberty and equality, between the interests of the individual and those of the group, between the similar claims of competing individuals or groups—which it was invoked to resolve in the first place. Nonetheless, the history of rights-talk shows that it becomes loudest in two types of social context. It is prominent where the state apparatus denies to all or some of its citizens those freedoms which are truly basic to autonomy, when the needs and desires of the individual are subordinated to a centrally determined and imposed 'collective' purpose. And, paradoxically, it also becomes prominent in libertarian societies where an individualistic ethos assumes the good of all to be simply the sum of the good of each, so that 'free choices' and rights to them become invested with value in themselves. Rights claims of this second sort, moreover, seem the more persuasive when they are put forward at a time when many societies are entering a period of liberalisation, and setting out to grant rights claims of the first sort.

Whatever the context, though, the purpose of invoking rights in moral or political argument is to make a claim with special status. This claim implies that whatever liberty or entitlement is so labelled should not be denied or overridden by the usual pragmatic considerations of the incidental effects of removing restrictions. Hence the power of appeals to rights in conflicts of interest between individuals, or between the personal and the general good, with rights trumping pre-existing priorities and pragmatic trade-offs. *Thus rights claims risk over-riding proper negotiation of the distribution of those very freedoms which rights are themselves invoked to secure.* In an individualistic context, therefore, such trumping moves must be treated with great caution, for unless the good of all is indeed truly no more than the sum of the good of each, those moves may not simply result in further advantage for those with already winning hands but also, paradoxically, inflict damage on the broader and longer-term interests even of those whose immediate interests they seem to serve.

Before this is elaborated, two separate confusions inherent in popular talk of rights must be noted, the first being the confusion between moral claims and legal entitlements, the second being the elision of differing orders of rights. On the first matter, in stressing the controversiality of rights talk, reference is of course to those moral entitlements which are claimed to be owed to individuals, irrespective of current conventional legislation in their societies. Polemic is bolstered by eliding claims to moral and conventional rights. And whereas to invoke the former is rhetorical and persuasive in intent, reference to the latter is uncontroversially factual. Despite the logical gulf between these two types of rights, popular debate and polemic frequently appeal to one of them to substantiate claims for the other. Thus when it is asserted that parents have a right to make choices and exert influence over their children's education, a demand is initially being tabled that social arrangements be modified to secure legal and institutional endorsement for a debatable moral entitlement, claimed to pre-exist though legally unrecognised. Once relevant legislation has been enacted, however, and the assertion becomes factually accurate, new conventional rights serve to reinforce the moral claims which they endorse. For to label social arrangements 'rights' rather than simply, say, 'opportunities', is not merely to report that certain courses of action are now possible. It is also to imply that wise and responsible individuals will avail themselves of those new opportunities, which are presented as redressing a prior, morally less satisfactory set of arrangements.

A second and more serious source of confusion comes from polemical failure to maintain distinctions between differing orders of rights. Once it is recognised that no rights are absolute, all appear on the same footing in popular debate, with little regard for the kinds of counter-claims required to over-ride rights of differing orders, despite the obvious point that what would suffice to over-ride a right to four weeks annual paid leave or to free medical attention is of a quite different order from counter-claims required to override, say, a right to freedom of thought. This last is perhaps the most basic of those general rights with greatest moral force, which protect those liberal immunities each requires to form and exercise rational autonomy. Were it the case that individuals, prior to the granting of legal rights to choice and control in education, had been deprived of such general rights, then the justification for newly-granted rights in education would be of the strongest sort. However, if none of the options for choice violates a general right, then choice between those options cannot be necessary to securing such rights. Conversely, if any of the options does violate general rights, they have no place within a free society and the question of rights to choose between them becomes redundant. The second example—the right to four weeks leave—is even more swiftly dealt with, being a contractual or special right which comes into being as a result of negotiation between contracting parties. Such rights may well arise between parties during the educational process (through participation of parents in school government, or in respect of religious education, for example), but they cannot exist prior to the transactions from which they would derive, and hence justify a market distribution of educational opportunities.

The remaining example above—the right to free necessary medical attention—offers the closest analogy with educational rights, being neither a general right, nor a contractual right, but rather a welfare (or social) right, arising from arrangements which individuals in a given society have collectively agreed for their mutual support and welfare. Being based on such contingent social agreements, welfare rights are socially relative, and are therefore more negotiable than general or contractual rights, which tend to lend them overmuch force by association. Precisely because welfare *is* socially relative, welfare rights are claimed by individuals against other members of the same society, and therefore they are only binding if certain conditions obtain. Broadly, individuals are entitled to claim such rights either if, without them, they would suffer direct disbenefit in relation to other members of the collaborating group, or if, by their obtaining them, the group as a whole also benefits. If, for example, we apply those ground rules to the matter of rights to health care or education, it seems clear that in a society such as ours that right could be justifiably claimed on both grounds—and most uncontroversially in the latter case. For in a society in which some receive education and in which personal development and life-chances in part depend on it, all individuals are entitled to demand access to that education without which they would be relatively disadvantaged, and whose outcomes also serve society. The welfare right *to an education* is thus doubly justified in a modern, democratic society. However, this argument cannot be simply extended for example to a parent's right to choice and control in schooling, for it would be over-hasty to treat all rights questions which arise *in connection with* education as if they were subspecies of educational rights: that is, rights *to* education.

It is clear that in response to talk of rights, what come first to mind are individual freedoms—of thought, speech, movement—which secure immunity from arbitrary interference by the state or fellow-citizens. We accord, unreflectively, the same persuasive force to those rights which claim not immunities, but powers—not 'freedom from', but 'freedom to'. This sleight-of-mind is most seriously misleading when the powers concerned can only be exercised in a context which is partially constituted by the similar competing powers of other individuals. And it is compounded when the good of all is also at stake and that good cannot be assumed to follow either from securing the immediate interests of some or even from responding to the immediate demands of all. This, I shall suggest, is precisely the case with individuals' rights to exercise consumer power and competition over the social practice of education.

RIGHTS TO EDUCATION: BENEFICIARIES OF EDUCATION

I have acknowledged unambiguously that all citizens have a welfare right to an education in a developed democracy. Within the educational process a series of rights issues may well arise, the most notable contemporary ones relating to matters of conscience or religion. These are not matters for consideration here. This section is concerned to analyse those justifications advanced, in practice and in principle (for as we shall see these cannot be neatly disentangled), for *consumer rights of choice and influence* on the public education system. Where these are rights for parents to choose schools for their children, these consumer rights, however, conceal a deeper rights question—to be addressed in the next section—namely, the relative rights and responsibilities of parents and the state in securing the welfare of the rising generation.

Given the public provision of education, funded through universal taxation, all are clearly entitled to equal rights of access to what they commonly provide. Where provision itself is common (with common standards of quality and as much commonality of experiences presented to learners as is possible in practice) those rights are met for all individuals without collision with the similar rights of others. *For the public, therefore, rights of choice are of interest in proportion as provision is or is perceived to be of varying desirability.* Now in the schooling context, where participation is compulsory, the existence of a universal welfare right to education implies that the state's response to any grassroots demand for consumer rights *to compete for access* should be not accession to those demands, but rather the overhaul of public provision to make such demands redundant. This type of response characterised educational change for three decades prior to market reforms (with increasing but imperfect success). Although recent changes have been popularly presented as a long-neglected restitution of individual rights, they are predicated on an ideological turning-away from attempts to realise that commonality of provision which would make such rights-claims redundant: a turning away which paradoxically, as we shall see, in fact threatens the universal welfare right to education.

The New Right blend of neo-liberalism and conservatism has three main objections to commonality of experience during the period of compulsory education. The first is that this neglects the freedom for each to develop capacities and interests which vary between individuals; the second is that general standards are thereby 'levelled-down' to the detriment of all participants and of society at large; and the third is that judgements of appropriate quality and experience are in the hands of professionals and bureaucrats who are not subject to democratic control. Consumer power offers a cure for all three ills. If these objections could be sustained, 'choice rights' would simply be a counsel of despair whose educationally unfortu-nate and socially inequitable consequences had to be lived with in order to avoid what is claimed to be even worse. If they cannot, then the only policy defence is the one of principle (the appeal to moral trumps) by which they are overtly promoted. We must first then examine the ideological rejection of common provision.

The first aspect of this rejection is clearly tendentious and makes a series of unwarranted assumptions. There is no reason to suppose that offering to all a similar menu of common quality means that all have to eat the same amount of the same dishes at the same speed. It need only mean that there is common quality of nutrition and an equal range of choices available to all at all stages of the meal, constrained only by appetite and what has previously been ingested. Nor is there reason to presume that digestive capacity and appetite differ inherently in individuals in ways which can reliably be identified in advance of participation, still less that these correlate neatly with cultural capital.[3] Underlying these assumptions is a confusion about equality which libertarians strangely share with 'flat' egalitarians and to which we will return in the next chapter. For just as the equality of opportunities to benefit from common provision cannot be judged simplistically by the sameness or otherwise of outcomes, so commonality of experiences equally offered does not imply identity of experience. Finally, on the basis of these linked assumptions rests the clinching claim that all will benefit if some develop extra strength thanks to a special diet. The lack of grounds for this in respect of the compulsory period of general education have already been noted, with nothing in common provision militating against differing emphases for individual interest during that period, still less against subsequent specialisation.

The second basis for hostility to common provision—that the general quality of education is compromised—seems more straight-forward, though the claim itself is ambiguous and, in its popular interpretation, false to the best of our knowledge. Whilst there are both conceptual and empirical obstacles to determining changes in general levels of education with precision, the best evidence available shows *mean* standards of achievement rising with common provision.[4] Lying behind the generalised claim that 'education' thereby suffers, however, is the publicly unacknowledged, popularly unpersuasive and democratically untested belief that general norms of achievement should not take priority over the opportunity of some to excel. Hayek, for example, questions whether it is desirable to make available to all "the best knowledge some possess",[5] adding that "the existence of an intellectual proletariat who find no outlet for their learning is a great danger to political stability".[6] These sentiments were echoed more crudely by New Right pressure groups in the UK at the start of the 'populist' reform period: "You don't need 'O' levels to be a road mender. . . . Too high a qualification is really a disqualification for a contented, competent employee".[7] This view of public education is far from novel, representing as it does a return to an *anti-liberal* strand in early nineteenth-century politics, well expressed then by Colquhoun: "Let it not be conceived for a moment that it is the object of the author to recommend a system of education for the poor which shall pass the bounds of their condition in society".[18] Moreover, it sits ill with claims that the object of consumer power is the raising of *educational* standards for all (though it is compatible, on the basis of dubious 'trickle-down' theories of economics, and questionable conceptions of welfare as non-relative, with belief in the greater *economic* benefit to all of a more stratified society).

The third basis of hostility to arrangements for common educational experience has the most serious implications for the polity, since it amounts to an implicit vote of no confidence not only in representative democracy but also in its participatory forms. When members of a liberal society endorse the view that it is hopeless to attempt publicly to negotiate the constitution and distribution of the one social good which exists to sustain and renew that society—when it is claimed that the market can be better relied on to 'deliver the goods' in forming the rising generation—this is truly a counsel of despair. Direct, individual action becomes the sole means for the expression of preferences, for although polemic presents change as a matter of consumers controlling providers, that is precisely what they cease to do in concert. When each exercises consumer rights individually, the aggregate outcomes of citizens' choices are removed from any deliberative process, which democratic control— whether central or local—of the conduct of education and of its distribution sought (however imperfectly) to realise. Whilst seeking to restrain the tentacular reach of the state, we shall see that the shift to control by market forces licences a "war of all against all" such as even the most 'minimal state' is designed to avoid.

It is thus clear that for the new ideological agenda, evidential support, which would make consumer power in education a pragmatic maximin device (adopted to avoid greater harms), is worse than flimsy: any persuasive justification must therefore rely on moral claims of principle. Of these, the most thorny question is whether arrangements which enable parents to select between schooling options on their children's behalf are legitimately considered rights to be accorded to each individual, to be exercised individually. That particular question raises all of the issues germane to the destructive power of consumer sovereignty on a society's educational provision. It is of special interest, however, as it contains more complex problems of principle than do, for example, the powers of consumers making choices on their own behalf about education post-school (though that too is more problematic than is popularly presented, treating subsequent learning as primarily a private good). Moreover, consumer power over basic educational experience has significant impact on the question of what arrangements for access to subsequent learning are both equitable to individuals and in the interests of society as a whole. For example, it has long been accepted in the UK that aspirants to higher education are in open competition with their fellows, and providers select openly from a pool of consumers whose custom they must court. Equity between individuals need not be compromised by that competition *provided that selection is based on lengthy past experience of conditions available to all*. However, as the effects of schooling choice over an extended period negate that proviso, with schooling deregulation making significant inroads on commonality of preparatory provision, compromised welfare rights to common schooling significantly alter equity questions in relation to higher education which become further compounded by associated deregulation of that sector. (In addition, what is directly compromised there are aspects of public benefit—the value education adds to social life. When providers under market pressure must court consumers, both the range and the standard of what is on offer become vulnerable to the ascendance of current market preferences, whether or not these correspond in aggregate to the spread and advancement of the range of knowledge and skill which has the greatest longer-term potential for enhancing the general good.)

Though these matters are important in themselves, the paradigm case of consumer rights to be examined here will be the putative rights of parents, acting individually, to select within and hence modify (for others as well as themselves) the provision of schooling. This case exhibits all of the problems which arise elsewhere in connection with public education (directly giving rise to some of them), and also raises special difficulties of its own. And it is this case which provided the beachhead for deregulatory policies not only in other sectors of education but across many areas of social life. Though having greatest intuitive appeal, this is also paradoxically the most problematic case, illustrating a series of intractable conflicts perhaps more starkly than any other social issue: conflicts between the neo-liberal desire to *satisfy* individual preferences and the liberal prior ideal of freedom for all to *form* unconstrained preferences, confusions within liberalism's understanding of the relations of freedom and equality to equity (further compounded in neo-liberalism), and clashes between claims to the good of each and the good of all, unresolved from both perspectives. And all of these matters, when examined in this practical context, provide backing for the growing insight within political philosophy that the salience of theoretical questions cannot be divorced from contingencies created in part by previous attempts at their resolution.

If we focus now on parents' rights in schooling, it must first be emphasised that *given commonality of provision* no rights are at stake other than those of choice and influence for consumers. Of course, if a parent required choice rights because some options were substandard, these would constitute welfare rights, though these could not by definition be accessed by all. As noted above, the only solution to that contradiction is that sub-standard options cease to fall to the lot of any individual, rather than that they fall to children whose parents—for whatever reasons—fail to act as effective agents on their behalf in a competitive situation. Indeed, the removal of options considered less desirable (for whatever reasons) provided the impetus for regulated educational change (however imperfect) in the past. If the supporting claim is that parents should be regarded as the appropriate educational decision-makers (of which more below), then in that case the consequent demand should be, not for each parent individually to select or bring pressure to bear on each child's school, but for parents to determine together what standards and ranges of experience should be common to all schools available to them collectively. It may well be objected that leaving control of educational decisions with the government of the day is no analogue for collaborative public negotiation (an incontrovertible objection in an adversarial political system where educational questions are not considered cross-party matters), but reasonable analogues are possible in principle and are widely found in practice in various systems in differing forms.

When, on the other hand, it can be assumed that all schools meet agreed common criteria—and there can be no other justification for any school's existence in a context of compulsion—then an individual parent's rights to choice and influence within existing educational options clearly does not merit the status of a welfare right under general equity requirements unless the pass has already been sold on those requirements. And it would only do so under a defence in terms of the greater general good if the empirical claims rebutted above—about the necessary poverty of any system where content and access are publicly controlled—could be established. So the argument thus far establishes that there are *no grounds in principle for jettisoning publicly regulated access to common provision in order to respect either general rights or a welfare right to education.* However, once consumer rights are conferred by legislation and sufficiently widely exercised, a new set of circumstances are produced. Once real diversity develops, freedom to avoid some options *presents itself to each consumer* as a welfare right on equity grounds, *despite the fact that what is offered is not a guarantee of benefit to all but a guarantee to all of opportunity to compete for benefit.* So once the process is set in motion, the principle's untenability becomes progressively harder to expose and those who initially opposed it in the political arena dare not propose stopping the clock. For to do so would not of itself reinstate previous conditions of (imperfect) equity but would now require additional state 'interference' to rectify fragmentation of the pre-existing system. Still less would it rectify the pre-existing deficits in equity, consequent on pre-existing diversity, which had initially lent the promise of choice rights their popular appeal. There is no question but that these did require further democratic attention, but a devil-take-the-hindmost policy is no substitute for that.

That said, we see that consumer rights for parents in schooling collapse into rights of choice. These constitute rights to express and fulfil autonomous preferences where those are self-regarding or where they are thought to aggregate to the common good. Within liberalism, respect for the autonomy of preferences follows unambiguously from equality of respect for the rational capacities of individuals which grounds the priority of freedom. But since this respect is universal, rights to fulfil preferences are dependant upon potential consequences for others and their preferences. These in turn vary with the objects of preference, as early liberal attempts to distinguish private and public goods made clear. Thus I have the right to choose to dye my teeth purple if I wish, not because I have a dental right, but because I have a property right over my own teeth; and I have the right to listen to Mozart rather than Elvis, when the sound around me concerns only myself. But I have no right to enlarge my garden at my neighbour's expense, nor to choose what side of the road I drive on unless I can persuade other road users to share the same preference and act in concert with me in our mutual interest. The nub of the question, then, is whether freedoms to exercise consumer choice in the schooling context are in fact private liberties whose exercise concerns only the chooser, or are social freedoms whose impact on others is either contingently or logically inescapable. In the education case, they are demonstrably the latter in both respects.

That this is so follows from the nature of the 'good' at stake, analysed in chapter three. Without rehearsing those arguments again, on the private dimension, in so far as any individual's experience of education develops them in cognitive, emotional and cultural ways, his/her growth and fulfilment would in principle seem neither to threaten nor to harm the similar growth of any other individual. But on the social dimension, public education in a complex and open society does not just further the private development of individuals, acting as a source of intrinsic value for them, but is also the primary mechanism for dispensing public exchange value, with performance and its credentials serving as currency of different denominations which can be cashed for access to life-chances of differing desirability. The complexity of educational benefit is crucial to *both the popularity and the untenability* of the rights-claims considered here. In so far as education promotes private development and benefit, it seems plausible to claim that individuals or their proxies should have the right to exercise choice and control over access and experience with a view to affecting outcomes for themselves. But in so far as the access and experience of each affects the access and experience of all, and as those in turn imply differing consequent life-chances for other present and future autonomous choosers, relevant preferences and choice rights to obtain them become far from self-regarding. Indeed they give rise to a series of deepening problems. These are basically of three kinds: the first entails inevitable disadvantage to some of the pool of consumers; the second makes what counts as benefit problematic for all of the pool of consumers; the third results from the consequent curtailment of wider preferences, in which even those who secure their immediate preferences also have legitimate interests. And all of these problems are compounded when rights of choice are not exercised by the rights-holders themselves, but are devolved to their individual proxies.

PARENTS' RIGHTS AND CONSUMER RIGHTS

At first sight it seems obvious that if rights were to be accorded to the consumers of public schooling, these should be exercised by parents acting as agents or proxies for the young. After all, these rights are claimed on the autonomy grounds which also provide the overarching legitimation in liberal societies for compulsory schooling. Since the young cannot be supposed to possess the requisite rational autonomy to choose and control the very process which aims to develop that capacity in them, surely the best alternative to state or interest group domination is to devolve proxy powers to their adult representatives, who can already exercise autonomous choice. And what better representative than the parent? These intuitions conceal a host of difficulties.

On that presentation, it seems that the rights at issue for parents are proxy rights (which as we shall see imply problems of their own), but the waters here are further muddied by direct rights-claims underpinning claims-by-proxy. This complication needs preliminary attention. Now whereas rights are normally thought of as straightforwardly protecting the actual or putative interests of rights-holders themselves, parents in this case are claimed to stand both as rights-holders and as proxies for further rights-holders; a combination of claims which apparently strengthens the case. To take the first aspect first, when it is argued that parents have rights over children which are designed to protect the parents' own interests, one or more of four claims is implied. The least sustainable of these is the biologically-based claim to ownership of offspring[9] (invoked still in contemporary debate on ethical matters in reproductive technology); the second concerns the parent's right to have the child perpetuate the parent's culture or religion (which, if that implies denial of access to alternatives, collapses into the ownership claim); the third asserts that the privacy and intimacy of the family and its close relationships have value in themselves against which the well-being of the child may sometimes be offset[10] (heard when the social agencies of the state are thought to be intrusive in their efforts to protect children within the family); the fourth sees the family as a valuable institution whose broad utility is diminished by encroachment on its power, even where this might benefit its members in particular respects.[11] All of these claims have been subjected to sustained critique, not least in feminist writings, and they sit oddly with priority for the liberty of the individual. Nonetheless, they continue to be invoked (often with cautious caveats) to support deregulation of public education, as if several dubious arguments added up to one strong one.[12]

The glue binding these disparate intuitions together tends to be an amalgam of a play on democratic fears of state oppression and a misunderstanding (or misrepresentation) of the issues at stake. Frequent reminders that "Abuse of the education process is something which has taken place under both fascism and communism and its prevention is central to the preservation of a liberal society"[13] cast parental consumer rights in education as all-of-a-piece with the need for a private sphere to guard against the "evil empire" of a potentially totalitarian state apparatus. Thus claims that the state should not have a coercive monopoly on education, that private aspects of upbringing should remain the preserve of the family, that matters of conscience should remain up to individual discretion, etc.—all matters which liberal states with regulated public education systems have not merely permitted but consistently insisted upon— are perversely run together with justifications for consumer choice rights. And all of these matters are set in the context of a caricatured dichotomy about forms of social organisation: ". . . should it be meritocratic and competitive, or egalitarian and welfare-oriented? regulated or libertarian?"[14] We are thus presented with a series of false choices in which monopoly, uniformity, coercion and flat equality are lined up on one side and choice, diversity, self-development and freedom stand on the other. Forms of popularly endorsed organisation for public education—painstakingly negotiated through the democratic process over decades in a plethora of liberal societies—are recast at a stroke as infringements of, rather than means to, the much-quoted demand in the Universal Declaration of Human Rights that: "Parents have a prior right to choose the kind of education that shall be given to their children".[15]

Given this pervasive misunderstanding (or misrepresentation) of the case, let it be stated here unequivocally that nothing in this chapter challenges the rights of parents to discharge their responsibilities for the welfare of their children. Nothing promotes the incursion of an all-powerful state into the private sphere. Nothing urges identical educational experiences for children, regardless of individual differences. Nothing suggests that parents have only a minimal role to play either in the education of their own children or in the constitution of schooling for children in general. Nothing is premised on the claimed desirability of egalitarian social organisation. And nothing places liberty at a discount: precisely the reverse. What is at issue in this analysis is *the appropriate mechanism for the organisation of public education in order precisely to allow parents optimally to fulfil their responsibilities to their children and to exercise those unchallenged rights necessary to do so.* My contention nonetheless will be that the granting of consumer rights to be exercised individually by each parent precisely frustrates that purpose. This can be seen if we now examine the role of parents as proxies for their children in securing those children's welfare and interests through education.

This is crucial, for although the waters are muddied by the claims noted here, it is parental proxy rights to promote the interests of their young which serve overwhelmingly to lend support to a market in schooling. Indeed even in matters of rights for parents over children, claims seldom argue that adult interests and welfare are overriding: rather they rest on supporting beliefs that the eventual welfare of children is also best served by protecting the present interests and wishes of their parents. (This may either be on the grounds that there is an identity of interest between parent and child, or on the assumption that the parent is the person best placed and/or most strongly motivated to act as trustee or agent until such time as the child becomes competent to choose and act autonomously.) So, even when parents' rights are to be exercised over children, they make implicit reference to those children's present or future welfare and interests, and therein lies their persuasive force. This is even more obviously the case when the rights in question are proxy rights, exercised by parents on a child's behalf. Such rights are unambiguously grounded in the parents' duties as trustees of their children's welfare and as agents for securing those children's interests. When proxy rights for parents are at issue therefore, we need to consider firstly whether the chosen proxies are in fact those best placed to choose and act in the interests of the individuals they represent.

Whereas it seems obvious at first sight that the most suitable proxies for children must be those closest to and most concerned about them—usually their parents—this is a hasty conclusion in the education case. For the ability not just of single individuals, but of whole categories of individuals, to make wise choices and obtain autonomous preferences depends not just on characteristics of the choosers, but also on logical features of both the objects of preference and the contexts of choice. To see this in respect of deregulated access to public education, we need only adduce the complexity of educational value, which I have shown to be both private and public, both individual and social, both inherent and instrumental, clearly positional as value-in-exchange and arguably positional on other dimensions of value. These complex characteristics bring in their train the three kinds of problem for consumer rights which the previous section flagged—problems which are compounded and can be seen most clearly when those rights are devolved to proxies or agents acting on behalf of individuals whose welfare is at stake.

Little space is needed to describe the first and most obvious of these problems. This results from a combination of the logical point that as regards positional value (however its parameters are debated) education has losers as well as winners, coupled with the obvious fact that some children have parents who are more effective as proxy-agents than are others. Given this, to increase the rights of proxies is to ensure that winning or losing in the education game is even less a result of characteristics inherent to the child than it tends to be under a regulated but imperfect system. (That those characteristics themselves may have origins partly social must be deferred to chapter six.) The consequent ratcheting of a spiral of cumulative advantage and disadvantage, passing from one generation to the next, is at odds both with the moral claims of equity, and the economic claims of human capital theory. Lest this point be again misunderstood, to take this position is not to argue for equality ('flat' or otherwise) of schooling outcomes, nor to support identity of educational process. At all times in educational policy, moral claims must of course take account of psychological, social and economic realities as well as questions of abstract principle: indeed consumer rights claims are vitiated precisely because they conspicuously fail to meet standards of argument on all of these dimensions.

The appeal underlying this first point is therefore not to equality (as it is caricatured in much educational debate) but rather to equity. A liberal understanding of equity requires that all have equal opportunities to develop the prerequisites to autonomy—a range of intellectual and affective capacities, understanding of a range of satisfying options—in brief, that all are on a similar footing with respect to the arena for *forming* preferences and subsequently exercising liberty. This requires that a liberal society seek the nearest possible approximation, not to identity of educational experience, but to equal breadth of options for all for as long in the process as possible (and at least until the end of the compulsory period). It was to this end that regulated common provision, with all of its shortcomings, was democratically negotiated. As noted earlier here, it was a chimera to suppose that public education might of itself iron out social inequalities: nonetheless, the least that can be demanded of schooling in a liberal society is that it not compound these where they (sometimes unavoidably, sometimes not) exist. Unless it is believed that, despite the logic of the case and in the face of all of the accumulated evidence, all consumers are equally effective on behalf of themselves or their wards, and that diversity of quality and product (thought required for any market to operate) are uniquely not features of a schooling market, then rights for consumers or their proxies offend not merely against equality but also against liberal conceptions of equity and hence against liberty itself.

Finally on this initial problem, even if a neo-liberal wished to discount the (liberal) equity argument on the (curious on his/her own terms) grounds that the good of all should take precedence over the equal liberty of all, and that that good was best served by letting the race be to the swift, any such defence of a competition for progressively less equal opportunities would require the rebuttal of volumes of research in education, in sociology, in genetics and in statistics, which combine to demonstrate that the potentially 'swift' are not stereotypically those with the swiftest proxies, unless we structure society so that that untenable assumption becomes a self-fulfilling prophesy. This being so, recourse to the economic argument is quite inadequate to rescue the neo-liberal. At any event, that rescue would come at a damning price, since an economic defence of schooling inequity would have to posit a particular conception of the good for all (increased overall prosperity) which was claimed to take precedence over liberty: a curious position for any libertarian to espouse.

The second type of problem with proxy consumer rights is more complex than this first, as it affects *all* parents acting as their children's trustees in a situation which has all the characteristics of a prisoner's dilemma in which individuals cannot achieve the best outcomes for themselves by pursuing their own interests directly and exclusively, but only by co-operating with other interested parties jointly to control the boundaries within which they make choices of available outcomes. Thus a market in education creates a competitive framework in which parents as consumers can seek relative advantage for their children. But it also creates a situation in which each child becomes vulnerable to the unspecifiable effects of the aggregate choices of other children's proxies. With consumer power presented as a right, the implication is that wise and effective parents should avail themselves, through their social purchasing power, of the opportunities made possible in that market. Whether this *is* the wisest move, however, depends on what moves other rights-holders make. Neither these nor their aggregate effects can be taken into deliberative account, except to assume prudentially that since all now have the right to compete and some are likely to exercise it (with varying degrees of effectiveness) competing now looks like the immediately rational strategy, despite the fact that this raises the stakes for all children, including the children whose welfare a given proxy seeks. Indeed, once this process (which democratic agreement to regulate was designed to obviate) is set in motion, its damaging consequences become an additional incentive to get an edge in a game with escalating stakes.

To endorse the consumer rights in question is therefore to suppose that proxies serve their children's interests *both* by competing *and* by raising the stakes in the competition. Both claims are problematic to say the least. It has already been pointed out that it is by no means obvious that the interests of children in general are best served by a ratcheting of the spiral of social competition, since some are bound to lose out. It should also be noted that it is perennially controversial whether the interests even of those particular children who are likely to come relatively well out of the competition are better served by securing additional personal advantage for them than by facilitating their eventual membership of a group with narrower educational (and social) differentials. These are matters of enduring political debate about the ability of differing forms of social organisation to promote the welfare of their members: and they are in no way adequately represented as a straight choice between egalitarianism and liberalism, nor, even more strangely, between a 'soft' liberalism and a 'realistic' neo-liberal libertarianism. They are rather part of liberalism's long-running and still unachieved attempt to realise its ideals of equitably distributed freedoms. This is clearly evident, provided only that the opportunity for all to *develop* autonomy and to *form* preferences is acknowledged to be logically as well as empirically prior to the cherished ability of each to exercise autonomy and enjoy individual freedom.

With all of that in mind, the appropriateness of the individual parent as prime trustee and agent for a child's interests in respect of education begins to look very problematic. However counter-intuitive it may seem, the parent turns out to be *particularly badly placed* to weigh alternative notions of the child's eventual interest even-handedly, and that not through any defect of agent motivation or ability. Since parents are not in a position directly to affect the social situation, but only the position of their own children within it, their best-available utility-maximising strategy becomes that of seeking the most advantageous outcome for their wards in the circumstances as currently given. When the context is inevitably structured like an n-person prisoner's dilemma, trustees have no responsible option but to make individualistic, competitive moves to avoid disadvantage which is clearly apparent, even though this lays their wards open to possible greater disadvantage which at the time is less apparent. I have argued that the exercise of consumer choice rights in schooling has three levels of consequence: it entails a worse direct outcome for some of the young; it will surely deliver an experience to all of them changed in unspecifiable ways (so that just what is being chosen becomes itself insecure); and it will entrain a changed social ethos and structure for society in the future which is clearly to the further disadvantage of some and arguably to the eventual disadvantage of all. This last matter, moreover, is not merely a concern for parents acting as proxies for their own children, as will be seen below. For it is not just current proxies who exchange new choice rights for broader political freedoms, but the polity as a whole.

All of this calls into question the intuitively plausible claim that consumers are best served by direct and individual choice and control over education's goods. It particularly undermines the claim that individual parents are best placed to claim these rights and exercise them as proxies for their children, since these are not simple opportunities to promote a child's welfare, but chances to enter that child in a lottery whose rules are changed outwith the control of individual players as the game proceeds and whose prizes are cashable in a context which alters their value. And once this becomes 'the only game in town' no individual parent can responsibly afford to abstain from play. Only by democratic collaboration (to negotiate mitigating regulation appropriate to particular contingencies) can the parent escape the horns of this dilemma. Nor is the individual's predicament the end of it. There are dilemmas, too, for society's interests as represented by the state whose democratic role is not just to secure the rights of each citizen, but to protect citizens from harms which may fall to them from the agency of other rights-holders.

Whereas the individual's predicament calls into question the role of individual parents as appropriate *proxies*, the consequent dilemmas for society as a whole call into question their role as legitimate *agents* in securing the interests of a child. It can be shown that even if the broader and longer-term interests of children were beyond dispute, so that individual trustees did not have a hidden hand twisting their evaluative arms, parents' rights of agency in securing those interests are far from axiomatic. For where social goods are at stake, each parent has no more rights to secure relative advantage on a child's behalf than any individual would have on his/her own behalf. In medical matters, for example, the rights of parents as agents for their children's welfare are granted only *prima facie* and can be overridden by the courts on the basis of both medical and moral argument. Where those medical matters concern not simply treatment of the child in question, but also imply concomitant changes in the health status or resources for treatment available to other children, parents' rights of agency are not granted even *prima facie*. Where these rights are given *prima facie* status, they relate to matters where the conflict of interests which potentially arises between individuals, each exercising their rights, is self-resolving. For example, under English law parents have the right to give or withhold consent to medical intervention where this is in the interests of their own child, as in some vaccination against infectious diseases. A parent who has good reason to suppose that a sufficient number of other parents will consent to vaccination, and who also knows that in rare cases it carries a serious risk, might rationally decide to withhold consent in the best interest of her/his own child. In doing so, however, she/he acts against the best interest of children in general, with the consent of the state whose duty is precisely to secure the interests which are thereby infringed. Parents' rights of agency are nonetheless democratically upheld in this instance, but only because this conflict is self-limiting in that if more than a small minority of parents adopted the 'rational' strategy, it would cease to be rational.

However, apparently similar conflicts in the educational context are not self-limiting, being more like a parent's right to obtain for a child, with resources not shared by all, scarce medical treatment which cannot be made available to all. For if the exchange value of education in a functionally diverse society makes the relative advantage of one child in part a function of the relative positional status of other children, and if the future nature of educational and social experience is changed by the aggregate effects of individual agency, then parents cannot seek to promote the interests of their own children without indirectly affecting the interests of other children. Thus, relevant legislation frustrates the duty of the state equally to protect the liberty and interests of all citizens. Far from being self-limiting, the dilemma posed by individual rights of agency in the distribution of public education (whether exercised by individuals from self-interest, or by parents from concerned trusteeship) is synergistic or self-exacerbating, with the momentum which is generated multiplying clashes of individual rights at the same time as practical appeal to them becomes ever more persuasive.

That dilemma arises from the state's duty to remain even-handed between the competing demands of individual citizens. These latter, however, do not have only private interests, though I have until now focused on those. Together, private citizens also have public interests, and they collectively provide a public education system to secure some of these. Unless we are to suppose that there is no more to the public benefit of education than whatever unknown outcomes result from the market's 'hidden hand'—from the aggregate outcomes of very imperfectly rational preferences expressed by the proxies of current consumers—then even the luckiest of current consumers risk being short-changed on the dimension of public benefit by any legislation which makes their private interests paramount. And education is a good which is not provided—bought and paid for—only by and for its current consumers. Therefore to elevate their perceived interests above all others once again places the liberal state in dereliction of its duty to remain agnostic between the interests and preferences of all.

THE GOOD OF EACH, OF ALL AND OF NONE

To gain public endorsement in a liberal society, the consumer-oriented deregulation of education would need to present a more satisfactory resolution of tensions between the good of each and the good of all than was exhibited by the arrangements it dismantles. It clearly does not do so. Supporting empirical claims are speculative or/and contrary to the available evidence. Polemical justifications appealing to individual rights promise to increase individual freedom for all, but in reality redistribute socially available freedoms between individuals. The granting of individual consumer rights of the kind examined here offers individuals the promise of greater control over some areas of their lives (deemed private interests) in exchange for loss of control on the wider educational and political stages. And the interests of the polity as a whole are placed at a discount when the preferences of current consumers of a social good—public and private in benefit—are given overriding priority. In popular political debate all of these considerations are eclipsed by persuasive talk of the interests of children and the rights and responsibilities of their parents in securing them. The previous section demonstrated, however, that the social embeddedness of education and the complexity of its value cast doubt both on the *legitimacy* of individual parents as agents and on their *capacity* as primary proxies for the broad interests of their children in these matters.

Consumer power in education, when this is exercised individually, compounds tensions between the good of each and the good of all in three principal respects which need brief elaboration. Firstly, relevant rights constrain the broader autonomy even of those individuals on whom they appear to confer immediate benefit. Secondly, the greater effectiveness of some in exercising rights—not to *obtain* benefit but to *compete* for benefit—produces cumulative social change with which not only the losers in the competition but indeed citizens as a whole will have to live. Thirdly, this procedural change brings about cumulative substantive changes in the nature and distribution of education and in the general political economy and takes such changes out of the democratic forum of debate. The first point here creates a dilemma for individual citizens, the second a dilemma for the polity, whilst they combine in the third to by-pass democratic deliberation about the social, cultural and economic benefits to all of public education.

On the first point, the one uncontroversial aspect of individual rights is that they are accorded to protect or increase freedoms. These rights, however, actually diminish freedom in an important respect, as they pre-empt more fundamental socio-political choices at the same time as they promise increased choices over education. For whilst neo-liberals may favour an individualistic social framework and an 'enterprise culture', not all citizens endorse the moral values and ideological commitments which are required to underpin this political option. Nonetheless, once legislative change creates a libertarian, consumerist context, the pressure is on individuals to behave, in their own or their children's interest, *as if* they endorsed such values, whether that is the case or not. And in so behaving, they place alternative options at a discount and strengthen an ethos which may be contrary not only to their own educational and social interests but also to their broader moral and political beliefs.

Indeed, this is the crux of both the strength in practice and the dubiousness in principle of creating a market in the provision and distribution of goods which are social and in part positional. For whether or not social consumerism has universal endorsement (and voting patterns till now show that to be nowhere the case), nevertheless deregulation generates a situation where individuals cannot prudently express dissent either from social consumerism itself, or from its repercussions, through the mechanism of consumer choice. Consumers have little option but to take part in a game which many of them have not chosen but which penalises those who do not actively compete, so that polemical claims that 'what people want is more freedom to choose' become self-fulfilling prophesy. When market conditions are introduced into public education, the private schooling dilemma of affluent parents (who perceive public provision, rightly or wrongly, to be inadequate) becomes universalised to all parents. The immediate losers, this time, are those lacking cultural rather than economic capital, but the long-term losers arguably extend to the polity as a whole. The substantive consequences of market reforms will be immediately regrettable, it is true, only to direct losers and to non-libertarians (whether direct winners or losers or simply the indirectly disenfranchised on educational matters). But even consistent neo-liberals, in so far as they are committed to the maximisation of choice and freedom, should deplore the decrease in political choice for all which increased educational choice for some necessarily entrains.

The neo-liberal rejoinder to this might be that if increases in individual opportunity do indeed result in decreases in socially available freedoms, then this consequence is not the responsibility of legislators. Since the only legislation involved is deregulatory, responsibility for its longer-term outcomes passes from policy makers and rests with the public as consumers, as the rights conferred on individuals consist only in the removal of hindrances, there being no compulsion on anyone to avail themselves of the opportunities they provide. What I have tried to show above, however, is that legislation alters circumstance, and circumstance has a compelling force. When individuals cannot directly affect either the structural constitution of society or the relation of social goods to that structure, then immediate private moral duties will be at odds, for all but neo-liberals, with broader moral and political values, placing individuals on the horns of a dilemma which, choosing and acting as individuals, they can only exacerbate. Though the consequences produced are in tune with neo-liberals' aspirations for social practice, the process itself runs counter to their philosophical commitments.

The waters are again muddied here by the undeniable point that educational choice for some has long existed in liberal societies, and choice for some but not all seems *prima facie* unjust. That oblique reference to the perennial private schooling controversy raises three points which might usefully be made in passing. First, any harms thought to result to the polity from private schooling options must be offset against potential greater harms from state monopoly. Second, the equity requirement on education policy can be no more than that it improve matters wherever possible and above all scrupulously refrain from making them worse. Third and most important, the issue of unfair advantage through private education is an artefact of the relative quality (or perceived quality) of public and private provision. There are therefore more appropriate responses to a *prima facie* injustice than to actualise, compound and institutionalise it. Indeed we see, however counter-intuitive it may seem, that to extend similar choices to all *is not to correct an injustice, but to foist on everyone implicit acceptance of a conception of justice which many do not share.* In consequence, the 'rational' resolution to a prior private dilemma creates a public dilemma for all citizens, and one for which those who design the parameters of choice, rather than those who have no choice but to operate within them, bear responsibility.

However, whilst the consumer's dilemma cannot be resolved by any of them acting as individuals, it is clear that society's dilemma is self-inflicted, being the outcome of prior political choice. It cannot be sufficiently stressed that given the complexity of value at stake in the social practice of education, the political choice in question sits ill not only with the ideals of liberalism, but also with the ideological commitments of neo-liberalism. The rights analysed here confer quasi-market freedoms on individuals, so that free exchanges can take place (between consumers and providers of education) designed to express citizens' settled preferences. Nozick has characterised such free exchanges as "voluntary acts between consenting adults"[16]—the paradigm of self-regarding acts with which none have the right to interfere. What I hope to have demonstrated is that the acts these rights initially permit and subsequently impel are only technically 'voluntary'. Moreover, they take place between adults who are only imperfectly 'consenting', since the goods their actions seek to secure accrue to them in a form and in a future changed in unspecifiable ways by those very acts themselves. Finally, the aggregate consequences of these imperfectly voluntary acts by imperfectly consenting adults entrain both procedural and substantive changes to the polity, which citizens other than current consumers have had no part in producing. The democratic deficit which is their procedural consequence is exposed by formal analysis. The substantive effects on the constitution of public education, produced when current perceived realities drive a social practice whose task is not merely to respond to circumstance but to keep options open for the polity as a whole, are foreseeable and confirmed by experience. Both of these considerations add further weight to my basic contention here that what is produced by prioritising rights of individual consumer choice in education is, in the economistic vocabulary of neo-liberalism, a classic case of 'market failure'.

CONCLUSION

It may be useful at this point to draw together the last three chapters before going on to examine the issues in political and educational philosophy and theory which they have thrown into sharp relief. In this part of my argument I have set out to dissent from both sides in the dispute which has now run on for almost two decades between liberal educators on the one hand and ascendant politicians and policy-makers on the other in those liberal democracies where the extension of the market into previously social distribution has found favour. I dissent from the belief of liberal educators that given more time, adequate resources and just a little fine-tuning, the original vision of emancipation for all could be realised through the greater spread of emancipation for each. I wish to question, in other words, the long-held liberal assumption that priority for the good of each eventually sums to the good of all. And despite post-Cold War rhetoric, to question that is not to pave the way for a demonised state-sponsored collectivity, but to suggest that the good of each and the good of all are *internally related,* rather than in political competition. To dissent in this way is therefore not only to point out shortcomings as much in the conception of the project of public liberal education as in its implementation: it is also to highlight significant fault-lines in the theory of much contemporary political liberalism.

I thus claim that there are more fundamental issues to be addressed by educational theorists than the merits and demerits of pedagogical method or curriculum content, important as these are. There are also more fundamental questions than those of educational access and distribution which appear at face value to have dominated the argument here so far. The particular interest of these latter questions is that they demonstrate the bankruptcy of attempts to evade the contradictions and paradoxes I have identified (puzzles highly germane to contemporary reconstructions of liberalism) by placing faith in the virtues of the market to deliver the good things which have eluded planned policy. These virtues are grounded in one of two ways and often, in public debate, in both. Either it is claimed, consequentially, that markets do as a matter of fact advance interests in a manner superior to planning or regulation, or it is claimed *a priori* that they are required to respect rights and protect the individual from the state. In both cases, justifications are ultimately grounded in the priority of freedom, so that "If that freedom is shown to be 'illusory', then the case for the market mechanism would be dis-established".[17] This chapter has sought to demonstrate that the freedoms conferred in the education market are indeed illusory since they directly harm some both educationally and socially, they indirectly damage all by pre-empting certain social choices, and they place in jeopardy even those direct benefits which some do obtain for themselves.

Of course the resurgence of faith in classical liberal precepts denuded of their social theses resulted from a host of contingencies all of which could have been otherwise. Nonetheless, it seems arguable that the ideal of liberal education for all, conceived as it has always been in individualist terms, carried within it seeds of disillusion ready to germinate in fertile ground. For it is not that educators have failed in the project of social progress through educational opportunity (as politicians claim), nor that they have been prevented by policy and resourcing deficiencies from fully developing the project (their usual rejoinder), though there may be elements of truth in either of those charges. It seems additionally (and more fundamentally) that we have *misconceived* this project in one very important respect. For throughout, we have simply tried to spread more widely the benefits that once only some enjoyed, on the (nineteenth-century) assumption that the welfare of all would accrue from the sum of the separate welfare of each. Our task now is to reconceptualise what we mean by education, by schooling and by training in a modern pluralist democracy, to acknowledge how individual and social benefit are mutually dependant and to rethink what we mean by emancipation *as a goal for all*. This task is part of the contemporary need to readdress rather than jettison the ideals of social reform which historically underpinned the development of mass liberal education as a project believed to be both worthwhile in itself and the royal road to greater equity in other social arrangements. As Dworkin has suggested, a reconceptualisation of society's educational project is a key element of contemporary efforts to establish an interpretation of liberalism in which neither liberty nor its equal distribution is compromised.

NOTES AND REFERENCES

1. This chapter is my fourth published attempt to address this problem. Previous attempts, elements of which are drawn on here in amended form, are: Jonathan, R. (1989), Choice and control in education: parental rights and social justice, *British Journal of Educational Studies*, 37. 4, pp. 321–328; Jonathan, R. (1990), State education service or prisoner's dilemma: the 'hidden hand' as source of educational policy, *British Journal of Educational Studies*, 38.2, pp. 116–132, and *Educational Philosophy and Theory*, 22.1, pp. 16–24; Jonathan, R., Parents' rights in schooling in: Munn, P. (Ed.), *Parents and Schools: Customers, Managers or Partners* (London, Routledge, 1993), pp. 11–26.

2. Dworkin, R. (1977), *op. cit., passim.*

3. See Jonathan, R. (1988), The notion of giftedness, or how long is a piece of string?, *British Journal of Educational Studies*, 26. 2, pp. 111–125.

4. Longitudinal evidence over many years of secondary pupil performance and subsequent experience has been collected and analysed by the Centre for Educational Sociology at the University of Edinburgh. Relevant reports and journal articles command widespread respect among both academics and the education policy community.

5. Hayek, F. A. (1960), *op. cit.*, p. 378.

6. *Ibid.*

7. Virgo, P., Learning for change, training, retraining and lifelong education for multi-career lives, *Bow Paper*, Nov. 1981.

8. Colquhoun, P., *Treatise on Indigence* (London, 1806), p. 17.

9. See Laslett, P. (Ed.), *Patriarcha and Other Political Works by Robert Filmer* (Oxford, Oxford University Press, 1959).

10. Schoeman, F. (1980), Rights of children, rights of parents, and the moral basis of the family, *Ethics*, Vol. 91, pp. 6–19.

11. Anscombe, E. (1978), On the source of the authority of the state, *Ratio,* Vol. 20. pp. 1–28.

12. As, for example, in Almond, B. (1991), Education and liberty, *Journal of Philosophy of Education* 25. 2, pp. 193–202, which draws on the arguments reported here.

13. *Ibid.,* p. 200.

14. *Ibid.,* p. 197.

15. Universal Declaration of Human Rights, 26, 3.

16. Nozick, R. (1974), *op. cit.*, p. 163

17. Sen, A. (1985), The moral standing of the market, *Social Philosophy and Policy*, 2.2, p. 5.

Chapter 5
Freedom and the Individual

A key element in any attempt to readdress those ideals of social reform which have underpinned the project of liberal education for all is a re-examination of the conception of individual freedom which has been dominant in liberalism for much of this century, sustaining linked beliefs about the permissible role of the state. That conception of individual freedom as immunity from interference in pursuit of chosen ends requires the state to stand neutral between competing visions of the good, ensuring that social arrangements privilege none above others. A neutralist liberalism as regulative principle for the polity thus offers a framework for an understanding of public education in which controversy is largely reserved for questions of what is to count as equitable access and what should be deemed appropriate content and process in order to realise the aim of keeping future options open for individuals and society. On the *outcomes* of education in terms of the beliefs and values individuals come to hold and of the knowledge and understanding which is developed for society, neutralist liberalism necessarily remains agnostic. The conception of freedom which underpins liberal neutrality can thus be seen resting on a view of persons as autonomous definers of their own ends, with the role of education being to promote that autonomy. Conflicts between the claims of liberty and equality in education, I shall argue, are at bottom disputes about how the liberal ideal of free agency for all is to be achieved.

I shall argue in this and the following chapter that the impasse which has been reached (for theory and for practice) after a long historical period in which the competing claims of freedom and equality have been juggled in the democratisation of education suggests that we should dig deeper into the premises of this theoretical framework. That re-examination requires that we move beyond asking how much social equality we may sacrifice to individual freedom, or debating conversely how far certain freedoms for some should be set aside in the name of particular equalities for others. A key area for enquiry will be liberalism's particular conception of the individual and of the formation of the self, for it is that conception which places commitments to freedom and equality in competition with each other when liberal neutralism, eschewing any social thesis, nonetheless relies on public education to realise a vision of the good society in which autonomous individuals severally determine what that good might be. I have argued that the contradictions exhibited by the liberal education project have been thrown into sharp relief (and hopelessly exacerbated in practice) by recent neo-liberal reforms in those democracies which now underwrite the extension of the market into the sphere of social provision. Popular debate presents this as a reversal of previous commitments, and indeed it is, in respect of a range of social values and priorities. In other respects, however, that shift can be seen as the latest social symptom of certain long-standing but inadequate metaphysical and ontological premises, deeply embedded in our conceptions of the individual and society.

Whilst an earlier liberal political quasi-consensus sought (with mixed success) to mitigate the social effects of a conception of the self which is fundamentally atomistic, successive attempts to realise social ideals based on that conception continued to mask the need to re-examine its philosophical premises. Today in neo-liberalism that conception—of individual agents as autonomous bearers of preferences in a social world constituted by freely-contracting persons who rationally construct their own purposes—is overt and unqualified. I am claiming that if we are to avoid a continual pendulum swing in policies for the ordering of society and education, it is not only the starkly atomistic neo-liberal conception of the self that requires theoretical attention but also the implicitly atomistic conception— which has a much longer history in liberal theory. Much contemporary theorising addresses questions which have their roots in similar conceptions of the self and society. This analysis follows a small but growing number of social theorists and political philosophers who sense that light can be thrown on these matters if they are also examined in the context of concrete circumstance. That return to an earlier, less fragmented mode of inquiry seems particularly apposite at a time when a neo-liberal revival, divorcing commitments of principle from social conditions as never before, on the one hand produces a strangely ideological version of the one world view which has long prided itself on being ideology-free, and on the other generates social practices with a curiously determinist flavour. I wish to take that turn to practice further, however, and claim that there is no more promising site for a socially-situated examination of relevant metaphysical and ontological premises than is offered by the theory and practice of liberal education. There are twin reasons for this. Firstly, education has been the practice primarily charged with mitigating those discrepancies in social equality between individuals which twentieth-century liberalism has identified as obstacles to its ideal of an equal distribution of liberty. And secondly, that mitigation is frustrated, and hence the ideal compromised, I shall argue, by an accompanying conception of the self which takes too little account of how persons become individuated, in part through their experience of education.

FROM PRACTICE TO THEORY

Sandel notes that liberalism, like any political theory, is more than a set of regulative principles: "It is also a view about the way the world is and the way we move within it. At the heart of this ethic lies a view of the person that both inspires and undoes it".[1] If we leave aside for the moment Sandel's verdict on that vision, there seems no better place to examine it than in the context of a social practice whose publicly endorsed function is the *formation* of persons. That liberal vision of the self and its relation to others, moreover, underpins a series of controversies—over whether the self is or is not prior to its ends, on whether autonomy is to be construed as an individual value or a social good, about where the boundaries lie between the public and private domains—which are thrown into illuminating relief in educational theory and practice. Related debates—on whether the state can and should be neutral between competing ideas of the good, on whether individuals 'own' their talents and attributes, on how far individual choices are auto-generated and self-regarding, over how the good of each relates to the good of all, etc., lie at the heart of disputes in educational theory and relevant policy. These disputes can thus usefully be brought to bear on any philosophical reconsideration of liberalism's vision of the self.

Liberal philosophy of education has long been imbued with the view of the person to which Sandel refers. This, in combination with the legacy of nineteenth-century liberalism's (now invisible) thesis about connections between freedom, reason and morality, gives rise to an optimistic confidence in social progress as a consequence of individual emancipation. That in turn underpins the social ideal of a liberal education for all which *both arises from and is designed to realise* the neutralist liberal vision of individual and social good. Thus the overarching aim of liberal education is the good of the individual and of society, with its content and process designed to enable individuals, through the achievement of rational autonomy, to determine what that good shall be. What makes liberal education liberal is precisely a principled agnosticism about the substance of its outcomes (though not about the procedural values through which those outcomes should arise)—an agnosticism grounded in implicit understandings concerning the relation of increased knowledge and understanding to an enhanced capacity for critical reflection, of this capacity to sound judgement, and of such sound judgement to moral value for the individual and society. All of these understandings are

rooted in a more or less atomistic notion of the individual in which
society is simply the sum of such individuals, negotiating with others
to secure mutual accommodation of individual preferences. The good
society, in consequence, is one which offers the optimal context for
differential preference formation and satisfaction, with continued
social progress to be realised through the emancipation of increasing
numbers of individuals who nonetheless remain separate, autonomous definers of their own ends.

This vision of individuals and society has increasingly been called
into question by theorists. Not surprisingly, its theoretical premises
run into intractable difficulties when they serve to guide, either
explicitly or by implication,[2] a practice which aims to institutionalise
the development of both rationality and autonomy in individuals. I
have discussed elsewhere how it bedevils debates internal to
education, for example on the selection of core educational content
in a pluralist context, the scope of teacher authority and pedagogical
neutrality, or controversy over the permissible content and procedures of moral and social education.[3] Here I am concerned to
highlight how the same assumptions and beliefs have long underpinned contested social policies for education and also public
expectations of those policies. The success of neo-liberalism in
finding a bridge-head of popular appeal initially in the education
context, despite (and paradoxically because of) the fact that there is
no more inappropriate arena for consumer sovereignty, is testimony
both to the pervasive power of relevant philosophical premises and to
their inadequacy. It may seem fanciful to see the same particular set
of beliefs underlying trends in policy which are apparently each
other's antithesis, but it is not for nothing that neo-liberals are often
seen (in educational matters as elsewhere) to have stolen the clothes
of the progressive reformers they repudiate and put on the defensive.
For in some respects, these are indeed the same ill-fitting clothes, only
with the addition of brass buckles, gold braid and the large shoulder-
pads of a more aggressive atomism which in the new dispensation
serves temporarily to disguise a still unresolved lack of fit.

To refer again to the UK as illustrative example, reforms of
education instituted there in 1944 reflected the urgent concern in the
post-war impetus to social justice with spreading the 'advantages' of
education more widely through the population. Accordingly, for a
thirty-year period thereafter, reforms focused on questions of access,
distribution and effective transmission, with the democratic and
democratising extension to all of an education which had historically
been associated with the possession and production of privilege
(intellectual, social and economic) seen as the key to both private and
public betterment. It was thus assumed that, were each individual
enabled to fulfil intellectual and creative potential and build a

personal system of values, then collective benefits would also follow, socially, culturally and economically. Improved collective economic performance and the social cohesion seen as its prerequisite and product remained the twin social goals of mass schooling: what changed with the institution of mass liberal education was the road to those long-held goals. Cohesion was to be achieved not by hierarchical order and obedience but through social mobility at least and social equality at best; similarly, economic advance was to follow, not from a pool of literate and numerate labour realising the intellectual and creative vision of the few, but from the maximal development of the talents and tastes of each bringing technological advance and greater efficiency to production, and finer discrimination and rising expectations to consumption, with both elements fuelling growth. This represented an ideal of individual development and social progress in which no trade-offs were required between the former and the latter, neither equity nor liberty need be compromised, and the good of all was to be realised through the separate good of each. In short, the project of liberal education for all can be seen as the social instantiation of the neutralist liberal ideal.

The real world stubbornly fell short of that vision, and successive educational reforms brought disillusion when they failed to realise it, as chapter three recalled. Overtly meritocratic arrangements lost allegiance when it became clear that these, even if they could be made to work equitably, offered emancipation only to the few. Common provision, however presented, was at bottom an attempt at a more equitable meritocracy, which in addition promised enhanced self- and social esteem to the losers in what logically remained in many respects an unacknowledged competition. As the instrumental pay-off of extending liberal education to all continued to evade some individuals, so it was also judged to have fallen short of expected forms of social progress in a manner and to a degree which would satisfy political demands for return on investment. The stage was then set for a backlash against earlier naive beliefs in the equal emancipation of all by means of a liberal education, and a backlash against the educational arrangements which had met with only limited success in achieving that among conflicting goals. The premises on which those goals were based were not called into question: instead battle lines were again re-drawn in the field of policy and practice over their implementation. At the theoretical level indeed, the assault on the challenged consensus was fuelled by an even stronger version of *the same metaphysical and ontological assumptions* as the earlier reform policies it repudiated. What disguises this fact beneath *radically revisionist practical policies* is the concomitant neo-liberal retreat from the moral and social ideals which had formerly held liberalism's ontological assumptions in check.

At the risk of some oversimplification for heuristic purposes, we see two approaches to the ordering of society and two approaches to the ordering of public education designed to reflect and realise those social orderings. If we list, against the educational context, the philosophical assumptions that neutralist liberalism and neo-liberalism share, and examine their opposing versions of similarly based mistakes, we may hope to throw light on shared inadequacies in background conceptions of the individual and society. For these conceptions, which remain as unresolved problems for contemporary liberals, have been elevated to articles of faith and triumphally re-embraced by neo-liberals. In the paper quoted above, Sandel is concerned to pursue theoretical enquiry into liberalism's vision of the self in order to throw light on a practical impasse: ". . . seeing how it goes wrong as philosophy may help us diagnose our present political condition".[4] This seems a necessary precondition to finding a coherent way forward. That enterprise will be still more effectively advanced, I believe, if we triangulate the exercise, letting the lessons of experience show up flaws in the theoretical map which has led us to this point. So this case study aims to contribute to the enquiry from the other end, in the belief that seeing how these assumptions go wrong when cashed out in practice in contrasting political conditions also helps us to see how they go wrong as philosophy. And by getting our premises clearer at that basic level, the ground can be cleared for headway in the practical field.

A listing of key relevant issues would go as follows. Both approaches to the forming of individuals and the re-forming of society through education subscribe to negative concepts of liberty, with which the claims of equality are seen as in potential competition: what differentiates them is how they resolve the competition between the two (discrete) values. Both see the individual as forming preferences through rational deliberation, with each individual ideally becoming the self-directed captain of his/her own destiny: what differentiates them here are divergent views on how autonomy is best expressed. Both envision individuals as having a 'property in their person' which extends to ownership of actual and potential talents and capacities: what distinguishes them here are empirical claims about how these are best developed. Both see the public and private spheres as discrete, with education ideally serving both and sacrificing neither to the other: what differentiates them is the forms of educational value—and its distribution—which assume priority when that balancing act cannot be maintained. Both seek to remain agnostic about substantive conceptions of the good, whether for the individual or the polity, though they differ on the forms of free exchange which will best guarantee a plurality of such goods for the future: here neutralist liberals rely on the maximal development of rational autonomy and the presumed synergy of freedom and reason, whilst neo-liberals turn to the executive power of preferences cashed as quasi-votes in a market of options. And both accord supreme priority to autonomy individually conceived, though liberals seek to safeguard its development through education as a prerequisite to its later exercise, whilst for neo-liberals its current exercise is paramount.

In setting out what these two contrasting approaches to social practice in general and educational policy in particular share as well as what very significantly divides them, I do not of course mean to suggest that there is little to choose between them as coherent theoretical positions, still less as approaches to guiding our social arrangements. No wholesale repudiation of either liberalism or liberal education as such is implied by this enquiry, only acknowledgement that, in the interpretation I have reported, both contain corresponding fault-lines which can be usefully scrutinised in tandem so that both liberalism and liberal education can be more adequately grounded. This has become the more urgent when neo-liberalism now pointedly exacerbates long-standing difficulties in many of liberalism's premises to a degree where they can no longer be ignored in theory, still less endorsed to guide practice. Since current alternatives to reformulating liberalism are neither defensible in theory nor promising for the guidance of public education, one way forward, for both theory and practice, may be to examine some of those fault-lines as they show up insistently in the context of public education. Many key disputes about education are intimately connected with liberal controversies over relations between freedom, equality and equity: those relations therefore present a primary focus for examining the "view of the person" which underpins them and vitiates debate over practice. I shall try to show that only with a richer understanding of how persons are formed, and of how their autonomy is enmeshed with that of their fellows, can society's arrangements for education be so ordered that they might contribute more successfully to the realisation of liberalism's enduring ideals.

LIBERTY AND EQUALITY

In *On Liberty* Mill famously stated that the only freedom worthy of the name consists in our "pursuing our own good in our own way". This is far from straightforward. Mill's adage is generally taken to mean that each should be allowed to pursue his own good except where that would frustrate the similar pursuit by others, and it is with that exception clause that the complications begin, as Mill himself was well aware. Clearly, the liberty principle is only unproblematic for pursuits which are entirely self-regarding and goods which are unambiguously private. However, controversy has always surrounded the former, and the latter diminish in number as the functional interdependence of social roles multiplies. Matters become still more complex if "our" refers accordingly to joint good as well as simply to a plurality of separate goods. Then freedom clearly requires that we collaborate both in defining and obtaining the good in question. This would mean that "we" would need an equal voice in determining not just what we each happen to value, but what is to count as value; and we would need common conditions for equally effective agency. *Liberty thus requires equality* in two respects for the liberal: on the individualistic interpretation of Mill's adage, liberty is a value equally for each; but on the more complex and comprehensive interpretation (which takes account of the fact that some goods are indivisible), some aspects of equality are prerequisites to any liberty which is constituted by all and available to each.

Despite this consequence, in much theoretical and most popular debate liberty and equality have come to be conceived as if they were in competition or even each other's alternative. It is a not unreasonable representation to note that: "The New Right contends that freedom conflicts with equality and should be preferred. ... the Old Left agrees that there is a conflict and contends that equality is to be preferred".[5] Nor is it new to set up liberty and equality in opposition, as if the more is had of one, the less can be had of the other. This can be clearly seen in the education context where disputes during half a century about appropriate policies (what constitutes acceptable content and pedagogy? does wider access conflict with the maintenance of standards? how do we prioritise 'academic' and 'social' outcomes? how should we balance private and public benefit? etc.) can be seen on one level as the playing out of a long tug-of-war between the apparently competing claims of equality and liberty. I shall argue that particular conceptions of liberty and equality have played a part in underpinning the tension between individual rights and social aspirations which public education sought to maintain in uneasy balance for decades until neo-liberalism staked an unambiguous claim in favour of the former. Analysis of that claim's appeal suggests that weaknesses in a conception of equality which many saw as too 'thick' (licensing state interference in the lives of individuals and thus compromising neutrality) opened the way for successful challenge by a conception of liberty which is certainly too negative (retreating from distributive oversight of social freedoms in the name of individual immunity from interference). Further analysis suggests that the 'thick' conception of equality driven into retreat was itself the reverse side of the coin of a liberal conception of liberty which has long seemed worryingly negative and insubstantial. And that in turn has arisen from a view of the self and its agency which is deeply problematic.

If we turn again to the education context, I argued in chapter four that consumer rights exacerbate the conflict between the good of each and the good of all. They can be seen as the latest policy response to the perennial tension arising from prevailing conceptions of liberalism's *two* key values. Education conflicts are often represented in terms of freedom and equality, with 'egalitarian' reformers seen to regard the sacrifice of some personal liberties as a price the right-thinking should be prepared to pay for a fairer social world, and libertarians claiming that posture to be both an unacceptable trespass on the good of each and self-defeating as regards the good of all. Neither position captures the complexity of the issues at stake. When, as with education, the good of all is not simply the sum of the good of each, so that the problem is not a purely distributional one (as it might be for example with the public provision of health care), the inadequacy of any conception of these values which sees them as discrete and potentially available for trade-off one against the other becomes glaring. When the good of all (public benefit) is *simultaneously* one of the goods that each requires, both for the sake of its own intrinsic and instrumental rewards and also to secure the framework within which any truly private good is constituted as an individual benefit, then conceptions of liberty and equality which place these values in mutual competition cannot but be destructive of the good of each *as well as* of the good of all. To understand how liberty and equality come to seem in competition, despite the fact that they cannot but be constitutive of each other, education provides the most illuminating practical context.

With regard to liberty, debate about the strengths and shortcomings of positive and negative concepts has been a staple of philosophical argument, with liberal neutralism seen to require the latter (the bad press the former has long enjoyed being underlined by Cold War rhetoric and now post-Cold War triumphalism). Debate has been less clear-cut on 'thick' and 'thin' conceptions of equality, partly because a 'thick' understanding of equality seems required to counterbalance a negative conception of liberty. The 'two concepts of liberty' debate has thus set the tone for our understanding of the relations between liberty and equality in a manner which is unproductive and only entrenches the dubious "view of the person" Sandel identifies—a view on which that long-running debate is itself predicated. I shall briefly examine these positive and negative concepts of liberty now, and 'thick' and 'thin' conceptions of equality in the following section, in order to show that the 'two concepts' debates give rise to misleading choices between false alternatives. It is not a matter in either case of deciding which interpretation is the more acceptable, since in each case both alternatives rest on a similarly inadequate view of the self and its relation to the social world.

I shall argue that liberalism now requires a more substantive conception of liberty, though not the crude positive concept which neutralist liberals of the post-war period were determined to keep at bay, nor its more benign variant currently proposed by some communitarians. That more substantive conception of liberty in turn contains within it a constitutive requirement to certain equalities in order to permit equity between all members of a liberal society. Again, just as the more substantive conception of liberty I shall argue for is not that covert coercion feared by neutralists, so the constitutive conception of equality which it requires will not be met by the simple removal of hindrances to opportunity, still less by the merely negative, formalistic equality-before-the-law which satisfies neo-liberals. I adopt the rather clumsy epithets 'substantive liberty' and 'constitutive equality' to avoid false identifications based on the disputes about positive and negative concepts or 'thick' and 'thin' conceptions (scare-quotes omitted from hereon), which I am seeking to recast. Throughout my survey of these questions the focus on education will reflect the unique salience of that practice for individual liberty and its equal distribution—a truism of liberal philosophy of education. My intention, however, is to give that truism more substance than neutralism can accommodate or individualism allow.

THE 'TWO CONCEPTS OF LIBERTY' DEBATE

Despite a history of debate over the complexities lurking behind the liberty principle's necessary qualifying clause, by the middle of this century contingencies of philosophical theory and political reality had significantly attenuated earlier caution. This gave rise to an unambiguous concept of liberty which regarded individuals as free to the extent that they are not coerced by other individuals or institutions. That interpretation was propounded in opposition to the kind of positive freedom against which Berlin argued and whose endorsement threatens to licence us ". . . to ignore the actual wishes of men or societies, to bully, oppress, torture them in the name, and on behalf of their 'real' selves . . . ".[6] With such a choice, who would not underwrite without further ado the negative conception championed by Berlin? There are, however, difficulties with both of those conceptions, much rehearsed over many decades. The crude positive concept seems to open the way for any dominant group to decide what is in the interests of the rest, with results which range from the obvious dangers of naked fascism, as in "Our concept of liberty is that the individual must be allowed to develop his personality on behalf of the state",[7] to the more insidious pressures of authoritarian conservatism, as in "The institution of marriage would be threatened if individual judgements were permitted about the morality of adultery; on these matters there must be a public morality...'.[8] Conversely, the stark negative concept relies on an untenable dichotomy between the public and the private spheres, ignores the social location of individuals, and opens the way to a libertarian social world which looks remarkably like Hobbes's "war of all against all". In that world we are all free to dine at the Ritz provided no-one bars the door, black South Africans are as free as whites overnight when they acquire formal voting powers, and the alienated and ignorant are as free as holders of substantial cultural capital.

Whilst no more need be said about the crude positive concept, rightly regarded as incompatible with liberalism's ideals, that repudiation should not thereby drive us straight into the arms of the stark negative concept. The first obvious difficulty lies in the conflation of constraint with coercion, which restricts sources of constraint to identifiable others or institutions and therefore implies a deeply conservative understanding of social relations. What this vision entirely neglects, moreover, are sources of constraint internal to the self. In its identification of freedom with the absence of identifiable obstacles to its exercise, it thus ignores the key question of how the individual's preferences and desires, which freedom is to respect and protect, arise. When Bradley pointed out that the developing individual grows within his social world "and when he can separate himself from that world, and know himself apart from it, then by that time his self, the object of his self-consciousness, is penetrated, infected, characterised by the existence of others",[9] he was drawing attention to the fact that, whatever the tenability of a sharp divide between individual persons and their fellows in the *exercise* of freedom, that dichotomy is entirely illusory when we focus on freedom's *development*. And these two dimensions must be considered in tandem by the liberal since *the parameters for freedom's development result to a large degree from its current exercise by others*. No more telling example is required than the 'freedoms' examined in the last chapter here. Green (who of all nineteenth-century theorists was perhaps the most concerned with the social policy prerequisites to liberalism's ideals) argued that "We do not mean freedom to do as we like irrespectively of what it is that we like. We do not mean a freedom that can be enjoyed by one man or set of men at a cost of a loss of freedom to others...We mean by it a power which each man exercises through the help or security given him by his fellow-men, and which he in turn helps to secure for them".[10] In insisting on the social parameters of freedom, Green was not opening the door to the totalitarian eclipse of the individual, but should be seen as underlining the mutual interdependence of individual agency in a social world.

He was also, like Bradley, calling into question a tendency within liberalism from its beginnings, to conceive of the individual as a free-standing, self-defining being who holds preferences related to self-chosen ends and requires of social arrangements merely that they permit to each the optimal exercise of personal choice consistent with the similar exercise by others. This attenuated vision of free agency and its parameters yields a conception of society as no more than the aggregate of its individual atoms: not only do these atoms remain always at the producing end of the individual/social interaction, but the role their preferences play in the production of social structure is itself discounted. Claims to self-regarding action often rely on given social arrangements being taken as data, with 'harm to others' requiring identifiable others. As Cohen argues in his analysis of freedom in capitalism, various unfreedoms are legitimated by invisibility, since those to whom they accrue are not "specified individuals".[11] This understanding of freedom rests on a view of the person which, as the work of Green and Bradley among others shows, has long been the subject of disquiet. Nonetheless, in the contemporary world, it remains pervasive, lying behind a series of difficulties within modern neutralist liberalism and now, despite that, being foregrounded to legitimate a resurgent neo-liberalism. For whilst this latter challenges neutralist liberalism on matters of social policy, it does so on the basis of a cruder version of philosophical inadequacies which have remained unresolved within liberalism. By focusing on those inadequacies through neo-liberalism's magnifying lens we can see defects more clearly.

Priority for the individual over the social, on the premise that these are discrete ontological categories, is unashamed in libertarianism, defined by Flew in his *Dictionary of Philosophy* as "wholehearted political and economic liberalism, opposed to any social or legal constraints on individual freedom".[12] It need hardly be repeated that this is deeply problematic. The previous chapter showed in the world of practice that when one half of a false dichotomy is prioritised, individual agency has social effects which in turn impinge on individuals, and so on. And that dichotomy is no more tenable at the level of general theorising. The individual freedoms which libertarians counterpose to social constraints must of course be established and protected by *some* social arrangements: and *any* that we select or protect cannot but commit us to some corresponding allocation of freedoms and unfreedoms between individuals across society. This was captured succinctly by Marx in the observation that "private ownership by one person presupposes non-ownership on the part of other persons".[13] It can be taken considerably further if we acknowledge with Taylor[14] that liberty has internal as well as external preconditions and hence potential constraints. Once that is admitted, it becomes evident that many social arrangements (most notably but by no means exclusively in relation to education) are crucial to the individual's freedom from *both* forms of constraint.

Neo-liberalism, then, rests squarely on ontological individualism and a narrow conception of constraint. More subtly, however, the individual/social dichotomy (with priority for the former) also implicitly underpins modern neutralist liberalism, giving rise to internal contradictions and unresolved tensions (particularly salient in educational theory and practice) which vitiate this pervasive contemporary form of liberal theory. Although most (but not all) contemporary neutralists depart from the purist version of negative liberty so clearly articulated by Berlin, in that formally they recognise internal constraints on individual freedom, the implications of that acknowledgement are not fully followed through. This becomes evident when the development of individuals as free agents is taken into serious account. The analysis needed to take better account of this will be deferred to the coming chapter: here, my concern is to show that prevailing conceptions of free agency and its development are indeed in need of revision. Though the theoretical position in question is standardly presented as straightforward, it seems far less so when carried over to liberal philosophy of education, where theory seeks purchase on practice. For the way in which modern neutralist liberalism attempts to reconcile the apparently competing claims of liberty and equality—and to accommodate pluralism in matters of moral and social value—is to require that social arrangements allow equal opportunities for each individual to espouse and exercise preferences. This approach prizes individual autonomy above all else, with that autonomy understood as the capacity to define one's ends and the means to them through rational reflection. In this respect its theoretical basis is sounder than neo-liberalism—which either takes preferences as brute data or ignores their provenance—for it allows a distinction between the individual's first- and second-order desires. This goes some way to meeting Green's caveat that what we seek through the exercise of freedom is not immaterial, without handing over decision about what our interests 'really' might be to anyone other than our more reflective selves. There are nonetheless real defects in this position, and these are associated with an under-specification of autonomy and its development—defects with which educational theory has long wrestled, with limited success.

Thus the aims and procedures of liberal education have long been justified by philosophers of education with reference to neutralist liberal conceptions of freedom and autonomy. And the public provision of education, with its successive attempts to remove or counteract internal and external hindrances to its benefit to the individual, represents, as I noted above, the social institutionalisation of this ideal. With hindsight, however, we can see how the ideal breaks down in practice when the greater freedom and autonomy of all is predicated simply on the greater freedom and autonomy of increasing numbers of individuals. In contingent conditions of social expansion, a prospect offered to all can be delivered to more than before, but no contingencies, however favourable, can provide for the equal distribution of opportunities to develop reflected preferences or to exercise them so long as the good of all *which is in part constitutive of the good of each* is conceived as no more than the sum of the separate goods of each. We need no better example of how the options available for preference are altered by their wider (or narrower) distribution, and no more telling instance of how the freedom and autonomy of each is enmeshed with the freedom and autonomy of others, nor of how the parameters of both circumscribe the good of all, than we get from a survey of the stubborn gap between our demands of public education and its ability to meet them.

Should the contradictions exhibited by this ideal for practice fail to ring the appropriate warning bells, they can now be seen mirrored in growing disquiet at the level of pure theory. Leaving aside the telling limiting case of education, or indeed any practical illustrations of the dialectical relationship between the individual and the social, recent work in political philosophy identifies a fatal internal incoherence in the notion that the spread of autonomous individual agency is of itself the royal road to increased liberty *and* its equitable distribution. To be tenable, the procedural ideals of modern neutralist liberalism would require that there be an indefinite range of co-possible liberties, for only this would permit each individual to pursue his own good in his own way without constraining the similar pursuit by other individuals. That we are social creatures in a finite world makes this empirically implausible, even if we ignore the fact that many of the means and ends we seek have positional characteristics. What is worse, this is a problem which liberals wedded to negative conceptions of freedom and to associated procedural neutrality can neither evade nor resolve in principle. They cannot evade the problem by advocating choices between competing sets of liberties, on pain of taking up an impermissible substantive position on the relative worth of preferences. However, if such qualitative judgements (which can only legitimately be made by each individual) are eschewed, the neutralist liberal is left only to posit an optimal set of co-possible liberties based on quantitative judgements about the amount of liberty available in principle to all, and its even-handed distribution.

Fatally, however, substantive judgements are also required to designate any set of co-possible liberties as optimal. To be sure, many different sets of liberties could consistently be assigned to each, but only by recourse to those impermissible substantive commitments which cannot be assumed to be shared by all, and cannot be imported by the liberal to over-ride preferences. The neutralist liberal is thus caught in a circular trap.[15] We might usefully ask how this predicament may have arisen.

It is worth recalling that this contradiction did not present itself starkly to nineteenth-century liberals. Their belief in causal connections between freedom, right reason and sound judgement made gradual social progress and moral harmonisation seem an empirically plausible hypothesis. Basic to a concept of freedom defined as the absence of constraint by individuals or institutions was the belief that preferences would tend to harmonise in proportion as freedom was extended. (Bellamy reminds us that "A view originally based on theological foundations, as in Locke and possibly Smith, became a secularised theory of progress about the evolution of society and the nature of human development".[16]) Since we cannot plausibly re-embrace the falsified assumption that under conditions of economic and political expansion the right-thinking will freely tend to make compatible choices (a thesis neo-liberalism resurrects only to controvert), liberalism now seems to have reached an impasse. With classical liberalism's social thesis whittled away by a century of democratisation, economic expansion and growing pluralism, the philosophical thesis it underpinned is left seriously exposed, requiring either a replacement social thesis or a non-empirical argument to ground the possibility of equally respecting the like liberty of all. There is now serious doubt among social philosophers that the latter is sustainable on neutralist premises, for the reasons I have reported. Thus a purely negative concept of liberty looks incompatible in principle with the requirements of equity embodied in Mill's demand that we should each be enabled to pursue our own good in our own way. I noted the contradictions which are embedded in liberal ideals for education: indeed the negative concept cannot help revealing its inadequacy when applied to the social world, where neutralist liberalism permits necessary inequities between individuals. (Where it differs notably from neo-liberalism is in remaining agnostic about where those inequities will fall, or with what characteristics or behaviours they will be associated.) Although resulting inequities have historically been mitigated by compensatory or redistributive policies which sit uncomfortably with liberalism's principles, as the coming section will show, the tensions they generate throw additional light on flaws in the conventional negative concept of liberty and the view of the person it reflects.

These begin with the under-specification of a conception which continues to reflect the preoccupation of Berlin (and others of his generation) with the protection of autonomous individuals from the predations of the state apparatus. For the negative concept of liberty is incomplete in the same respects as the positive concept which has conventionally been seen as its only alternative. Firstly, both the stark negative concept and the crude positive one it holds at bay are based on dyadic relations: the former restricts itself to x's freedom *from* y (remaining agnostic about the substance of individual preferences), whilst the latter is concerned with x's freedom *to* y (denying priority for the individual in judgements of worth). Secondly, in both cases x is atomistic and either, in the negative concept, separate from and *acting on* the social world, or, in the positive concept, separate from and *acted on* by society. Neither of these conceptions permits an equal distribution of liberties in practice and neither stands up to theoretical challenge: their unacknowledged weaknesses lie in what they share. Neither can take account either of the interdependence of personal agency in a social world nor of the social context as both product and producer of consciousness. And both of those shortcomings are grounded in the view of the person which Sandel identified as in need of revision. Many commentators have argued that there is an implicit third relation in formulations of liberty as either 'freedom from' or 'freedom to', with the distinction between the two therefore less clear cut than it seems. Once it is acknowledged that liberty cannot be anything other than a *triadic* relation, we can begin to move beyond disputes about which of two (similarly grounded) concepts is the true one and towards a consideration of "what persons are, and...what is to count as an obstacle to or interference with the freedom of persons so conceived".[17] That insight of MacCallum's (and of thirty years ago) should enable us to reconnect theory with the world of circumstance and leave behind not only sterile old debates for example about whether the struggle of colonial peoples can properly be called a fight for freedom[18] but also contemporary arguments about whether all are free to obtain goods which are positional, provided that none are barred from the competition. And moving beyond "the 'artificiality' of a borderline for distinguishing freedom from other human values"[19] (semantically) we can ask, not whether social arrangements which interfere with freedom are the result of deliberate intent, but "whether the difficulties can be removed by human arrangements, and at what cost".[20] These insights are welcome concessions to the complexity of personal agency and the freedom of the individual, but they still do not take us far enough.

If that triadic relation in freedom's elements is taken seriously, it requires more than a broadening of what counts as external constraint, together with formal recognition of internal constraint. *It further requires that the notion of internal constraint comprehend internal barriers to the formation of preferences as well as to their satisfaction.* This in turn demands that we call into question a view of the person which sees the self as 'prior to its ends', a view which characterises the problem of freedom in terms of hindrances to the expression of preferences and the exercise of choices whose provenance remains a mystery. With the conventional negative concept, such preferences and choices are seen to issue from autonomous rational deliberation, as if the knowledge and information on which they are apparently based were givens, and as if the process of deliberation itself were unaffected by those attachments, ranges of options and pressures of circumstance which lie at least to some extent beyond the control (and often the awareness) of the 'autonomous' chooser. Neutralist liberals have recoiled from these considerations for fear of opening the door to others deciding for us what is in our real interests and what we ought to want, but this implication need not follow. Indeed, if the liberal conception of autonomy does not at least admit of Taylor's distinction between weak and strong evaluation—with both still the preserve of those whose preferences are at issue—then preferences become not merely immune from over-rule by others, but also from correction by the self. And where preferences are in principle incorrigible, liberalism admits relativism in theory and licences in practice any social arrangements short of known harms to specified others.

When we attend more carefully to internal constraints on liberty, the focus shifts from necessary conditions for freedom's exercise to necessary conditions for its development. A focus on these places a premium on a conception of the self which sees persons as neither simply the active producers nor merely the passive recipients of ends, meanings and circumstance. Clues to that conception can be found in problems with liberal education's designated tasks at both the individual and the social levels. At the former level, liberal education aims to initiate the individual into a culture and its values whilst also enabling her/him to dispense with the ladder of understanding and commitment once it has been climbed. At the latter level the system of public education is required to maintain and reproduce society for all at the same time as each is enabled to stand aside from or rise above existing social arrangements. Some of the ensuing practical contradictions have already been described: their theoretical implications will be returned to in the coming chapter where an examination of how the self and its capacity for free agency develops will offer grounding for a more substantive concept of liberal freedom. First though, conceptions of equality which have muddied both the practical and the theoretical waters need re-examination, since the disputes they entrain put flaws in the negative concept of liberty (and associated neutralism) under the spotlight.

'THICK' AND 'THIN' CONCEPTIONS OF EQUALITY

Just as the standard debates offer a (Hobson's) choice between two concepts of liberty, the one too positive but the other too negative, so the ensuing polemic and social policy debates have offered two conceptions of equality, the one too thin and the other too thick. It is useful to recall those parallel developments briefly here, since attempts to reconcile them have preoccupied modern liberalism, as the closing section of this chapter will show. For early anglophone liberalism a thin conception of equality matched an understanding of liberty as absence of constraint, since, given its social thesis, no more was required. Liberty was a value equally for all, and opportunities for the exercise of individual preference should be equally available to all. Extended suffrage, the economic conditions of free market capitalism and the spread of education would bring the conditions of freedom equally to all on the social thesis referred to above. Over time, circumstance belied the empirical assumptions supporting this thesis. As chapter two recalled, rather than bringing increasingly perfectly-competitive market relations, the development of industrial capitalism (through capital concentration, the profit mechanism and the development of organised labour) tended towards the destruction of ideal markets, widening rather than progressively ironing out the initial differences between contracting parties. Urbanisation and the agglomeration of both capital and labour rapidly negated the free market's role as rewarder of moral merit and engine of moral progress. And the development of fully representative political structures, which Mill had advocated as "an agency of national education",[21] failed to embody the rise and workings of a moral meritocracy in which a public-spirited initial elite would foster social conditions for the moral advancement of the rest. Instead, the political elite tended to support the economic interests it was expected to control, thus exacerbating rather than moderating the dangers foreseen from the start in the unregulated workings of the market. When confidence in an evolving coherence in preferences lost its empirical basis it nonetheless lingered on invisibly, supported only by philosophical assumptions about connections between freedom, right reason and sound judgement.

A twin-track development ensued thereafter which has given rise to much confusion in liberalism's response to equality issues. During the first half of this century, as liberalism ceased to be a patterned theory of justice in which the pattern criterion was moral merit, both political conditions and philosophical developments made this shift from perfectionist social theory to neutralist meta-ideology seem like an advance to be celebrated. In philosophy, the rise of positivism underpinned the triumph of procedure over substance in questions of moral and social value. In political thinking, this triumph gave rise to the 'end of ideology' thesis which legitimated liberalism's claims to superiority not only over various totalitarian systems of thought but over any form of political and economic organisation with substantive and explicit moral and social goals. A negative concept of liberty and a thin conception of equality were central to these claims (the position classically represented by Berlin's analysis). Meanwhile, however, in the real world of social policy, from the time of the first Factory Acts to the 1944 Education Act and beyond, *the failures of the free market to live up to perfectionist moral and social expectations were progressively mitigated by compensating social and legislative arrangements*. These sought to modify structural conditions which hampered the realisation of formally equal opportunities to exercise individual freedom, but the ideal remained elusive. Postwar reforms of education initially addressed external obstacles to equal liberty, but the limitations of that project soon placed internal constraints firmly on the practical agenda. Social practice attempted by these means to acknowledge just those realities which much political theory at that time explicitly denied.

By the 1960s, the public provision of liberal education for all aimed also to address inequalities in internal obstacles not simply to the *exercise* of freedom, but to *the development of its prerequisite capacities* in the individual. By this point, the discrepancy between the thickening conceptions of equality invoked to address structural constraints on freedom, and the thin conception of equality required by liberal commitment to non-interference in the lives of individuals by the state, were set on a collision course. Nowhere is this more apparent than in the debates which have raged over equality issues in education for the past half century. Indeed it is as if nineteenth-century optimism about the ability of free exchange to distribute freedom equitably *was replaced in the mid-twentieth century with belief that the extension of liberal education to all might do so in its place*. Two dimensions can thus be seen in policy debates, reflecting dual concerns with education and equality. The first is relatively straightforward. As a source of private benefit, whether intrinsic or instrumental, the demands of equity required that none be debarred from opportunity to avail themselves of the goods of education. All should have equal freedom in this regard. Reforms instituted immediately post-war in the UK were accordingly designed to enable all to have access to differentiated intrinsic goods and to compete openly for positional goods. Social and economic status were no longer to operate as barriers. In this respect such reforms presented no more difficulties in justification (whatever their empirical shortcomings) than did the provision of health-care or retirement funding to all. What complicates matters in the education case, however, is that this social practice is not merely a suitable *object* for social reform along with others: uniquely, education is also looked to as a powerful *engine* of wider social reform, in virtue of its power in principle to mitigate both internal and external constraints on individual freedom. What complicates matters still further, however, is that just as education policy affects social structure, with the former influencing though not determining the latter, so social structure mediates educational experience for the individual. And this last feature tends to frustrate the very emancipatory aims which made education the repository of liberal optimism during this historical period.

In chapter three I argued that education's relation to social structure is not quite what post-war reformers hoped, being asymmetrical. Inequalities in educational access and experience do indeed reproduce and perpetuate structural inequality in society, but their removal does not of itself remove it. (Their re-introduction, of course, as chapter four indicated, exploits and exacerbates existing inequalities.) The primary reason for this asymmetrical relation lies in the question of cultural capital. When availability of educational goods depends upon ability to pay, economic capital is a key determinant of access: when those goods are publicly provided and freely available to all, then cultural capital remains as a powerful modifier of educational experience and hence of any access which depends upon prior experience. Successive reforms therefore sought to mitigate the effects of cultural capital differentials by abandoning selection, by delaying or disguising differentiation and, where this still did not seem to be enough, by various compensatory programmes. These latter were of two kinds: some aimed to give a leg-up to deserving individuals in the social competition, on a deficit model of the losers' ability to compete.[22] The more radical approach rejected this deficit model, advocating far-reaching changes in curriculum and pedagogy to acknowledge the culture, values and aspirations of those who under-performed in a competition seen to be not merely stacked against them, but so stacked because it embodied norms and beliefs which many did not share (arguments put forward in the 1960s for reasons of class; in the 1970s and 1980s, of gender and ethnicity[23]).

Both avenues of reform met with strong opposition, with all contenders invoking equality to support their positions. Those who resisted going more than a short way along the first avenue of reform invoked Aristotle's adage that injustice results just as much from treating unequals equally as from treating equals unequally, whilst proponents of compensation urged that equality or inequality in potential was what ought to be at issue and that apparent ability as reflected in current performance was no adequate measure of this and hence no criterion for differential treatment. Advocates of equalisation had disappointment with the distribution of private benefit and hence with the structural effects of reformed educational access on their side. Those holding the line, however, were on theoretical grounds which appeared the more compelling as their opponents tended to over-extend their arguments in response to unyielding circumstance. Thus when, for example, equality of opportunity remained elusive, and advocates of more far-reaching reform wished it measured by equalities of outcome (identifying hindrances to individual achievement in factors further from the individual's control and hence requiring further intervention to modify), their demands for truly equal opportunities for all became very vulnerable to attack. As those demands threatened to slide into the impossible requirement that education prefigure and produce that social equality which could never be the simple product of redistributing a good by its nature partly positional, they lost practical credibility and theoretical defence.

So, in the face of arguments which were sometimes over-extended and could always be presented as such for polemical purpose, the two positions tended to polarise in policy disputes. Those operating with too thick a conception of equality sought to measure the acceptability of process against their disappointment with its results, and those operating with too thin a conception tended to downgrade the importance of outcomes as one important touchstone for evaluating the fairness of procedure. The more radical wing of egalitarian reform (whatever the force of its claims) only exacerbated this polarisation. Demands by 'excluded' groups for the overhaul of content and process were sometimes seen to imply that public education should not only *respect and take account of* but also *reflect and reproduce* the values of its participants, whether categorised by class, ethnicity or some other group designation, sounding alarm bells for the liberal aiming to free individuals from constraining circumstance. Moreover unless suitably qualified, the relativist implications of some of these demands seemed to threaten education's intrinsic value for individuals in their efforts to spread its exchange value more widely between them. From the radical viewpoint, however, the traditional liberal educator's position offered precisely an affront to personal liberty.

Thus both wings of the social equality debate have grounded their positions in *commitments to liberty and equality in and through education*, with these commitments invoked to support opposing policies whose underlying aim remains the simultaneous achievement of equitably distributed individual freedom and overall social welfare.

This is not the place to examine the (interesting and important) intra-educational disputes over just which practices might best mitigate existing barriers to emancipation for individuals: what is significant here is that these deep disputes about means share agreement on ends. They can all be read as taking place within the framework of ongoing attempts to 'pass the buck' to this social practice for the accommodation of contradictions embedded in the liberal ideal of an equal distribution of liberty to all—contradictions which, as I have shown, cannot be overcome at the level of theory. They can be read, one might even suggest, as *contending versions of a replacement social thesis for liberalism*. On one wing of relevant dispute, a negative concept of liberty and thin equality seek to protect the individual from state interference (in the form of compensatory or affirmative action programmes for access or process) with the free play of personal talent and effort. The negative and thin formulation seeks also to protect and promote the public good by safeguarding what is to count as ability, by providing educational structures which recognise intellectual achievement and by ensuring that none are debarred on external grounds of race, religion, economic status etc. from access to a good which requires fair distribution not only on moral grounds but also for the effective exploitation of a pool of human capital to the benefit of all. In so doing, these negative and thin conceptions underplay the role of the social in defining, identifying, providing for and rewarding individual ability and achievement, and thereby risk frustrating both the moral and the pragmatic dimensions of social benefit.

The thick formulation, on the other hand, in overcoming some of these obstacles, risks incompatibility with cherished liberal ideals. Whilst social structure is taken seriously as a potent force in individual aspiration and achievement, stark divisions between external and internal constraints are refused, and opportunity becomes more than a matter of procedure, these welcome admissions also bring problems in their wake. For in this formulation, what is inherent to the individual risks eclipse by a vision which invites us to see the self, with its achievements and its failures, as primarily the product of external forces. So strenuous have efforts to set all on the road to liberty become, that the very capacity for personal agency seems challenged. When thick equality is relied on, public as well as private benefit is located in a more far-reaching removal of barriers to opportunity and the concomitant better use of human capital to the benefit of all, together with the anticipated evolution of a fairer social world. However, the first of these outcomes is premised on the egalitarian not carrying compensatory principles further than can be supported by empirical warrant (and it is hard to see how evidence can restrain what often looks like an 'unsinkable' theory), whilst the second requires limits to the discounting of individual responsibility, which this position finds hard to ground.

When we look at how disputes underpinned by those thick and thin conceptions of equality have been played out in the education context, therefore, the lessons of practice show neither to be theoretically sustainable. Whilst the thin conception *cannot realise* the ideals of liberal neutrality, the thick alternative *risks compromising* those ideals. The thin conception is clearly too thin, offering the kinds of formal equality which claim freedom for all to dine at the Ritz provided no-one bars the door. Where relevant freedoms concern access to experiences which are constitutive of autonomy and the development of free agency itself, formal equalities of access are practically hollow and theoretically circular, having all the hallmarks of a classic 'catch 22'. (Counter-claims which would suggest that, provided no fees are charged for education, all have not only formal freedom to dine but an actual meal voucher, depend on assumptions about the provenance and ownership of personal capacity which will be addressed in the next chapter.) Conversely, the thick conception is too thick, discounting individual differences and impossibly seeking equal outcomes from the distribution of a good which is in part positional. That position is therefore unable to set limits on public interference with individual effort in pursuit of a goal which can only recede for all, the nearer some approach it.

It seems that the appeal of each of these opposing positions is drawn to a large extent from weaknesses in the other. To escape from misconceived debate and fruitless battles about how much liberty may be sacrificed to equality or vice versa, and to avoid the practical counsel of despair offered by a neo-liberal backlash in which new policies throw out the baby with the bath water, two things need to be done. One of these, which cannot be pursued further here, is to get clearer about the asymmetrical relation between educational and social equality, so that the problems of theory and practice illuminate rather than compound each other. The other is to step aside from sterile disputes about true meanings of equality (which mirror deadlock in the 'two concepts of liberty' debate) and analyse the individual and social preconditions to an equal distribution of liberty. That enterprise, however, requires a problematising of liberalism's ontological and metaphysical premises, and before embarking upon it in chapter six I shall now try to show in the closing section here that neutralist liberalism does indeed leave no alternative to that further enquiry.

LIBERTY, EQUALITY AND EQUITY

I have shown that in education's policy and practice disputes, liberty and equality seem at odds with one another, with the moral and practical issues coming down to how much either may trump the other in particular circumstances. This practical impasse in education shines a spotlight on an ontology which is at odds with experience. We see this when, across the spectrum of opinion, a conceptual dichotomy between the individual and society creates contending conceptions of liberty and equality which then underpin competing prescriptions for the just distribution *to individuals* of a good which is *clearly social*—and in part positional. And to make matters worse, a primary function of that good for individuals is their own development: the foundation of their autonomy. Three positions seeking an equitable outcome can be identified in relevant debates, and none can be sustained. I have already conceded that when that outcome is sought on the basis of too thick a conception of equality, it risks giving rise to an unsinkable theory which places individuals so firmly on the receiving end of social forces that their personal attributes seem to disappear into thin air. Carried into practice, this risks licensing potentially endless regulation by the state to mitigate the presumed effects of those social forces, as the goals which would satisfy proponents of these reform programmes continue not merely to elude them but necessarily to recede. That feature of claims which, in their strong form, are open to the charge of social determinism, lends credibility to liberal critics who argue that too much liberty is thereby sacrificed to the demands of equality. I have also shown that those strong claims draw their appeal in part from the failure of earlier, weaker demands to deliver an equal distribution of liberty. That they did not do so in practice, however, does not of itself entail that they might not do so in principle.

The key question therefore becomes whether the liberal can redeem the claim that, *despite the theoretical paradoxes already noted, neutralist liberal ideals can nonetheless in principle be realised through appropriate social arrangements.* In sketching liberalism's twin-track development above, I described a collision course between theory and practice, in which education was the practice delegated to realise the ideal of equal negative liberty for all. There are broadly two accounts within neutralist liberalism of how that is to be achieved. Each of these understands social arrangements for education as central to an equitable society which respects and promotes free agency, but since they differ in what is to count as constraint, they yield rather different prescriptions. I shall examine a well-known (and well-argued) case for each of those two positions, in order to show that neither a strong nor a weak interpretation of negative liberty will permit the necessary balancing act which the opposition of liberty and equality demands. If negative liberty (and neutralist liberalism) cannot be rescued even in principle by the social arrangements to which that task has been delegated, then that is vindication for my claim that its supporting ontology needs recasting.

The premises of the strongly negative position are set out and defended at length in Cooper's *Illusions of Equality*.[24] There, removal of external constraint is seen as essential to permit equal access to education as a good which has value in itself and which indirectly gives access to other goods. Beyond that, equality in education is seen as a threat to liberal ideals in two respects; both through too much interference with what is recognised as necessarily a competition and also as a danger to educational quality, which must be defended as both a private and a public good. Cooper's liberalism—like the educational arrangements it defends—is reliant on strongly negative liberty, a narrow conception of constraint and a sharp dichotomy between the individual and the social. In support of that position and its implications he aims to show (by reference to two fictional schooling systems) that even where inequalities in provision are manifest, there is no *prima facie* justification for redistribution on for example Rawls's 'difference principle' since "Before an inequality which does not benefit the least advantaged can be subject to criticism, surely the following condition must obtain: if the better-off were less well-off then the worst-off would be better-off. If this causal condition does not obtain, it is impossible to understand the rationale for making the better-off worse-off".[25] There are two avenues by which this strong claim and its implicit supporting assumptions should be challenged. The obvious one would make reference to education's exchange value for the individual, pointing out that in respect of this unambiguously positional good, the causal condition must always obtain as a matter of logical necessity, such that "does not benefit" should read 'harms'. The inequalities concerned thus fall foul of the 'harm to others' criterion. Anti-egalitarian proponents of strongly negative liberty might well be unmoved by that, however, concerned as they are to focus on the intrinsic value of a practice they see as in danger of subversion by extraneous policies of 'social engineering', with that subversion objectionable in terms of both private and public good. A second, supporting challenge would therefore invoke the fact that whether or not education's intrinsic goods can be shown also to be positional, they too are certainly irredeemably social. Their unequal availability sacrifices the good of all to the privileged good of some unless we assume, illiberally, that only some are to determine and deliver what is good for all, whether all share those judgements or not.

Indeed, when Cooper looks at threats to educational quality from equality, it is clear that he is not concerned with the education of the public as a social practice, nor with 'public good' in the sense of something available to all, but only in the sense of something whose availability to some is deemed to be in everybody's interest. From that perspective, what matters (to all) is how people "at the top" are educated, on the grounds that "...it is a 'distributional' fall—collapse towards mediocrity—which is typically connoted by the news that quality has fallen".[26] The "fundamental human concern" with outstanding performance is seen to outweigh "the lesser concern that there should be an evenly spread, general improvement in the quality of a practice".[27] Now this claim may sometimes happen to be true, though certainly not without challenge, for attitudes to quality in the luxuries of life—sport, opera, painting etc.—but it is manifestly untrue in respect of justice, health care, or building standards. And that is not just because those things affect everybody, but more importantly because standards for those goods are in an obvious way publicly constituted and socially defined. So indeed, if less obviously, are the products of culture and their standards. To overlook this goes with a conception of agency which discounts the social as much as the 'thick' equality under attack discounts the individual. Cooper does allow that "When a practice, like building or education, has an important effect on everybody, another concern arises—that quality should not fall below a certain minimum".[28] This is a somewhat back-handed concession to the social, however, for it sees quality from the perspective of those who are *indirectly* affected by the education of the masses, with the general public seen to benefit at one remove from "Resources and methods devoted to fostering talent [which] cannot, at one and the same time, be employed to raise the average person's performance or ability".[29] This position must be challenged not because it might be politically unacceptable to some, but because it is quite misconceived theoretically. And to challenge it is not to be driven into what Cooper sees as the alternative camp, peopled by those "without any enthusiasms" except "the second-order enthusiasm for frustrating those of others",[30] and who perversely contend that mean levels of achievement matter more than excellence.[31] For what is at issue here is not respect for excellence, but the ontology underlying elitist claims.

That view of cultural excellence and the way to promote it educationally rests on a series of assumptions which accord with the narrow conception of constraint implied by strongly negative liberty. Two things are overlooked. The first is due attention to how the abilities, tastes and motivations which sustain cultural practices develop as attributes of the individual. Matters here are far more complex (as chapter six will show) than is admitted by a view which assumes a given hierarchy of capacity for cultural production and appreciation. The second (related) point is that when a good is socially constituted and socially defined, then the standards of a practice at given points on its range are partially constituted by performance across that range. And this is true not only for our subjective evaluations of the practices in question, but also for their objective outcomes. What is to count as the highest standards of justice or building is socially defined, and high standards and excellent artefacts are in part produced by public expectation, peer example and institutional arrangements. So too for other cultural goods. Even if we take cases of the clearest individual achievement, Mozart was a great composer not just because he happened to be better than others and we judge him as such, but also in part because of the standards of musical production and appreciation around him: conversely, the former Soviet Union invested heavily in sports facilities not just to improve mean levels of fitness, but to secure a disproportion of Olympic gold medals".[32]

How much the more true for the goods of education, when *public education in a democracy,* where all are providers of this good and all its direct and indirect consumers, is at issue. For what differentiates those who interpret equitable access to educational experience as requiring removal only of external barriers, from those who accept the case for a measure of regulation in educational opportunity, need not be (despite polemic) that the former care about standards and quality whilst the latter do not, or that the former are concerned with learning's intrinsic value whilst the latter see it merely as a currency exchangeable for social position. What legitimates advocacy for strongly negative liberty and concomitant formal equality in relation to education is an implicit notion of a series of differentiated publics within the polity, with what is to count as 'standards' defined by and relative to levels of performance in only some of these.[33] That notion, like the assumption of a given hierarchy of cultural capacity on which it is based, reflects a strongly atomistic view of the person, licensing a narrow definition of constraint and hence further reinforcing the strongly negative concept of liberty. These premises together seem to legitimate "a defence of a selective, mixed quality system of education"[34] which offends not merely against equality (as its proponents accept) but also against the liberal ideal of the democratic distribution of equal liberties, unless its lynch-pin conception of the self can be sustained.

The extended examination here of the strongly negative liberal argument has two purposes. First, it provides an example of how what appear in debate as positions grounded only in commitments to principles none would rush to challenge (here liberty and excellence), in reality draw on a whole nexus of interconnected philosophical and empirical premises. When that nexus is disentangled, leverage on supporting premises and their interconnections can give purchase on the principles themselves. Secondly, examination of a case grounded in strongly negative liberty alerts us to more subtle difficulties which are also to be found in the weaker interpretation of negative liberty. In this more subtle form of neutralist liberalism, which accommodates a more generous conception of constraint, we see that attempts to hold liberty and equality in tension, walking a tightrope to avoid sacrificing too much of the one to the other, are again vitiated by an inadequate conception of the self.

That position was set out by Williams in his seminal paper "The idea of equality".[35] Williams saw education as crucial to the realisation of liberal equality (required by the ideal of equitably distributed liberty) not only because education serves both as an object and as an engine of social reform but also because that context highlights the fact that handicapping conditions to liberty for individuals take many forms. In this way his position, with its broader conception of constraint, is more sensitive to reality than Cooper's. It is also theoretically better grounded than the egalitarianism under attack in that account, for Williams recognises that the availability of many desired goods is limited, either "by their very nature" (positional goods where status or prestige are attached), or "contingently" (where some happen to lack the attributes necessary for access), or "fortuitously" (where availability could be greater if supply were increased)".[36] What is at issue for Williams is therefore not equality but equality of opportunity to secure desired but not unlimited goods. The world beyond the individual is therefore acknowledged, with the equal distribution of liberties being the goal. Moreover, his analysis rejects the claim that equality of opportunity is established once the rules of entry to a competition are changed so that none are debarred from access, and he allows that *even individual capacities, on which the competition for benefit is itself decided, are themselves in some degree the product of social forces.* The availability of desired goods is thus under social control in respect of the two latter kinds of scarcity he notes. If access to desired goods is to be increased, we would thus be justified in intervening to modify both the good in question and the individuals who seek it. This is where Williams sees his analysis become worrying, offering the thin end of a potentially illiberal wedge: "We have seen that there is good reason to press this further, and to allow that the individuals whose opportunities are to be equal should be abstracted from more features of family background. Where should this stop?"[37] On speculating about possible practical consequences, he wonders whether his analysis implies that "our notion of personal identity itself was beginning to give way", but rejects this, concluding that "Our objections against the system suggested in this fantasy must be moral rather than metaphysical".[38]

In this, I believe, he was wrong. The tension between liberty and equality does indeed present a metaphysical problem, which requires a metaphysical solution. Williams's impasse, I wish to argue, is at the heart of liberalism's dilemma in accommodating the claims of equality, which it cannot refuse if liberty is to remain an ideal which can realistically be endorsed by and for all. Williams rightly declined to take up a position at either end of the spectrum of debate but remained uncomfortably marooned in the middle, aware that on one side lay the "quite inhuman society" he saw as the logical outcome of thoroughgoing attempts to achieve real equality of opportunity, and on the other the "futile Utopianism...having no rational effect on the distribution of goods, position and power that would inevitably proceed" if equality collapses into empty talk about equal respect despite individual differences in social position".[39] He was therefore obliged to conclude uneasily that we "should seek, in each situation, the best way of eating and having as much cake as possible", hoping that "new forms of social structure and education" might reconcile conflicting claims.[40] A problem unresolved in liberal theory thus gets handed over to the public practice of liberal education to ameliorate. Thirty-five years since the publication of that seminal paper, the results are as we see. Disappointment with attempts to have our cake and eat it, both individually and socially, have now elicited the policy response described in earlier chapters here.

There seem to be two ways forward from this impasse. The one, outside the scope of this enquiry, involves belated recognition that education cannot be the royal road to social reform merely through the equalising of educational opportunity, due to the asymmetrical relations between equality in education and social equality. That admission prompts enquiry into the relation between various kinds of desired goods, and the distributional principles which would ensure that advantages and disadvantages do not arbitrarily stack up together. (Walzer's notion of 'complex equality', in which different goods are distributed for differing reasons and some goods are not convertible for others, is interesting here.[41]) The admission that education cannot of itself deliver social equality, however, should not lead us to think of society's arrangements for the formation of persons as just one (important) good among others. Williams's insight that this, of all social goods, is of special significance for the equal distribution of liberty was indeed correct: *what his analysis lacked was an adequate account of how the formation of the individual is enmeshed with that of their fellows during that process*—an account which negative liberty and liberal neutralism cannot accommodate.

Perhaps the most influential enquiry into distributional principles to underpin a liberal theory of justice in which unavoidable inequalities are fairly shared out is found today in the work of Rawls.[42] This project for resolving the competing claims of liberty and equality by recourse to regulative principles rather than social practices has generated two decades of intra-liberal exegesis and critique, which cannot be addressed here. However, one observation should be made, since no enquiry relevant to contemporary attempts to give an adequate account of how an equal distribution of liberties is to be achieved can ignore this work. Few will need reminding of the two principles which make up Rawls's "special conception of justice": notably that each person is to have an equal basic right to the most extensive liberty compatible with a similar liberty for others; and that inequalities are to be arranged so that they are to the greatest benefit of the least advantaged and are attached to positions open to all under conditions of fair equality of opportunity. These principles, it is claimed, are objectively even-handed, since they would commend themselves to anyone behind "the veil of ignorance" and unaware of the natural and social advantages which would accrue to them personally in concrete circumstances. Standard objections are equally well-known: most notably that the advantages accruing to individuals from their own attributes cannot be considered on a par with contingent social assets, and that the self so 'unencumbered' and abstracted from its characteristics and situation has no identity from which to make judgements on any distributional agreement. It is the second of these objections which requires brief comment here, though to do more than that would take me too far from the case I am sketching.

Now Rawls is firmly a neutralist liberal seeking regulative principles to underpin state neutrality between competing ideas of the good held by free and equal citizens and supportable by "what are publicly recognised as sufficient reasons".[43] Such reasons, publicly recognisable in a liberal democracy (for he denies universal applicability for his theory of justice) will respect both individual liberty and the equitable distribution of unavoidable discrepancies in advantage (arranged to spread liberties as evenly as possible). In these latter, Rawls includes discrepancies which arise from an individual's attributes as well as from their circumstance. He therefore readily acknowledges (as Williams did) that a person's attributes can act as constraints on their freedom, constraints which should be taken into account in the just ordering of a liberal society. His earlier work, however, does seem to be open to the interpretation both that these attributes are simply given and that the individual can stand at a reflective distance to them: his later work elaborates a more complex position but still one which takes insufficient account, not so much of what persons are as of how they are formed. I am therefore not simply echoing the familiar criticism that since the 'unencumbered self' must put aside knowledge of its talents, tastes, attachments and motivations while assenting to just distributional principles, this device for fair contracting relies on a conception of the self which is prior to its ends. For Rawls has been at pains to explain, in the two decades since such criticisms were first made, that his conceptions of the individual and society are "political not metaphysical".[44] He thus makes clear in *Political Liberalism*[45] that he is making no ontological claims about persons as persons, merely urging what is a necessary negotiating posture for persons in a democracy which is both liberal and pluralist.

Leaving aside difficulties with that divide between the individual-as-person and the individual-as-citizen (which raise again the metaphysical problems seen in his earlier work), Rawls's reformulation, I would suggest, still falls short of the substantive liberty and constitutive equality I am seeking to ground in one very important respect. He argues that the "'difference principle' should regulate the distribution of "primary goods", comprising basic liberties and "basic social institutions". In these latter he includes "a society's main political, social and economic institutions",[46] not only because these directly affect the exercise of liberty but also because "these institutions can have decisive long-term social effects and importantly shape the character and aims of the members of society, the kinds of person they are and want to be".[47] Rawls thus sees that if society is to be organised as a fair system of co-operation between free and equal citizens, then attention must be paid not only to arrangements which enable all equally to exercise their agency, but that *that* equal distribution has an effect on free agency itself. What is notable is that along with institutions *not included* in the basic structure such as— unremarkably for a liberal—families and churches are, together with hospitals, museums etc., *society's institutions expressly charged with the education of the public*: schools, colleges, universities.

Now on one level educational institutions—which socialise and train the young and transmit a cultural heritage—can be characterised as belonging to the categories of public service or cultural practice and hence seem to merit designation among the "secondary goods" of society. However, and more importantly, given the justifying aims of *liberal* education—the development of individual autonomy and the maintenance of an open society—I would argue that public education is a prime candidate for the category of "primary goods". It merits that designation on the very grounds that Rawls allows for his "basic institutions": that it plays an inescapable part in setting the parameters for freedom's exercise and, moreover, influences the development of agency itself. Where I would depart from Rawls' criteria for a "primary good" is in putting my emphasis on the second of these considerations, which becomes logically prior to the first if we abandon the conception of persons as self-defining authors of their own ends. I thus share the view of many of Rawls's critics that his regulative principles rest on a metaphysical position and that that position is unsatisfactory, but I am less concerned with the basis for assent to the difference principle than with what should fall into the category of goods to be distributed by that principle, less exercised by how that agreement relies on an insubstantial characterisation of the self and its interests than by the fact that any political theory seems to require a richer notion of the self and its interests *including consideration of how these evolve.* That richer notion, I suspect, would itself undermine the explicit distinction in Rawls's later work between personhood and citizenship, and a blurring of that distinction would in turn require a more substantial category of primary goods comprising not only equal opportunities for the exercise of individual liberty, but *the equal availability of opportunities to develop the prerequisite capacities for free agency, most particularly through the arrangements made for public education.* Whilst the asymmetrical relation between equality in education and social equality requires recognition that education cannot of itself be the royal road to social reform, it also implies that any modelling of principles for the more just ordering of society cannot treat education as if it were just one among many of the benefits an individual might seek. To develop a critique of Rawls is outside the scope of this analysis: debate surounding his position, however, has resonance for my claim that modern neutralist liberalism relies on a problematic conception of individual agency, and that this inhibits an adequate account of how an equal distribution of liberty is to be achieved. Secondly, it suggests that regulative principles alone cannot furnish a way out of that impasse, bypassing an ontology which requires reexamination.

That second avenue of enquiry turns not to relations between various goods (as in Walzer) or to just regulative principles for their distribution (as in Rawls), but rather to internal relations between liberty and equality which are both conceptual and empirical. For this, the liberal ideal must be concerned as much with the formation of preferences as with their exercise, as much with an equal distribution of opportunities to develop the prerequisites to liberty as with an equal distribution of opportunities to secure desired goods. And whereas the latter equal distribution requires us in practice to mitigate handicapping conditions which may be internal as well as external to the individuals concerned, in the pursuit of what are frequently goods limited in one or more of Williams's three respects, the former equal distribution places different demands on us. For the provision of equal opportunities to develop the prerequisites to liberty, which liberty itself demands, does not just call for palliative measures intended to rectify or mitigate conditions which give rise to internal constraints—a stance which still takes the self and its attributes as given. *Instead of corrective measures to remove obstacles, it requires constructive measures to develop capacities—a stance which takes the self as always in process of formation and reformation.* From this perspective, our liberty ceases to be purely negative and becomes substantive: and free agency is a capacity we achieve, not something we safeguard or reclaim. Certain equalities—those which pertain to the development of the self—are therefore unambiguously constitutive of liberty itself. In our social arrangements, it is thus a matter of ensuring that, insofar as conditions for the development of freedom's prerequisites are socially constituted, they are equally provided to all.

This change of perspective is of obvious pertinence to a liberal theory of education and to relations between any such theory and liberal social philosophy. In the world of practice, it offers clearer implications for relations between education and social equality than can be drawn from Williams's analysis. That already implies, of course, that liberty as well as equality—indeed, an equal distribution of liberty—cannot be served by any educational arrangements which have recourse only to the strongly negative concept of liberty and concomitant formal equality based on the narrow conception of constraint, for this licenses a distribution of (not unlimited) benefit— *and of liberty*—which is differentially correlated with initial social position. The unacceptable result of those arrangements is that liberty as well as equality becomes cumulative. So the educational arrangements which, for example, Cooper favours (for a selective schooling system of mixed quality with meritocratic competition within it) are clearly ruled out. And so, even more obviously, is a market distribution of educational goods, in which allocation of mixed quality options on the basis of premature judgements about the capacities of the developing young is replaced by the even more arbitrary mechanism of parental acuity in obtaining goods on their behalf. Such arrangements clearly offend as much against liberty as they do against equality. In this respect, public education must represent the limiting case of the market even for the consistent neo-liberal, never mind the neutralist liberal. But the case I intend to develop in the final chapter here can take us further than this, with implications not merely for what society's arrangements for public education in a liberal democracy should avoid, but to what they should aspire. And those arrangements will require more substantive aims than the neutralist commitment to the development of autonomy, individually conceived, which both reflects and compounds the problems of liberal neutrality.

The necessary lines of enquiry (conceptual and empirical) can be sketched once we move beyond Williams's position (representative of neutralist liberalism, of much liberal philosophy of education and of educational policy and practice prior to neo-liberal market reforms). Once we cease to see liberty and equality in opposition to each other, we can leave aside arbitration about the priority of competing values in the abstract, where the bottom-line, being ideological, confirms rather than challenges the ontological premises which place those values in competition. When certain social equalities are understood as prerequisites to liberty in so far as they embody public, institutional provision for the equal development of those individual capacities which are constitutive of autonomy, we are no longer impaled on the horns of Williams's dilemma where we can only suck it and see and hope for the best on questions of how much intervention or compensation we can afford in the name of equality before we offend unacceptably against liberty. When particular social equalities, most notably in relation to public education, are understood as *constitutive* of personal freedom (and hence are seen as central to the "primary goods" of a liberal society), we are led to consider, with reference to equality, where individual talents and tastes come from, and, with reference to liberty, where the boundary may appropriately be drawn between the public and the private spheres.

On the basis of theory, research and experience associated with the social practice of public education, we can thus enquire into the tenability of liberalism's "view of the person" by examining both empirical and conceptual attempts to get insight into how individuality might evolve. The coming chapter will address these issues. That enquiry, together with this analysis of freedom and equality, has three purposes. For education, it may offer grounding for policies which do not involve an invidious choice between liberty and equality. For liberal theorising, it may provide additional support for contemporary insights that individual and social development are in dialectical relation, and may thus ground a conception of autonomy which does not "...collapse into the human will [with the consequence that] The idea of the good remains indefensible and empty so that human choice may fill it".[48] If more substance is to be given to the conception of agency at the heart of modern liberalism, which Murdoch tellingly characterised as "a shadow clinging to a shadow",[49] then we must question our ontological premises about the second of those shadows if we are to understand the first and make appropriate social arrangements for all to develop it fully.

CONCLUSION

From one aspect, this monograph has offered a case study illustrating the changing fate of one social project aiming at liberal education for all. It began by exploring the relation between education policy and the social order. It then presented recent key reforms of education and the social order in the light in which their proponents wish to cast them—that of the neo-liberal restoration of individual freedoms and responsibilities in an area of personal endeavour and social aspiration where the state was claimed to have previously over-extended its powers. A survey of the practical effects of relevant policies for both 'providers' and 'consumers' in the new market-oriented ethos, and of the confused and confusing demands which the public in a democracy makes of the social practice of education, brought the analysis to an examination of the kind of good that education is. That analysis revealed long-standing tensions between the good of each and the good of all, tensions which are only exacerbated by neo-liberal policies which overtly (indeed deliberately) individualise the distribution—and indirectly the constitution—of a good which fails to fit standard categories of public/private, individual/social, etc. When analysis turns from liberal and neo-liberal commitments and policies to the ontological and metaphysical premises on which they are based, we see that contending solutions of a long-running battle between the claims of liberty and equality are rooted in a conception of the self and its formation which requires further scrutiny. A more satisfactory view of persons and their formation is needed to ground an account of how the liberal ideal of an equal distribution of freedom is to be achieved—an account which relies neither on over-optimism about social practice (and in particular, education) nor relies on regulative principles which take too little cognisance of social realities (and in particular, of education). The relation between any such conception and the practice of public education in a liberal society is reciprocal: since education at the same time reflects and produces both the social world and our beliefs about it, we require a sounder liberal ontology to ground our theories for practice; we also require that regrounded practice as a touchstone by which recursively to conceptualise our selves and our social world.

NOTES AND REFERENCES

1. Sandel, M., The procedural republic and the unencumbered self, Avinieri and de-Shalit (eds.), 1992, *op. cit.* p. 14.
2. As in much of the work of philosophers of education such as R.S. Peters in the 1960s, who claimed to reveal through conceptual analysis, not how things ought to be, but how they cannot but be, provided only we clearly understand what we are about.
3. In Jonathan, R. (1995a), *op. cit.*
4. Sandel, M. (1992), *op. cit.*, p. 14.
5. Hollis, M. (1990), Market equality and social freedom, *Journal of Applied Philosophy,* 7. 1, p. 16.
6. Berlin, I. (1969), *op cit.* p. 131.
7. Rocco, A., The political doctrine of fascism: in *Readings on Fascism and National Socialism* (Chicago, University of Colarado Press, 1952) pp. 35–36.

8. Lord Devlin, (former high court judge), 'The enforcement of morals' (1959) a response to the Wolfenden Report on Homosexual Offences and Prostitution (1957), p. 10.

9. Bradley, F. H., *Ethical Studies* 2nd edn. (Oxford, Oxford University Press, 1927), p. 172.

10. Green, T. H., Liberal legislation and freedom of contract, *Works of T. H. Green, III,* (Longmans, Green and Co., 1888), p. 370.

11. Cohen, G. A., Capitalism, freedom and the proletariat: in Miller, D. (Ed.), *Liberty* (Oxford, Oxford University Press, 1991), p. 181.

12. Flew, A., *A Dictionary of Philosophy* (London, 1979), p. 188.

13. Marx, K., *Capital, III* (London, Harmondsworth, 1978), p. 812.

14. Taylor, C., What's wrong with negative liberty? in: Ryan, A. (Ed.), *The Idea of Freedom* (Oxford, Oxford University Press, 1979), pp. 175–193.

15. This key flaw in neutralism is particularly succinctly analysed in O'Neill, O. (1979), The most extensive liberty, *Proceedings of the Aristotelian Society*, 80.

16. Bellamy, R. (1992), *op. cit.*, p. 3.

17. MacCallum, G. C. (1967), Negative and positive freedom, *The Philosophical Review*, 76, p. 320.

18. cf. Berlin (1969), *op. cit.*, p. 159.

19. MacCallum, *ibid.*

20. *Ibid.*

21. Mill, J. S., *Considerations of Representative Government:* in *Utilitarianism, On Liberty and Considerations of Representative Government* (London, 1972 2nd edn.), p. 177.

22. The Head Start programme for pre-schoolers from underprivileged backgrounds, and positive discrimination policies in college entrance in the US, are perhaps the best known examples of that type of compensation.

23. Radical demands for changed content and process were based on class considerations by the 'new sociologists of education' in the 1960s (with associated experiments for curriculum change in "educational priority areas" in England and Wales at that time). Demands with an ethnic basis (and to a lesser extent, gender and class) are represented in 'the battle of the books' in secondary and higher education in the US during the 1980s.

24. Cooper, D., *Illusions of Equality* (London, Routledge and Kegan Paul, 1980).

25. *Ibid.*, p. 36.

26. *Ibid.*, p. 54.

27. *Ibid.*, pp. 54–55.

28. *Ibid.*, p. 55.

29. *Ibid.*, p. 56.

30. *Ibid.*, pp. 56–57.

31. Though the World Bank seems to find that a persuasive position for many developing economies.

32. I have elaborated these arguments in Jonathan, R. (1982), *op. cit.*

33. For discussion of the connection between academic and political elitism, see Jonathan, R. (1986), Cultural elitism explored, *Journal of Philosophy of Education* 20. 2, pp. 265–277.

34. Cooper, D. (1980), *op. cit.*, p. 63.

35. Williams, B., The idea of equality: in Laslett, P. and Runciman, W. (eds.), *Politics and Society* (Second Series), (Oxford, Blackwell, 1962), pp. 110–131.

36. *Ibid.*, p. 123.

37. *Ibid.*, p. 128.

38 *Ibid.*

39. *Ibid.*, p. 131.

40. *Ibid.*

41. Walzer, M., *Spheres of Justice* (New York, Basic Books, 1981).

42. Rawls, J. (1971), *op. cit.* and Rawls, J., *Political Liberalism* (Columbia University Press, New York, 1993).

43. Rawls, J. (1980), *op. cit.*, p. 561.

44. See particularly Rawls, J. (1985) Justice as fairness: political not metaphysical, *Philosophy and Public Affairs,* 14. 3.
45. Rawls, J. (1993), *op. cit.*
46. Rawls, J., *op. cit.* (1985), p. 224.
47. Rawls, J., *op. cit.* (1980), p. 538.
48. Murdoch, I., *The Sovereignty of Good* (London, Routledge and Kegan Paul, 1970), p.80.
49. *Ibid.*, p. 50.

Chapter 6
Persons and their Preferences

The previous chapter examined the liberal conception of individual freedom in which persons determine their own ends and choose the means to them, with constraint permissible only to prevent harm to others. As a political theory designed to maximise freedom of belief and action between consenting adults, liberalism's conception of the individual thus posits an autonomous bearer of preferences whose agency is exercised in a social world made up of similar individuals. I have argued that any resolution of liberal tensions between the competing claims of freedom and equality must accord not only with the protection of freedom but with its equitable distribution. This follows from recognition that effective agency is a function of conditions both external and internal to the agent. Whereas the individual's freedom is obviously constrained if external conditions prevent or hamper the exercise of autonomous preference (whether by simple force, through coercive regulation, or by social arrangements which negate some options), it is no less seriously constrained if internal conditions prevent or hamper the exercise of autonomous preference (whether these are psychological or cultural barriers). Interpretations of liberalism which recognise both internal and external constraints on freedom—as neo-liberalism does not—therefore go some way towards acknowledging the social location of the individual. In this chapter I shall attempt to make good my claim that they do not, however, go far enough. For in so far as both sources of constraint focus primarily on the exercise of freedom by persons bearing existing preferences, too little attention is given to the development of those persons and the evolution of their preferences.

Individuals do not of course come into the world bearing preferences. Nor do they come into the world with a developed capacity for autonomy. Nor does the world exhibit a range of options for preference as part of the natural order. Both the subjects and the objects of freedom—the choosing and the chosen—evolve through a process of development in which the individual and the social are in dynamic interaction. Thus the world's range of options for differing forms of human flourishing and the means to them is largely structured by past agency, whether that of individuals acting severally or in concert. And the individual's disposition and capacity to choose between or reconstruct them—their relative autonomy—is even more evidently a product of personal development in which individual and social factors are inextricably entwined. Social attitudes to and arrangements for an individual's potential for autonomy combine with existing social conditions to influence both its development and its exercise. That being so, an atomistic conception of the individual, which understands the social world as merely the backdrop to individual agency, with freedom for each to determine ends for themselves and secure the means to them, is clearly deficient. Supporting conceptions of individual autonomy, understood simply as a capacity to be exercised are similarly deficient. Their deficiency becomes quite clear when we focus on where that capacity comes from and how individual potential for it is developed. When that broader focus is adopted, it is evident that the freedom of the individual cannot be a purely negative concept, but requires substantive content and reference to enabling social conditions, most obviously in public education. And in turn, those persons whose freedom is at issue cannot be understood as if they were factored into the social world only through their agency, since the enabling conditions in question are social in multiple respects. Thus the liberal conception of the self 'prior to its ends' requires revision if we are to develop a better understanding of what criteria those enabling conditions must meet.

I have noted that this traditional liberal conception is currently the subject of controversy in social and political philosophy, with its coherence now challenged. Certain puzzles which tend to be considered largely the business of philosophers of education might well throw light on these questions. (It is, of course, no accident that it is in the field of educational theory that an asocial conception of the individual gives rise to so many intractable problems: that in itself should alert us to something fundamentally amiss in our understanding of the social features of free agency and its development.) This analysis aims, therefore, to bring insights from currently disparate fields together, drawing on differing branches within philosophy's current division of labour and blurring the edges of what counts as a properly philosophical consideration. The evolution of personhood is just the kind of question which demands this, since it poses empirical as well as conceptual questions, with both kinds of question best addressed in relation not just to 'consenting adults' bearing existing preferences but also to developing individuals who are in process of forming preferences. My analysis therefore turns now to some of those questions, drawing on disputes about learning and education (familial, institutional and social), in order to tease out social factors in the evolution of individual consciousness. The individual's attributes—talents, tastes, values, personality characteristics—and their operative force in the formation of preferences will be the first focus. This will trace the complex origins of features which become internal to the 'consenting adults' of liberal theory—features in virtue of which they are individuated. Next, analysis of the respective rights and roles of the family, the state and the individual in the formation of persons will review the central liberal dichotomy between the public and the private spheres. Disputes over that boundary reflect the view of the self I wish to recast, and how it is drawn in relation to education has significant implications for a substantive concept of liberty. With a more complex and qualified picture of how persons become individuated, of how the development of each relates to the development of others, and of how the capacity for freedom is in part socially constituted as well as socially exercised, we can begin to recast liberalism's problematic view of the self. And only then can intractable disputes about the equitable distribution of freedom—and the educational arrangements without which that cannot be achieved—be better addressed.

PERSONHOOD AND SOCIAL CONTEXT

Before my claims locating selfhood and free agency more firmly in their social context are backed up by evidence and argument in later sections, some initial elaboration may be helpful. If we first take the *exercise* of freedom by individuals, this has both preconditions and consequences. The consequences consist in repercussions which are both self- and other-regarding. (Even in the limiting case where claims to self-regarding choice can be most fully sustained, the chooser still modifies his/her own future options and relations with others, except where choice is entirely trivial.) The consequences of freedom's exercise are other-regarding in two respects: in their direct repercussions on the immediate freedoms of others, and in their indirect repercussions for an amended range of future options available to others as well as the agent. Preconditions to the exercise of freedom are also both internal and external to the self. Free agency requires the possibility of choice between options, and these—the *possible objects* of freedom—may indeed be external to the agent. But to constitute options for choice—*actual objects* of freedom—whether in respect of values, beliefs, social arrangements or artefacts, options must be recognisable as such by the agent where they exist, or be conceivable by her/him where they do not. And, to this extent, *the objects of freedom are partially internal to the 'free' subject.* Nor is acknowledgement that in principle the conditions of free agency are both external and internal to the subject the end of the matter. For that subject to be free in practice, effective agency either to secure desired existing options or to create and secure desired new options (whether alone or in collaboration with others) must be a real possibility. So effective agency in practice doubly depends on features some of which are external to the agent, some internal. This explains the asymmetrical relation between the individual self and her/his free agency: we may not be as free as we believe or would wish ourselves to be, but we are never *more* free than we believe ourselves to be. To conceive of ourselves as free subjects is therefore the first precondition of free agency.

This elaboration may then be taken further, from the dynamic of internal and external conditions which permit or hamper the exercise of freedom to a similar dynamic at work in the *development* of the individual's prerequisite capacities. At this point matters become even more intractably complex. To understand the personal prerequisites to free agency we must look within the agent and analyse how the internal/external dynamic—the interaction between what is 'individual' and what is social—creates both the disposition to autonomy and the capacities and preferences which that disposition expresses. The first point to be made is that a person's disposition to autonomy is itself a product of that dynamic (which in turn it reinforces). Awareness of other times and places reminds us that the necessary disposition to conceive of ourselves as persons with a capacity for autonomy and the right to exercise it is not an inescapable fact of nature. We learn in the course of our development to be more or less autonomous. We learn to value autonomy more or less for our own lives. We learn our rights and expectations about the scope for our autonomy in relation to the claims of others. We learn all of that to a greater or lesser extent (or we can learn the opposite) from relations with individual others, from the messages conveyed through social and material circumstance and from the social arrangements explicitly set up to guide learning as individuals develop.

It is stating the obvious to note that autonomous individuals do not develop from human babies as daffodils do from bulbs. In the latter case, the end result is inevitable provided relevant conditions are sufficient to sustain continued life at all. In the human case, outcomes for individuals are radically various, depending on relevant conditions interacting with inherent tendencies. Those conditions are at first wholly external to the individual; then, as development continues, they are constituted by the dynamic interaction between external conditions and internal factors, with these latter being themselves the result of past similar dynamic interactions. What is true for the disposition to conceive of ourselves as free agents is the more evidently true of the knowledge and understanding we require to become aware of alternative ends for our lives and of appropriate means to those ends. The developing individual does not start out with that awareness; only (under normal internal circumstances) with the capacity to acquire it (under favourable external conditions). It is acquired by learning from those same three sources as development proceeds: from relations with individual others, from the lessons conveyed by the material and social environments, and from society's institutional arrangements to guide individual development. (Liberal philosophers of education have long been preoccupied with how the last of these contributes to individual autonomy. Some of the difficulties they encounter in analysing how persons and agency develop have their roots in the view of the person I am challenging, as a later section will argue. It seems strange that theorising about education should merely reflect the prevailing premises of social and political philosophy, when it should rather be drawn on to evaluate and modify them.) Thus, although the capacity to deliberate, choose and act freely is undeniably an individual characteristic, it is the outcome of a process in which social factors and 'inherent' factors are in dynamic interaction. Since the interaction itself takes place in a social context, it is clear that any individual's capacity for freedom has causal antecedents which are social in multiple respects.

The brief analysis sketched here moves away from the standard liberal view of persons as acting on society and acted upon by it, but existentially separate from their context. That view presupposes an individuality which social forces may either empower or frustrate— the model of a norm which generates a deficit model for those who fall short of it. I argued in chapter five that protracted trench-warfare on the battle-ground of education over how much liberty should be sacrificed to the claims of equality or vice-versa are grounded in this view of individuality. In an attempt to break this deadlock in theory and the pendulum swings of policy which mirror it, my analysis suggests that the dynamic interplay between the personal and the social in development is a dialectical process. This is a view of the person in which *the initially external becomes progressively internalised through a process of mediation by the already internal*; a self in which 'the inherent' is what currently actually inheres, not what nature (or genes) mysteriously might allow potentially to inhere; a self in which the inherent meets and is modified by the external for as long as that self remains capable of learning from experiences of all kinds. This, I wish to maintain, is what the self and his/her individuality amounts to; no more, no less. It is therefore not enough to allow that we are social creatures on the grounds external to ourselves that we interact with others in a social world. We are social creatures in the much stronger sense—and on grounds internal to ourselves—that our individuality (what makes us different from others) results from an interaction between the internal and the external which is a continuous feedback loop. Neo-liberalism is clearly defective both as philosophical analysis and as prescriptive social theory to the extent that it denies even the weak claim that we are social creatures. Liberalism, as understood in its modern neutralist form, is inadequate to the extent that although it rightly accepts the weak claim (with differing interpretations of its implications, as chapter five reported), it does not allow the strong case outlined here and supported below.

That strong case does not drain meaning from our concept of the self (as Williams feared in respect of the potentially unlimited excusing conditions for personal deficits advanced by some egalitarian reformers[1]). In moving beyond a conception which dichotomises the individual and the social, it avoids an invidious (and incoherent) choice between prioritising liberty over equality or the converse, depending on which of two apparently independent variables is considered primary in the construction of persons and preferences. In the strong case I am advancing, individuality does not 'disappear' or 'evaporate' as neutralist liberals fear (with some justification) that it does when 'structure' is conceived as so powerful that agency pales beside it. (Such over-extended claims indeed can be seen as the reverse side of the neutralist liberal coin.) Nor, however, is individuality in the strong case 'fixed' as we might fix a photograph once it is developed. We are indubitably who we are, constituted by our own attributes, at any given point in our lives. Each of us at any given point has preferences in respect of our ends and the means to them. Each of us has the same liberal rights to express and obtain those preferences with due accommodation for the similar rights of others. What changes with a changed conception of the self is *what will count as due accommodation*. This in turn implies a changed analysis of free agency; of how the freedom of each relates to the freedom of all; and of the social conditions (most particularly in relation to education) which a substantive concept of liberty presupposes.

I have characterised liberalism, uncontroversially, as a political theory designed to maximise freedom of belief and action between 'consenting adults' and made the very obvious point that no one starts out in life as one of these. Liberalism does not (impossibly) ignore this fact, but it does draw astonishingly few implications from it. Mill of course did give attention to the child and its development through education, staking out a position which liberals have broadly followed since. For Mill, the child was a little bearer-of-preferences in the making. Educators should promote the child's eventual autonomy by fostering knowledge and understanding in pursuit of rational development, by refraining from indoctrinatory pedagogical techniques which might erect internal barriers to freedom, and by promoting development of personal value commitments. By and large, modern liberal philosophers of education follow this position with respect to the development of rational autonomy (though dispute arises over what is to count as moral autonomy in the modern world), and these commitments of principle have been reflected in practice to a greater or lesser degree. This is significant, for it should alert us to the existence of another feedback loop—from theory to practice, from the world to our beliefs about it. Thus, *our conception of the person informs how we guide development; how we guide development is a part of that development; that development becomes part of how individuals understand themselves.* In the sections that follow, therefore, I do not intend to bring the tenets of liberal philosophy of education to bear upon liberal theorising in order to illuminate the latter, nor indeed to set out on the reverse process. Rather, I am seeking to bring together the intractable puzzles of both areas of enquiry, looking at the practice as well as the theory of education, in order the better to understand the theoretical problems which both areas share and which each seems fated to compound in the other.

In calling into question, in this and the preceding chapter, liberalism's conception of the self, I should perhaps have referred throughout to its conception of the adult self. For in liberalism, there are on the one hand developing individuals, children, selves-in-the-making, and on the other developed individuals, adults, achieved selves with ends of their own. The latter have all the rights of the free agent to freedom from constraint short of harm to others. The former have similar rights short of harm additionally to themselves, with what constitutes both of those harms determined by others. In everyday life this works well enough as a rough and ready heuristic principle for the upbringing of the young child. It is fraught with difficulties in legal theory, in social practice, in education in school and upbringing in families in respect of the not-so-young but still developing individual. And it is entirely inadequate as an ontological and metaphysical categorisation of individuals. For there it is not, as with the heuristic principle, a matter of difficulties in drawing an appropriate line in particular cases between the two distinct kinds of selfhood: it is rather that a dual conception of the self in respect of individuals whose development is continuous cannot be theoretically coherent. Such a conception takes insufficient account of the complex sources of individuality—of the particular set of attributes which constitutes personal identity—and allows liberal theorising (and the social practices it justifies) to overlook the fact that persons are ineluctably 'all members of one another'. Clues to these matters can be gleaned from aspects of the developmental process and the claims of competing agencies to guide it. For reasons already noted, the stubbornly unresolved problems of educational theory may offer the most telling clues.

INDIVIDUALS AND THEIR ATTRIBUTES:
TALENTS AND ABILITIES

As individuals evolve and grow, they develop talents, acquire tastes, endorse values and form preferences. The modern liberal premise is that our attributes and commitments are our own: that whether or how we choose to develop, modify, express or repudiate them is up to us. The only proviso there is harm to others—failure to benefit others does not justify interference with personal agency. (We might note that this intuition is historically contingent. Though formally taking that position, early liberalism also embodied an implicit duty to self improvement which, combined with a belief in the morally meritocratic nature of a free society, implied indirect benefit to others than the agent. Alternative positions coexist uneasily in societies informed by liberal premises. Thus the Biblical parable of the talents, like many non-secular visions of personal freedom and responsibility, views an individual's attributes as loaned rather than owned, with the hire repaid by benefit to others.) Nonetheless, the modern liberal premise guides our everyday thinking. Talents and abilities seem to be characteristics with which we happen to be endowed and which appear simply to emanate from our individuality, like our tastes and values and the preferences to which they give rise. Accordingly, the liberal vision of a self which is prior to its ends forms a cornerstone of our understanding of persons and society— and of education. This last is informed by notions of the duties and interests of one generation in developing the (individual) attributes of the next. Since talents, tastes and values are considered to influence free agency in different ways, the question of their development gives rise to a series of particular debates within the liberal perspective. In each case intractable problems arise for educational theory and practice, as they do for philosophy. The first focus here will be on talents and abilities, since those attributes seem most basic to selfhood.

We might begin from Locke's uncompromising statement that "Though the earth and all inferior creatures be common to all men, yet every man hath a property in his own person; this nobody has any right to but himself".[2] That person is more than a material organism: it is also a repository of talents, abilities, skills and the disposition to make more or less of them. Across the spectrum of contemporary liberal philosophy, the rights of ownership of these personal attributes rest firmly with the individual concerned. This is most explicitly asserted by libertarian theorists such as Nozick who, though claiming to advance an 'entitlement theory of justice'[3] which escapes the theoretical and practical defects of 'patterned' theories[4], arguably champions an implicit patterning criterion for fair distribution—that of personal merit. For libertarians like Nozick, each is fairly entitled to enjoy without redistributive interference whatever has been obtained through personal talent and effort, together with whatever has come their way by good fortune (winnings, gifts, inheritances). And these two avenues by which goods can be fairly gained and individually owned are linked, since talents and abilities, like affluent and/or capable parents, are simply unevenly distributed in the lottery of life. Though that unevenness may be unfortunate for some, interventionist attempts to remedy it are seen as indefensible. To interfere with the naturally uneven distribution of talent and good fortune is claimed offensive because it compromises Locke's basic precept, allowing public intrusion into the private sphere: it is doubly unacceptable in damaging everyone's interest, since "fair and open competition, though understandably uncongenial to reluctant and sluggish competitors, is... the surest means of maintaining or raising standards...".[5] (This position, which sees individuals as endowed with particular attributes or the potential to acquire them, seems to underlie two positions in educational policy debates. It is seen in measured form in advocacy for rigorous meritocracy—as, for example, in Cooper[6]—and it is adopted with fewer scruples about "fair... competition" in libertarian endorsements of a market in educational goods.)

Towards the other end of the contemporary spectrum of social and political theory, those same rights of ownership are implicit in the analyses of philosophers who seek defensible parameters for redistributive measures. Thus Dworkin bases his redistributive arguments on a distinction between 'natural' and 'willed' inequalities, with the primary case for treatment constituted by the latter.[7] Additionally, since "There is no combination of abilities and skills and traits that constitutes 'merit' in the abstract"[8] (because judgements of worth necessarily reflect social ratings of particular attributes), Dworkin allows that individuals might legitimately arrange social affairs so that those less fortunate in the natural lottery are not disproportionately disadvantaged by society's contingent valuation of their attributes. Nonetheless, he still needs "to retain the belief that those aptitudes and traits we do possess are 'natural' and are not themselves socially constituted",[9] for without the basic distinction between 'natural' and 'willed' inequalities, intervention to redistribute seems open to just the kind of charges (of potential lack of limits) levelled by Nozick *et al.* (We saw in the previous chapter that Williams's argument ran into precisely those difficulties when he cast doubt on that distinction by allowing that the process of education powerfully influences not only what individuals compete *for* socially, but also what they compete *with*.) Clearly, the extent to which a person's attributes may be socially constituted—the interplay between what is individual and what is social—is as crucial for liberalism's social implications as it is for the metaphysical premises on which these are based.

In order to throw some light on that interplay, we must turn from the 'consenting adults' of liberal theorising to the processes by which they—with their "abilities and skills and traits"—develop. To do so is not to turn from philosophy to psychology, for although conceptual and empirical questions are involved, the latter tend to be addressed within the framework of the same metaphysic which ideally we might expect them to test. There are thus four standard positions on the vexed and hoary question of the extent to which talent and ability is inherent or acquired. Much time has been expended on this question, reputations made and lost, educational arrangements defended or attacked. Answers are various but fall into three broad categories: either abilities and traits are basically inherent (in the sense of innate or naturally evolving from the innate), with the questions for psychology and education being how best to identify and nurture valued inherent characteristics; or, abilities and traits are basically environmentally produced, with the questions for social policy and education being how best to distribute social opportunities to acquire valued characteristics; or again, abilities and traits result from both nature and nurture, with the task of psychology being to establish causal variables and their proportional effects, and the task of education being to maximise potential by responding to what is inherent and optimising the learning environment.[10] A fourth response draws its skirts aside from those messy disputes, declaring nature/nurture debates to be metaphysical questions, to which answers are neither verifiable nor falsifiable in principle. The question is of undoubted practical importance, but debate is deadlocked.

These four categories of response exhaust the possibilities offered by the conception of the self challenged here. None of them is adequate, as I shall try to show. In so doing, my intention is to demonstrate that nature/nurture debates, premised on a dichotomy between the individual and society, are radically misconceived: their intractability shows up the falsity of that sharp divide. I hope to establish that only a view of personhood which refuses such a dichotomy can allow us to accommodate the insights about individual abilities and traits which we obtain from our three most reliable sources: practical wisdom, lessons from upbringing and education, and the exigencies of conceptual coherence. On a revised conception of the self, where the individual and the social are dialectically related, it does not make sense to ask questions about nature and nurture as they are standardly posed. For in conventional debates, inherent and environmental factors are seen as discrete: they interact in a unidirectional manner, with the environment either fostering or frustrating a mysterious endowment which each individual brings with them into the world.[11] In the standard conception, what is inherent to the individual is that endowment: the inherent is what we start out with and carry through our lives. In the revised conception I am arguing for, the internal and the external—the individual and the social—are in *dynamic* interaction, in a relationship which is *not causal in one or the other direction, but dialectical.* What is inherent to the individual is simply what currently inheres in that person—whatever abilities and traits they actually exhibit at a given point in their lives, including of course the current capacity and disposition to develop these further. Though minor at first sight, that modification to our conception of the self has significant implications.

It enables us (against those who would discount 'nature' in order to strengthen claims for the social importance of 'nurture') to retain the common-sense conviction that when we look at any group of adults or of children, some strike us as patently cleverer, more dextrous, more tuneful, more diligent, more energetic than others. It enables us to treat them 'accordingly', whatever we may decide that to be. It lets us do this, though, without positing some mysterious *potential* inherent capacity as part of a causal explanation for what we see currently inhering in the individual. Such a mysterious additional extra may or may not exist (and the fourth response above is correct in noting that this is something we will never know): what matters about this ghostly abstraction is that we lose nothing by setting it aside, but we lose a great deal by making it part of our conceptual baggage. If we set it aside, we have to base our judgements about appropriate educational experiences only on the individual's current abilities and skills and the motivation to take them further: that is anyway all we had to go on, other than wishful thinking, even with the extra mysterious premise. More importantly, in setting it aside we avoid the strong element of self-fulfilling prophesy which attaches to all of our (fallible) judgements of better or worse when response to the individual before us is based on strangely teleological explanations for current attributes. Conversely, the revised conception also enables us (against those who seek limits to the explanatory force of 'nurture' for fear that the self with its attributes be downgraded) to retain the countervailing common-sense insight that life can surprise us: that individuals can achieve what we did not dream they were capable of, just as they can disappoint our best-founded expectations and our most well-intentioned efforts. These are only the gains for practice. For theory it allows a more adequate account of the development of autonomy—one which acknowledges that this has distributional aspects and hence pertinence to an equal distribution of liberty. And for policy it has substantive implications for a system of public education whose justifying aim is autonomy's development. These matters will be returned to below.

The revised conception thus accommodates the practical wisdom of educators in home and school. However, it seems at odds with certain 'expert' claims from systematic studies of individual traits and abilities and their development, and these might be thought evidence against the view I am proposing. I therefore need to show (too briefly) that such empirical enquiries fail to test liberal premises about natural endowment, but rather extrapolate from them. Moreover, that extrapolation stultifies debate, seeming to confirm false underlying premises. In all such systematic enquiries, a series of implicit assumptions are at work: that each individual has a (real but unknown) level of 'potential'; that such levels differ between individuals; that there exists a range of causal factors which may facilitate or impede progress towards (but not by definition beyond) that level in any given individual; that the best empirical indicator of an individual's potential is careful judgement of their current developmental position in relation to that of their fellows (sometimes with allowance for past deficits in stimulation). It should be evident that where practices are based on these assumptions, nothing will succeed like success—and of course the converse. Indeed there could be few clearer examples of how the world can seem to confirm our beliefs about it: if a social practice for the formation of persons is based on empirical findings whose premises are metaphysical, it tends to confirm the assumptions which lie behind those enquiries.

It is not difficult to see that with the discontinuous or dual conception of the self, in which development towards maturity is a matter of realising or failing to realise what individuals have 'in' themselves, these assumptions can scarcely be avoided. Accordingly, education (and indeed upbringing, in an age when all practices are believed enhanced by technical expertise) is pervasively understood to require recognition of latent or nascent talents and levels of ability so that these may be optimally brought to fruition. At the populist level, self-help books on 'parenting' conflate current developmental progress with innate levels of potential ability, and urge additional stimulation for the currently 'advanced'.[12] (The same publications do not advocate that evidently physically sturdy children should be better fed and housed and given extra exercise.) At the academic level, psychometric testing procedures rely on the same equating of measured pace of early development with predicted level of ultimate development, for the 'intelligence quotient' is a measure of precociousness in children, with a high IQ score on test showing that a given individual is able to perform certain mental tasks that are ordinarily performed only by those chronologically further along the developmental track. One might expect that a set of purportedly empirical assumptions about how development proceeds, assumptions which have grounded educational debate and policies for practice over more than half a century, would be subject to rigorous empirical testing. In the nature of the case, however, and given the metaphysical basis of those assumptions, this cannot be done.

From the earliest attempts in the nineteenth century to measure innate abilities,[13] through work at the start of the twentieth to trace their development in children,[14] seminally operationalised by Terman in the 1930s,[15] psychometric tests of ability of increasing sophistication down to the present day have remained reliant on two basic premises: that talent and ability are measurable as a function of mental over chronological age, and that their variation through the population follows a normal curve of distribution. The first of these premises, when operationalised, may be a more or less useful device for measuring current performance, but it clearly cannot be used to throw light on the relation it posits between current and eventual achievement (the realisation of 'potential'), for it is based on a determinate hypothesis concerning that relation, presupposing its existence and regularity. Still less could testing procedures be used to question the second, supporting, hypothesis—that ability is indeed 'normally distributed' along a spectrum of endowment.[16] For in order to devise tests with items of increasing difficulty and to score these, it is necessary to operationalise some determinate hypothesis concerning the nature and distribution of the factor under test. In sum, since a 'normal' distribution of a characteristic quantitatively varying between individuals is precisely the hypothesis operationalised in psychometrics, that work cannot be used either to validate or to seek evidence for matters which constitute the assumptions on which it is based. Empirical work on individual endowment thus extrapolates from the conception of the self at issue, rather than providing evidential support for it.

Further supporting evidence is nonetheless also claimed from the fact that test findings and educational outcomes reveal significant correlation between levels of individual achievement and those of others with shared genetic makeup. Again, however, there is no empirical means of investigating the vexed question of whether this correlation has a social or a biological (individual) explanation. The barriers to this are again both empirical and conceptual. Despite an extensive literature on the proportionate contribution of environment and heredity to traits and abilities, the complexity of the genetic/environmental interaction remains unaddressed. Those complexities are typically disentangled more subtly by geneticists studying very simple organisms than they are by social scientists studying the most complex creature of all in the most widely varying material and social environment. Geneticists take account of three, interacting complexities: genetic endowment, the range of environmental variation and *the processses of interaction themselves.* Classic findings (too complex to summarise here) identify a host of non-inherited factors influencing apparent genetic variation, compounded by multiple environmental factors and resulting in unspecifiable individual outcomes.[17] Those analyses—of hair on fruit flies—should be compulsory reading for anyone wishing to make authoritative claims or even plausible guesses about endowment (and potential) in persons. Indeed, such work in genetics points to something very like the dynamic concept of individuation which I am proposing.

Once the processes of interaction between the external and the internal are taken seriously, it is clear why there can be no resolution to disputes over the interpretation of educational research literature which repeatedly shows correlation between socially valued traits and abilities and favourable social environment. Again, dispute which centres on whether these findings result from class-biased teaching and testing or whether they reflect 'real' individual differences (genetically correlated with class) cannot be resolved within the paradigm which gives rise to it. For there is no way the correlation can be examined without operationalising in the research design one or other verdict. As there can be no such thing as a 'culture-free' measurement of traits socially manifested, the search must be for a 'culture fair' investigation, lest the correlation be an artefact of measurement procedures. Sadly, the only way to produce and standardise an instrument to test that hypothesis is to devise one which progressively eliminates the phenomena to be explained. With any instrument not so standardised, class-correlated individual differences remain evident: equally, the explanation for them remains entirely obscure. We cannot know whether such differences result from favourable endowment, from favourable environment, or from the two variables interacting with or synergising each other in unknown and empirically untestable ways.[18]

The most important upshot of all this is that we do not have, *nor could we have,* any basis derived from empirical studies of developing individuals to support a conception of the self as the owner of attributes or potential attributes which are independent of, or determinately separable from, the social processes which are a logically inescapable part of their evolution. The evidence adduced from psychometrics cannot serve to confirm that conception, since it could not possibly be disconfirmed within a research paradigm to which it is central, and the same is true for the relevant findings of empirical educational sociology. The lessons of educational practice show that accurate prediction cannot be distinguished from self-fulfilling prophesy, with consequent dubious claims running through disputes about freedom and equality and the relative claims of meritocratic and compensatory rationales in public education. When hypothesised 'potential' serves to justify practice, there is no way of arbitrating between on the one hand advocates of meritocracy who see current attributes as evidence of eventual attributes and therefore as justifying differential treatment correlated with predictions about the eventual outcome of inherent capacity; and on the other hand, advocates of compensation who see current attributes as evidence of past favourable treatment which would conversely justify compensatory measures to remedy deficits presumed to result from deficient treatment in the past. As so often, *when no rational progress can be made on a matter of such evident practical importance, we are impelled to suspect that the problem itself may have been wrongly construed.* And again, we cannot rely on evidence from implementation, since both contradictory hypotheses are confirmed by practices based on them. When schools select, stream or band, 'high flyers' fly higher still and 'under-achievers' achieve relatively further 'under' the mean. When schools adopt common curricula and 'mixed-ability' pedagogies, one end of a notional spectrum is 'levelled-down' and the other is 'levelled-up', producing a raised mean of achievement with lesser variation across the range. And in neither case can it be shown whether the practices in question run with the grain of a posited endowment or whether they run against it.

The dialogue of the deaf between disputants thus results from the fact that both sides are correct in their observations, but neither is entitled to their explanatory inferences and the advocacy based on them. It is primarily the conception of the self under review here which defines the problem as a matter of determining whether or how much developing individuals are 'inherently' different as a matter of brute fact, with the consequent practical choice being whether to treat them during development either as if they were all (potentially) different or conversely as if they were all (potentially) much the same. The inadequacy in this dichotomous choice lies in what is implied by 'inherently'. If by 'inherent' we understand attributes with which the individual is endowed, and which lie dormant like future features of the flower in the bulb, there is no escape from the theoretical impasse and no way forward in the practical dispute. For once we posit *potential* abilities and traits, an individual's attributes can as surely be frustrated as fostered by circumstance at whatever relative level we envisage them. Claims that favourable treatment (and investment) should correlate with perceived high 'potential' cannot be adjudicated *on grounds which make reference to the rights and freedoms of individuals* (though they might on non-liberal economic grounds of cost-effective investment), against claims which argue precisely the reverse. The only way off the horns of this dilemma is to reconceptualise the ontological status of the individual's attributes—those traits and abilities which inhere in the person. I am arguing that if by 'inherent' we rather understand simply whatever attributes *currently* inhere in a given individual, then social practices can take account of actually existing identifiable individual differences without overdetermining future development whether for better or for worse.

The practical implications for how the development of specific individuals should be separately responded to are limited but nonetheless clear and significant. They are limited, because in fostering individual development, in homes or classrooms, doing the best we can for differing individuals cannot mean aiming at invisible (potential) targets, but only making the smallest number of mistakes in our judgements of what is appropriate current response, burning the fewest possible bridges to their later repair. Any parent of several children has a hunch that humans come into the world significantly different from each other in unfathomable ways, and that to try and treat developing persons as if they were all the same would be as foolish as it is impossible. The same parents also know, however, that the more our behaviour is guided by judgements of perceived difference, the more divergent development becomes. In families, 'the clever one' may well get cleverer, 'mother's helper' grow more alert to the needs and approval of others, 'the difficult one' become more of a cross to be borne. Practical wisdom reminds us that names, bad or good, influence a dog's development: to institutionalise that long-recognised hazard in the arrangements a society makes to guide the development of its future members is wilfully to compound its dangers.

The substantive implications for public education in a liberal society are, of course, much more far-reaching. For although in day-to-day practice we are simply concerned with doing the best for the individuals before us, our concern at the level of educational policy is for all of the rising generation. And this does not, as is so often supposed, simply present the problems of upbringing or educational practice all over again, but now multiplied by 'n' or a very large number. Indeed, to suppose that it might is to wear just those individualist blinkers which constantly vitiate our understanding. At the policy level we must of course remain concerned with the individual's experience: but part of that concern is an understanding of how each person's experience affects and is affected by the experience of others. Since the educational experience of the individual is a social experience; since the outcomes of education are in part positional; since those outcomes (and their distribution) affect each person both individually and as one of the category collectively affected, so public provision for individual development is more than a matter of responding to what seem like the contingencies before us (and *a fortiori* more than a matter of meeting consumer demands). How we conceptualise the process of development is therefore crucial not only to good teaching but to developing policies for public education that are appropriate to a society inspired by the ideal of an equal distribution of liberty. An atomistic view of the person functions as a significant obstacle to relevant understanding and hence frustrates the search for appropriate policies and the realisation of that ideal. (More detailed discussion of this will be deferred to my concluding chapter.)

This section has attempted to chip away at that obstacle. Even in the case of a person's traits and abilities—those attributes which seem most central to selfhood, most basic to a person's capacity to acquire understandings, develop tastes, endorse values and form preferences—we see that it is impossible to separate a notional endowment from social components of development, whether these be informal, structured or fortuitous: impossible to disentangle the internal from the external. And this is as much the case conceptually as it is empirically. Once we set aside the lurking belief that individual minds are somehow 'furnished' in the process of development by the learning and experience which come their way, with 'potential' making different approaches to interior design more or less appropriate; once we understand that minds are *constituted* during the developmental process rather than somehow brought to fruition by it, then the traditional liberal conception of a self which is prior to its ends begins to crumble away.

UNDERSTANDINGS, TASTES, VALUES AND THE FORMATION OF PREFERENCES

What has been argued for the individual's talents and abilities can be shown the more so for her/his understandings, tastes and values and the preferences arising from them. On the conception of the self challenged here, we are in some sense 'stuck with' our talents and abilities, but we choose what to like, admire or believe. The plausibility of both halves of this taken-for-granted perspective again depends on a focus on the static, achieved selfhood of liberalism's consenting adults. When the focus is shifted to the developing individual, the dichotomy between what characteristics persons posses whether they like it or not and what they can take on board if they like—between who we are and what we choose—begins to break down. On the dichotomous notion of dual selfhood, where there are on the one hand developing individuals and on the other achieved selves—embryonic bearers of preferences and fully-fledged free agents—liberal theory (and liberal philosophy of education) has no difficulty laying down the distinct rights and responsibilities of persons in each of those categories. The latter are free to choose how to think, feel and act short of harming others; the former need to be constrained in the present in order to equip them for future free thought, feeling and action. The neatness of that formulation is matched only by the contradictions it belies.

Even leaving aside the practical consequences of empirical problems which arise from this neat dichotomy, to do with pinpointing the moment (which historically recedes with social development) at which members of the first category metamorphose into members of the second in various areas of life, there remain serious conceptual problems associated with this 'look, no hands' view of a person's progress towards the status of free agent. The goal is that achieved selves should be free to choose, but we cannot choose (or rationally reject) what we do not know about. What counts as 'knowing about' something depends upon what that something is. How persons acquire whatever counts as sufficient knowledge, understanding or acquaintance will vary with what options are put in their way. When time, energy and resources are finite, those options themselves must be selected. Criteria for their selection will be necessarily controversial. Controversy will reflect the preferences of 'developed' selves. Those selves themselves underwent a process of development in which their undeveloped inclinations required to be constrained or nurtured... The regress could continue. And the practical consequences of the puzzle are obvious. They range from the hapless parent's "Eat up your greens: you will learn to like them, then later you can refuse them," to the Plowden Report's famous declaration: "Children should not be taught to doubt until faith is firmly established".[19]

That bald statement has been much lampooned, but it merely reflects in a particularly sensitive area the uncomfortable reality that many of both the good things and the bad things in life—from spinach, piano-playing and diligence to tobacco, compulsive shopping and domestic violence—are acquired tastes. And quite often tastes for things in the former group are more arduous and rebarbative to acquire and we do not necessarily 'pick them up' willingly. Most of all it reflects a fact of life which sits ill with the liberal aim of keeping all options open for the developing self. Much of what we pick up through no choice of our own becomes part of us: though we may later choose to reject it, we do not thereby remake ourselves as if the process of induction into 'possible future options' had not occurred. This will be returned to, but the pertinent questions here are how persons acquire understandings, tastes and values, how what is internal and what is external to the individual interact in that process, and how during it, the development of each is enmeshed with the development of others. The most illuminating focus is again the young, but it is part of my contention that similar considerations can be extended with appropriate modification to all (developing) individuals. In the dynamic evolution of individual abilities, it is evident that a society's arrangements for education—how it is constituted and how it is distributed—are powerfully influential. The same arrangements also significantly influence (whether by positive guidance or by default) the particular understandings, tastes and values which evolve, and how these come to be distributed through a population of developing individuals. The first part of this claim is relatively uncontroversial: indeed when they are not being philosophically self-conscious, most parents, teachers, taxpayers and politicians would say that that is precisely what families and schools are for. Philosophical caveats arise less in relation to knowledge and understanding than to tastes and values, so it may be useful to take each of these in turn.

On knowledge and understanding, Hirst's work on an epistemological foundation for the content of a general, liberal education[20] attracted controversy in proportion to its influence. What stands above controversy, however, is Hirst's basic claim that the mind is constituted by the conceptual schemes individuals form from the modes of reasoning, forms of understanding and claims to knowledge put before them. Equally securely founded is the supporting rationale for the curricular implications Hirst draws from his (in some respects controversial) epistemological claims: that if public education is to be liberal, then all developing individuals should be introduced to whatever modes of reasoning and forms of understanding together constitute current standards of rational thought and enquiry. (Some see Hirst's recent emphasis on the social nature of education as a practice to be a radical departure from his earlier position, but it is hard to see what could have greater implications for the social constitution of consciousness than those basic contentions.) If we set aside proper and inevitably non-definitive debate about precisely what forms of reasoning can be identified as mutually discrete, about where claims to knowledge shade into claims to belief, and about what informational items in particular circumstances and for differing individuals best illustrate the current building-blocks of rational understanding, one thing remains clear: none should be deprived, by action or default, of access to those building blocks, lest some be short-changed in the equal development of free agency.

That a primary purpose of public education is to develop knowledge and understanding would be generally accepted, with disagreement reserved, as noted in chapter five, for how this should be distributed between individuals. The development of tastes is somewhat more problematic. The liberal educator avowedly takes up an agnostic position about the tastes which individuals might eventually adopt, but this sits uneasily with the brute fact that some options for the development of tastes will not come into the path of many individuals in an accessible manner unless they form part of the educational process. Moreover, it sits even more uneasily beside the conceptual truth that all teaching beyond the impersonal purveying of information implies a non-relativist stance to the worth of varying interests and pursuits (and even in the limiting case, information must be selected). This dilemma for the liberal educator has generated much debate: here it is sufficient to note that taste, like understanding, is not auto-generated. It is both caught and taught from the three sources referred to earlier, of which the institutional structured source is public education. And whatever the pretensions of educators to agnosticism in this regard, the process logically cannot be neutral. Taste is inevitably parasitic on understanding and contingent on circumstance. The tastes individuals develop can of course be nothing other than 'their own', but their provenance nonetheless represents an unambiguous case of the dialectical relation between the internal and the external in the evolution of the self.

The development of value commitments is yet more problematic, exhibiting all of the empirical and conceptual problems which arise in respect of tastes, and compounding them. Given the liberal educator's commitment to fostering rational autonomy, the aim in moral matters is neither to inculcate the values of tradition nor of any particular creed or ideology, but to foster critical reflection on values and a capacity for autonomous moral judgement. In recent years, confidence in this substantively agnostic vision (underpinned by an implicit notion of moral and social progress through the spread and increase of rational autonomy, inherited from nineteenth-century liberalism) has come under attack from two quarters. On the one hand, philosophers and educational theorists have called into question the adequacy of critical reflection as a sufficient response to the value fragmentation of the modern world, variously urging the claims of shared normative frameworks and of virtue ethics in the formation of moral dispositions.[21] On the other, politicians and public call for directive moral guidance in education to combat a perceived decline in personal conduct and a claimed erosion of the moral fabric of society.

I have argued at length elsewhere that the weakness of the liberal educator's neutral position on value development arises from its grounding in the conception of the self challenged here, which offers an inadequate view of the development of moral motivation and disposition.[22] Since social structure and personal relations are far from neutral sources of influence, a principled neutrality in the third source—education—risks exacerbating the power of contingent circumstance in the development of value commitments. An atomistic view of the individual, backed by overemphasis on the power of reasoning (as if what is taught were separate from and more powerful than what is caught) misconstrues how values are formed, as a consequence of ignoring the dialectical relation between individual and social evolution. Thus neutralist liberal educators set out to foster moral autonomy as if that were analogous to the capacity to make informed critical judgements on, say, scientific or historical questions, striving for an objective presentation of moral claims and the skills and attitudes needed to evaluate them, so that considered personal judgements can be made. Unfortunately, this careful neutrality is least likely to achieve its goal of cool appraisal, just where—in order to avoid undue influence—it is thought most necessary. For value appraisal and endorsement is not analogous to scientific or historical learning, where the young are led, within a structured environment, to climb a cognitive ladder which they then may extend or rebuild to the benefit of their own cognitive development and the ongoing falsificationist project which advances collective understanding. In the development of value commitments, where structured experience is but a minor mediating element in what is learned, and where emotion as much as intellect acts as filter and reinforcer, values are not analogous to the facts, hypotheses, procedures or skills which are intentionally passed on in other areas of learning. For beliefs are not the rungs in a ladder developing individuals ascend, but the view from the height they are at, just as dispositions and attitudes are not equipment they use in the ascent, but the muscles they acquire along the way, which cannot later be discarded by purely rational decision. Priority for rational appraisal in the development of values therefore cannot secure the goal of unconstrained self-definition by which it is justified—a failure which reveals conceptual problems with that goal.

Teachers and parents of course have always been aware that 'outside influences' affect the tastes, values and attitudes of the young, often more powerfully than the processes of public education. That insight, however, reflects a similar conception, in which the social and material parameters for individual development are seen as mere frustrating intervening variables which may stand in the way of autonomous judgement, to be fostered through the structured learning of formal education. What I am arguing here is that all three sources of learning are inescapable constituents of the raw material which goes into the construction of the self. (In the next chapter I shall argue that such a conception of selfhood implies that education must have a broader transformative purpose than the emancipation of the individual, as that emancipation itself depends in part upon the transformation of social structures and practices into forms which can become part of the educative process.) Here it is sufficient to sum up this section so far by noting that in their understandings, tastes and values, individuals should be seen neither as products of their environment, nor as rational appraisers who survey that environment and its influences in order to espouse options consonant with traits and capacities which they simply happen to have. Nor indeed can individual development be adequately characterised by some kind of middle position, which attempts to accommodate an element of both unidirectional causal explanations for how people become what they are. A view is required, as in the earlier case of talents and abilities, which sees the individual and the social, the internal and the external, in a process of dynamic interaction whereby the self evolves and modifies itself throughout a continuous (if perhaps decelerating) process of development.

Such a view of the person has substantive implications both for the nature and importance of structured learning, and for how access to educational experiences should be distributed. Since each individual's development is enmeshed with the development of others, educational arrangements significantly affect not only how autonomy develops in any individual but also how its prerequisites—and hence liberty itself—are distributed between individuals. Given the liberal ideal of an equal such distribution, coupled with the substantive concept of liberty for which I have argued, corresponding educational arrangements are fundamental to the establishment and maintenance of a liberal social order. Again, disclaimers may be required. I am not suggesting that people develop inexorably along paths laid down for them, still less that they become what formal education seeks to make them. What a dynamic, socially interactive conception of selfhood implies is simply what corresponds to our experience: that we are not born with settled attributes, tastes and values; that they do not come from nowhere, nor do we acquire them solipsistically; and that the primary arenas for the intentional mediation of the contingent messages which come from the world around us are the home and the school. (In a largely secular society I do not include religious institutions among the sources of mediation common to all.) Of these arenas, the schooling system represents society's arrangements for fostering talent and ability and guiding the development of understandings, tastes and values. Thus the policies and practices of public education necessarily have—by intent or default—substantive effects on the attributes, abilities, tastes and values developed in a population of individuals. Furthermore, *the distribution of those characteristics and commitments through that population is also consequent on educational policies and practices.* Thus, through the mediating influence of public education as through the political structuring of the social world, the abilities, tastes and values of each, though 'their own', are inextricably enmeshed *in their development as well as their exercise* with the talents, tastes and values of others.

In education they are doubly so in that this source of learning is social in the strong sense elaborated in chapter three. In society's institutional nurture of individual development, response to the perceived characteristics of each carries implications for response to the perceived characteristics of others. The individual's attributes may be her/his own—how could it be otherwise—but they cannot be the basis for the kind of propriatorial claims envisaged by Locke and latterly Nozick, simply because their development cannot be a purely self-regarding matter, whatever we conclude about their exercise in particular circumstances. As chapter three suggested, talents and abilities, as well as the merit that society attaches to them, evolve to a significant extent as a result of social arrangements, which advantage some individuals over others: particular educational policies affect the range of differentials in benefit as well as position in the range. A similar case can be made for outlooks, tastes and values: though again the individual's 'own', endorsed by him/her from a range of possibilities, these commitments evolve to a significant extent from social arrangements, and given educational policies affect the availability of particular developmental trajectories to differing individuals. When the relation between the good of each and the good of all in a liberal society was examined in chapter three, I concluded that defects in liberalism's metaphysical and ontological premises vitiated attempts to resolve a clash between those two goals in respect of the expression of preferences and the exercise of freedom. I have further argued here that similar difficulties are also involved in the formation of those preferences and the development of freedom's prerequisites. The implications for an equitable distribution of autonomy and freedom alert us both to what constitutive social practices should avoid and to what they should facilitate. That being the case, it is hardly surprising that the respective roles, rights and responsibilities of the public and the private spheres in the formation of the individual are hotly contested.

THE FAMILY, THE STATE AND THE INDIVIDUAL

Of all social practices, upbringing and education, as frameworks for individual development, highlight perhaps most strongly the contestable boundary between the public and the private spheres. The existence and protection of a private realm is central to liberalism, as is dispute about its boundaries. As Berlin reported, liberals of all traditions hold "... that there ought to exist a certain minimum area of personal freedom which must on no account be violated",[23] as that is essential both to the development and the exercise of autonomy.

Therefore, "It follows that a frontier must be drawn between the area of private life and that of public authority. Where it is to be drawn is a matter of argument, indeed of haggling".[24] Libertarians emphasise this the more strongly, not only asserting that "Freedom thus presupposes that the individual has some assured private sphere, that there is some set of circumstances in his environment with which others cannot interfere",[25] but also insisting that pre-eminent among these is parental or familial primacy in the formation of the young. One of the features which distinguishes neo-liberalism from less 'hard line' interpretations of the liberal ideal is that it settles this significant boundary dispute by fiat. Historically, the boundary between the public and the private spheres has thus been basic in a liberal society to the protection of individual freedom from encroachment by the power of the state. In modern times, the boundary has been challenged from within liberalism from two quarters. Feminist theory objects that 'the private sphere' serves as a smoke-screen for patriarchy: that to treat the traditional family as an entity is not in the equal interests of all of its members. Those arguments will not be examined here (despite the fact that the slogan "the personal is political" echoes disquiet with atomistic conceptions of the self[26]) because they tend to focus less on the boundary as such than on just what should lie within the protected area. The second source of challenge, however, arises precisely from the matters in hand, and presents liberalism with another paradox.

The boundary which is seen as basic to the liberal conception of a free society must be maintained to allow individuals to exercise their freedom without interference. Nonetheless, it is seen to permit potential threats to the *development of constituents of freedom* in respect of the formation of the young. Where the boundary dispute is not settled by *fiat*, upbringing and education are increasingly the site of two main issues for contemporary intra-liberal dispute about the respective rights and responsibilities of the family and the state. The first of these issues concerns the distribution of available goods; the second their constitution. The first concerns how opportunities to realise individual preferences might come to be distributed across society; the second concerns the nature and development of those preferences. Both of these disputes present intractable difficulties. That they underlie liberalism's attempts (as in Williams' account) to arbitrate the claims of liberty and equality, and also to guarantee accommodation of moral and cultural pluralism, might be taken as evidence that in the world of social practice, the notion of persons as straightforward owners of individual attributes runs into serious trouble. Notwithstanding those messages from practice, on the conception of individual development which is here subjected to critique, the two disputes in question are formulated as theoretically separate, though they impinge on the same interface between the public and the private spheres. On the conception of individual development—and hence of the self—for which I am arguing, the two disputes are no more separable in theory than they are in practice. Amendment to the liberal conception of the self may therefore suggest ways forward from the impasse reached in both disputes.

The distributional dispute can be outlined as follows. Among the imperatives of a liberal society are on the one hand, the freedom of each to conduct personal relations of intimacy without interference of the state except to prevent harm to the individuals involved in those relations, and on the other hand, to provide social arrangements which offer equality of opportunity for all to develop the preconditions of autonomous agency. The primacy of family relations is a key guarantor of the first of these: it is also a key inhibitor of the second. Rawls notes that equality of opportunity requires that "those who are at the same level of talent and ability, and have the same willingness to use them, should have the same prospects of success regardless of their initial place in the social system".[27] For this to be possible, of course, social arrangements must be agreed which mitigate the fact that some families, for both internal and external reasons, can and do offer their members a 'better start in life' than others. Pre-eminent among redistributive measures to mitigate initial handicapping conditions to the equal development of autonomous agency is the provision of compulsory public schooling. (Indeed this form of state encroachment on the role of the private sphere seemed unobjectionable even to Pareto, who asserted that "compulsory education should rather be called freedom of education, since the parent who does not educate his son harms him greatly and in a direct way".[28])

Public education is provided both to fulfil the goals of social reproduction referred to earlier and to foster emancipatory individual development: both purposes presuppose that all adults in a liberal society have obligations towards that society's future members in general. Disputes about the distributional effects of public education therefore can be seen as clashes between private obligations to one's own and social obligations to the rising generation. Publicly-financed schooling meeting minimum agreed standards represents, in developed liberal societies, a relatively uncontroversial buffer between an individual's prospects and his/her familial circumstances.[29] Controversy enters the debate over what level of provision beyond that minimum should be dependent upon the motivation and means of the family and what should be the responsibility of all, realised through the state. Disputes over private education, vouchers and parental choice within a diversified public sector are all practical manifestations of that controversy. So indeed are various social programmes for compensatory intervention in the upbringing and educational support which families provide both pre-school and during schooling. Champions of the rights of parents to pass on to their own children the cultural capital (and social advantage) which are constituents of the family's self-identity rightly point out that even with strongly interventionist policies, it remains the case that concerned, wise and motivated parents are an asset to individuals which could only be legislated out of existence at the price of tyranny. Advocates of a more comprehensive role for the state in the distribution of education counter with the observation that whilst that is admittedly the case, no social arrangements are neutral with respect to the penalties which attend lack of relevant initial assets. Those differences cannot be constructively addressed without bringing to bear on them a view of free agency which understands individual and social factors as combining dialectically in development. For on the view of the self here subjected to critique they remain deadlocked, buttressed by contending (but equally misconceived) beliefs about parameters for the development of persons and thus on where responsibility lies.

The second area of dispute has rather different features and can be outlined as follows. Here, the obligations of a liberal state are potentially in conflict with the inviolability of the private sphere, not through its duties to insulate individuals from differentials in benefit which arise *between* families, but from possible harms which may arise *within* them. That the state should intervene to protect members of families, particularly the young, from obvious harms of physical abuse and neglect is uncontroversial (with disagreement reserved for what counts as a relevant harm and how it should be remedied). Controversy enters with respect to the cultural, ethical and religious understandings and commitments which are powerful influences on individual development. Families tend—and often seek—to pass to their younger members those outlooks and values which are constituents of the family's self-identity: the liberal state is committed to acceptance of a co-existing plurality of such outlooks and values, and is further committed to fostering through public education the rational autonomy which will enable each individual to endorse, modify or reject the outlooks and values they encounter, including those of their families and communities of origin.

It is immediately clear that two types of clash will be waiting in the wings. Where the outlook and values of the family is not consonant with the secular pluralism of the liberal perspective (as in families with fundamentalist religious commitments, or with cultural values which do not admit of equality between the sexes or between particular culturally defined classes, or which seek to insulate their members from the technological or epistemological stage of development the wider society has embraced) then public liberal education will be seen as a direct threat not only to the values of the family and what it perceives as the best interests of its developing members, but also as a threat to the continuity of the cultural option which those values and interests represent. Where the outlook and values of the family *is* consonant with liberal secular pluralism, the potential conflict is less stark but in consequence more pervasive. For despite the fact that they may endorse pluralism as a political principle, particular families remain existentially singular. In matters of spiritual, moral, social, health or sex education, whether formal or informal, in standards of conduct, in attitudes to authority and on acceptable types of sanctions for the young, the liberal educator's theoretical commitment to agnosticism (short of demonstrable harm) falls at the first fence of practice. Whether in prescribing a curriculum or 'delivering' it, in determining the institutional structure or working within it, in actively guiding the young or serving as 'facilitators', neutrality is logically not an option for educators. Specific actions and reactions are called for in the face of real contingencies. Those cannot but embody substantive judgements, which imply greater or lesser endorsement for the commitments of particular family perspectives. Families who believe that what they hold to be important is being threatened, discounted, challenged or insufficiently buttressed by public education will therefore feel badly served by the state in matters of fundamental concern to them.

In the case of both types of clash, families will demand either that they be enabled to educate their developing members according to their own lights outside the state system, or that they be permitted sufficient choice and control within that system, or that the system as a whole conform to the values and standards they are prepared to endorse. The measures which accede to these demands are, respectively; the coexistence of 'independent' provision alongside a state schooling sector and/or legislation to allow 'home-schooling' under certain conditions; denominational schooling within the state sector or latterly choice between and direct 'consumer' influence over options within that sector; and in the third case the existence of effective democratic negotiation about the values and ethos of public provision. All of these measures contain a deal of fudge with respect to the underlying clash between the rights of families to pass on their own values and commitments and so to perpetuate themselves culturally, and the duties of the state to put a range of worthwhile cultural and personal options before developing individuals and thus to protect them from acquiring internal constraints to later autonomous commitment. The formal position, for example (typically) in the UK, is that the state retains responsibility for ensuring that the education of any individual be adequate and appropriate, wherever and however it is conducted. However, if the criteria of adequacy are taken to include the liberal respect for pluralism, not simply as a constitutive principle for the polity but also as an outlook which provides the framework for individual development, then extra-state provision to permit cultural or value diversity on the grounds of respect for pluralism will be defensible only in direct proportion to its redundancy. That, of course, is on the assumption that state provision itself reliably meets relevant criteria of adequacy and appropriateness. Thus the neutralist liberal dilemma remains unresolved.

Part of the popular appeal of neo-liberalism is its apparent resolution of this problem through consumer choice within and influence over state-provided schooling. Whilst those proposals are clearly defective in ways reported in chapter four, their apparent plausibility can alert us to defects in the neutralist liberal construal of boundary disputes between the public and the private spheres. What the neo-liberal perspective underplays is that our understandings, tastes and values are constitutive of our identity: *they are not options external to the self which can be surveyed with rational detachment.* So indeed are our self-understandings about personal desert and social position. To acknowledge this enables us to take full account of the tenaciousness with which individuals in families seek to defend the private sphere, as well of as the stubborn tendency of social hierarchies to work for their own perpetuation at all levels of advantage and disadvantage. It also implies, as MacIntyre has forcefully argued,[30] that a liberal education cannot achieve its aim of fostering the development of autonomous individuals by agnostically placing before them a cafeteria of cultural understandings, ways of life and options for judgement, from which they are to form preferences in the light of reasoned appraisal. Such an approach clearly neglects MacIntyre's useful distinction between goods which are internal to practices and those which are external to them; more importantly, it ignores the dialectical relation between what is internal and what is external to the self.

Most of all, therefore, acknowledgement that a range of constituents of selfhood—aspirations, abilities and achievements as well as understandings, tastes and commitments—result from a continuous dynamic interaction between the individual and the social throughout the process of development, leads us to set aside the notion that the private and the public, the personal and the political, the individual and the social are conceptually discrete, such that practical disputes must centre on where precisely the lines between them should be drawn. With acceptance that each defines and gives form to the other, the two liberal disputes over the respective rights and responsibilities of the family and the state which I have outlined become a single dispute. How identities are constituted and how they are distributed become inseparable issues, and *the transgenerational construction of identity becomes a matter at the heart of democratic deliberation, not one that should be granted immunity from it.* When public education is seen as both continuous with and productive of the role of families in upbringing, then perennial clashes between its reproductive and emancipatory functions appear in a different light, to be taken up shortly. And when our conception of the self sets aside the duality implied by the neutralist liberal perspective, the ideal of individual autonomy which is the educator's priority will need some recasting in the light of a revised conception of what that complex capacity involves and requires.

AUTONOMY AND INDIVIDUALISM

That necessary revision has three aspects. One entails rejection of a notion of free agency in which persons can question all roles and commitments in a manner which seems perilously close to the existentialist's criterionless choice. As Taylor notes, this is self-defeating, since "...complete freedom would be a void in which nothing would be worth doing, nothing would deserve to count for anything. The self which has arrived at freedom by setting aside all external obstacles and impingements is characterless, and hence without defined purpose, however much this is hidden by such seemingly positive terms as 'rationality' or 'creativity' ".[31] The second aspect requires a move beyond a rights-based fixation on the protection of the individual from constraint, which reserves concerns about the social dimension of autonomy for relatively simple questions about how the exercise of one person's autonomy impinges on that of others, to the neglect of more complex questions concerning how each person's development of that capacity relates to the development *and* exercise of autonomy in others. These two aspects, I shall try to show, are intimately connected, in theory as in practice, with both resting on a construal of autonomy which is over-individualistic. That construal supports and is supported by the commitment to state neutrality on the worth of human ends and the preferences to which they give rise.

It is on the relation between these two ideas that the third aspect of that necessary revision can be built. I reported in the previous section that the boundary around the private sphere is standardly justified by the requirement that the liberal state remain neutral between competing ideas of the good. That position, as I shall show below (of necessity somewhat schematically), is sustained not simply by the pervasive belief that the fact of pluralism and the claims of individual freedom require it, but also by the view of the person I am challenging—a view which puts a particular gloss on individual freedom. The crux of the matter here is that any debate about whether the public sphere must stand above substantive conceptions of the good presupposes that it can so stand. And if persons are seen as simply having the attributes which individuate them, forming and exercising preferences in a largely asocial process of self-definition, then this is clearly the case. If the formation of the self were indeed a process of self-definition by rational reflection then, since that process is essentially private, the preferences which issue from it would require immunity from public interference in order to maintain priority for individual liberty. If, on the other hand, persons become individuated through an inescapably dialectical interaction between the individual and the social, such that the public sphere is ineluctably implicated in the construction of the self and its preferences as well as in their expression, then demands that the state stand above conceptions of the good become otiose, on the familiar grounds that 'ought implies can'. This, I shall try to show, downgrades neither freedom nor autonomy. It does, however, imply that autonomy should be conceptualised as a capacity to be achieved, and to be valued as constitutive of free agency itself, rather than, as in neutralist liberalism, that it should be conceptualised and valued as the individual expression of freedom.

These matters are extremely complex and can only be given indicative treatment here. To address them adequately demands a full length analysis of its own. However, they must be briefly outlined in order to ground the arguments of my concluding chapter in which I shall try to demonstrate not only that the retreat of the state in relation to education's distribution (with inseparable consequences for its constitution) is wholly incompatible with liberal ideals but also that those ideals can offer a firmer basis for society's educational arrangements than neutralist liberalism provides. With that in view, I shall first try to show that contemporary unease with modern liberalism's lack of substance in respect both of the nature of individual freedom and autonomy and of the worth of human ends can be vindicated. We would expect the context of public liberal education to be as well placed to illuminate these matters as it is in need of their revision, being both animated by these neutralist ideals and charged with duties to serve them. For education aims to secure the protection of individuals from external and internal forms of constraint by equipping them to develop and deploy the capacities which free agency requires, whilst remaining agnostic about the values and preferences which may result—and all of this whilst contributing substantively (like it or not) to the understandings, tastes and values which come to individuate the person. The contradictions in that position should add further weight to the case developed here against the purely negative conception of liberty, the atomistic view of the person and the agnosticism about values and preferences which together characterise modern neutralist liberalism—and *a fortiori* neo-liberalism. Just as this cumulative case is needed for a better understanding of autonomy, so that in turn is essential to any justifying theory for the social practice which aims to foster that valued capacity.

From its beginnings, a strand in liberal thought warning against the dangers of individualism has coexisted beside its celebration.[32] Thus de Tocqueville feared that self-sufficiency might be destructive of the civil society on which it depended, leading its members to forget their interdependence. Democracy, he observed, should enable people to gain control over their own lives, but "Such folk owe no man anything and hardly expect anything from anybody. They form the habit of thinking of themselves in isolation and imagine that their whole destiny is in their own hands".[33] Recognising that habit of thought reflected in contemporary theoretical and practical disputes, it might be argued that liberalism, like its practical manifestations in representative democracy and public education, has begun to fall victim to its own success. I have noted that the individualist emphasis in liberal freedom is associated with a notion of self-ownership which legitimates a barricade around the private sphere. Formed in a context of growing tolerance and secularisation, that view of the person implied public neutrality on the worth of differing ends, and abstention from interference (subject to the harm condition) with individual preferences on ends and the means to them.[34] To exercise preferences, individuals require that their autonomy be respected. To form them they require that the capacity for autonomy be developed. The first demand sits happily with negative liberty, but the second does not, unless the two disputes outlined in the previous section are to be dismissed out of hand. When the disjunction between these two demands is examined, it is the notion of autonomy at work which seems to lie at the heart of the problem. A more coherent conception would see autonomy not merely as an attribute of individuals, but as a social good: as something that has to be developed and provided for socially since, without that, it cannot be exercised individually, except at the expense of others and within a range of options thrown up by chance. Such a conception suggests a social order where practices constitutive of liberty, and structures forming its parameters, require more of the state than abstention from interference and more of liberal education than the agnostic emancipation of individuals.

This is not the place to trace philosophical arguments for the primacy of individual autonomy as grounding for immunity from interference (which of course predate classical liberalism and have deep metaphysical roots—to be seen, for example, in Kant's 'transcendental subjects'). Nor is it the place to rehearse debates over the tenability of, for example, Rawls's claim that neutralist liberalism's 'unencumbered self' can be understood not as a metaphysical claim but merely as a pragmatic device for negotiation between persons which transcends self-interest. I have indicated (too summarily) above that the pragmatic device itself seems to rely on implicit metaphysical support: indeed, when the development and not the simple exercise of autonomy comes into focus, we see that the contradictions which arise are themselves metaphysical. Thus the standard rationale for a pragmatically-based analysis is that since there is no public authority on ends, the state should maintain a just framework for coexistence between individuals with differing purposes and views of life. Individuals, however, do not start out with views and purposes, but acquire them during their development through personal attachments, environmental influence and institutional guidance, with the latter furnished through public education. This is defined as liberal in so far as it, too, remains neutral on outlooks and ends: as Ackerman observes, "A liberal school has a different mission: to provide the child with access to the wide range of cultural materials that he may find useful in developing his own moral ideals and patterns of life".[35] Liberal philosophers of education continue to wrestle with the paradoxes contained in this apparent solution. Thus the same writer also allows that individuals can only develop views of their own against a background of "cultural coherence" provided by the family and cultural community.[36] Autonomy's development therefore seems to require just what it exists to transcend; liberal education's agnosticism on all but procedural values seems to institutionalise the conflict of interests between public and private spheres; and the liberal state's commitment to neutrality on the relative worth of differing commitments and preferences seems to collapse into contradiction when the social practice which is supposed to foster that neutrality in the next generation can only do so by interference with the settled commitments of this one.

These contradictions are on the face of it disguised by liberalism's dual conception of the self, which licences dichotomous interpretations of liberty's implications for the individual before and after the achievement of autonomy (and acknowledgements that this is always a matter of degree sit uneasily here). Liberalism's consenting adults have ostensibly been enabled, by the development of individual autonomy (in part through a liberal education), to pull themselves up by their rational bootstraps and adopt perspectives for themselves from which to review the cultural and moral options available. From that appraisal issue preferences which a liberal state must neutrally respect, short, as always, of harm to others. Developing selves, on the other hand, must be constrained in the present in the name of their own future liberty. They should be enabled to develop talents and traits, and be introduced to tastes and values, so that later they can refashion themselves through critical refection. Sufficient has been said in earlier sections here to cast doubt on this dualism. Not surprisingly, how that transition from potential to actual autonomy is to be understood and effected has presented intractable problems for educational theory and practice. Until recently, theoretical debates focused on whether or how far the exercise of autonomy was necessary to its development—debates reflecting the conceptual problems addressed here.[37] And perennial dispute over the role of precept and example in the development of moral autonomy shows the same problems echoed in practical concerns. More recently, some philosophers have begun to turn from deadlocked debates about how individual autonomy is to be understood and developed, to the underlying questions of how selves are formed and what conceptions of free agency can be defended as conceptually coherent. That enquiry is urgent, as the dual conception of the self required to juggle these contradictions is as untenable in theory as it is hopeless for the guidance of practice.

MacIntyre's critique of liberal neutrality and individualistic autonomy has provoked considerable interest among educational philosophers, partly because he recognises that matters of education are where paradoxes become impossible to ignore, and also because the choices he presents are alarmingly stark. He is surely correct in arguing that it makes little sense to think of developing individuals as engaged in a process of reflective self-creation, guided only by reason and the unbiased presentation of alternatives, for this is "more like the freedom of ghosts—of those whose human substance approached the vanishing point—than of men".[38] His understanding of the transgenerational transmission of identity as a process in which people are formed in communities with particular traditions, at least reinstates the social as an important constituent of individual development: it need not, however, have the consequences he claims for education. On the one hand, he is right to insist that a liberal education cannot be seen as offering a menu of knowledge and belief for rational evaluation by individuals who are a combination of natural characteristics and acquired (but expendable) attitudes and commitments. On the other, to reject that picture need not imply that the education of the public is impossible in modernity, on MacIntyre's grounds that learning and development can only occur on the inside of traditions which modernity fragments.[39] That stance seems to jettison too much of the liberal ideal, opening the door to forms of communitarianism which buy conceptual tidiness at the price of potential threats to individual autonomy. In the third chapter of this analysis it was argued that failure to realise the conflicting social and individual aims of liberal education point to flaws in our conception of those ideals, and the coming chapter will return to this. Public liberal education *premised on a defective conception of the self and its development* may indeed seem condemned to deadlocked debates and practical impasses: but we cannot move forward from them by looking for solutions nostalgically, either to the nineteenth century, as neo-liberalism proposes, or to the pre-modern condition which communitarians evoke.

To move forward does not require that the ideal of autonomy be abandoned in favour of the security of traditional frameworks, but rather that autonomy be differently understood—and this requires tenable metaphysical premises. In contemporary political philosophy, two conceptions of autonomy are at work in re-interpretations of liberalism. The strand which refines the neutralist conception remains thoroughly individualistic in the sense called into question here. Dworkin's characterisation states its implications: "The value of autonomy ... lies in the scheme of responsibility it creates: autonomy makes each of us responsible for shaping his own life according to some coherent and distinctive sense of character, conviction and interest. It allows us to lead our own lives rather than being led along them, so that each of us can be, to the extent that a scheme of rights can make this possible, what he has made himself".[40] The autonomy of the individual is thus both a precondition of liberal neutrality and a source of its justification. That conception leaves unresolved the pressing question of how the self who does that shaping created itself in the first place, and the consequent developmental puzzle of how, with the achievement of autonomy, that which the individual encounters (understandings, tastes, values, etc.) ceases to be a component of evolving identity and becomes instead an object of appraisal, with autonomous appraisal somehow disentangling the components which earlier went into the appraiser's development and resulted in individuation. Despite Dworkin's concern with the equal distribution of individual liberty as well as its primacy, the view of the self and its autonomy which he retains vitiates his attempts to take adequate account of the social preconditions to equal liberty. In this respect if not in others, the strengths and weaknesses of his interpretation share similarities with those of his fellow neutralist, Rawls.

An alternative conception informs the work of Raz.[41] There we find the acknowledgement (which MacIntyre's insights require) that forms of life are logically prior to the individual—that selves do not create themselves—without the communitarian inference that they may therefore be morally or politically prior, meriting greater deference than the chosen commitments of individuals. For Raz remains firmly a liberal, for whom autonomy is of central importance: where he diverges from, for example Rawls or

Dworkin, is in his more substantive (and sustainable) conception of autonomy and in rejecting as incoherent the liberal commitment to state neutrality on questions of worth. He does so on the grounds that that particular commitment, like any other which is to serve as a constitutive principle for social arrangements and political agreements, requires the maintenance of substantive social forms to sustain it. In this, Raz echoes the early awareness of liberals such as Mill that free exchange and liberal freedoms required the establishment of pre-requisite social conditions and moral commitments, without relying implicitly on the accompanying social thesis which then made social progress and individual development seem a dual-purpose perpetual motion machine, once given its start. Where he diverges from those early liberals (apart of course from not echoing their social thesis) is in his view of the person. Raz's position is both complex and subtle, and no attempt will be made to do justice to it here. I draw summarily and selectively on his arguments only in order to ground my claim that liberalism does not presuppose the kind of state neutrality that neutralists adhere to as an article of faith nor consequently the kind of agnosticism for public education that has justified liberal education in theory and vitiated it in practice and which now is more crudely manifested in policies for individual consumer rights and control over this social good.

Raz values autonomy then, not for its power to enable us to re-invent ourselves, but for its importance in that reflective expression of our preferences which contributes to the continual evolution of individuals and their social worlds—an evolution in which agency and contingency are intertwined. His re-interpretation accords with (indeed requires) the continuous view of the self argued for in this chapter. Such a self does not have two phases—the pre-autonomous and the autonomous—nor does the second phase exhibit radically free choice: for Raz, individuals have personal and cultural attachments which are constitutive of identity and only partially negotiable. Whilst "autonomous persons are those who can shape their life and determine its course, they are not merely rational agents who can choose between options after evaluating relevant information...".[42] On the contrary, "Persons who are part creators of their own moral world have a commitment to projects, relationships and causes which affect the kind of life which for them is worth living".[43] A person's past does not determine what he/she does or chooses, but nor is it a carapace that can be shed as a matter of existential choice: it is part of the raw material from which autonomous individuals review and reconstitute their projects for the future. Such a view of the person accords with our experience and avoids many of the contradictions of liberal political and educational theory explored in this chapter and the one before it. We learn to be autonomous (to understand, to value and express our agency), and then we continue learning.

This conception of the self implies a rather different role for the liberal state. It no longer entails a neutralism requiring the state to abstain from intervention, except to protect the rights of autonomous individuals to pursue their chosen ends and the opportunities of pre-autonomous individuals to achieve that protected status. Rather, it suggests a substantive role for the state in relation both to the exercise of autonomy and to its development. When the view of the person ceases to be that of asocial individualism, however, *this changed role for the public sphere is not a threat to individual freedom, but its essential precondition.* The outlines of the position I wish to argue for, and which are broadly similar to that advanced with great subtlety in *The Morality of Freedom,*[44] can be summarised as follows. (I should emphasise that I am not attempting to *précis* Raz's analysis, since my concern is not the general one of the political constitution of a liberal society but the specific one of the role of public education in reflecting and sustaining the ideals of such a society.) Free agents require that their autonomy be respected, if individual freedom is to be society's guiding principle. In order to be autonomous, they must be independent—free from coercion, constraint and manipulation, whether by other individuals or by institutions. That is the accepted, negative specification. Autonomy requires more than this, however. Without a range of inner capacities—cognitive and emotional— autonomy is empty. These capacities evolve socially, in ways I have sufficiently described: they do not develop in a vacuum of neutrality, nor can the agent rise above them with an autonomous bound. It further requires an adequate range of options for autonomous endorsement or rejection, or freedom to make choices is empty. Many of those options are very obviously dependent on arrangements in the public sphere: none of them can be entirely independent of that sphere, once it is allowed that persons are partially socially constituted. It is therefore not the case that in our social and political arrangements we have the choice either, liberally, of excluding considerations about the availability of options and the worth of differing preferences or, illiberally, of allowing a non-neutral state to acquire a licence to intrude on the development of autonomy and to interfere with its exercise. It is rather that, willy-nilly, the 'look no hands' neutralism which seeks to stand above or aside from conceptions of the good is either incoherent, or it is an endorsement of relativism. And if it is the latter, then the very priority for individual freedom, which has seemed to entail neutralism, itself evaporates.

I shall return to these claims in my concluding chapter, in order to argue that in a liberal society the state may—indeed must—concern itself with *providing for,* as well as *protecting* the autonomy of persons. It hardly needs to be said that there are far-reaching implications for public education if this re-interpretation of liberal theory can be sustained. I have repeatedly noted that in a liberal society education is charged with fostering autonomy, for all of its members. Where it is not so charged, or *where an incoherent conception of autonomy and its development frustrates attempts to discharge that duty,* the view of persons and their autonomy I am propounding here implies that educational arrangements will not merely fall short of that aim but must actually frustrate it. The contemporary intra-liberal dispute about the legitimate role of the state, which cannot be adequately represented here, is clearly central to the renewal of liberal political theory. It is equally central, I am claiming, to the renewal of the theory and practice of public liberal education. And that second set of concerns can usefully be brought to bear upon the first, since the core dispute requires an amendment of liberalism's metaphysical premises, which the problems of education, I believe, can materially advance.

To sum up, a growing number of political philosophers (Raz prominent among them) maintain that the individualist perspective of modern neutralist liberalism conflates two commitments. With the valuing of autonomy runs the accompanying belief that the conditions for autonomy can be secured negatively by the simple absence of internal and external constraints on individual agency. And it is thus mistakenly supposed that to reject the second belief is to betray the first. (I have sufficiently elaborated how these have come to be run together.) Philosophical critics of that conflation argue that a political culture centred on individual rights carries the seeds of its own destruction within it: I hope to have illustrated how readily this can be seen in relation to education and its distribution, which reflects and renews the political culture. Thus Taylor notes that although "the rights model goes very well with a more atomistic consciousness," it also implies a willingness to turn aside from commitment to the shared form of life on which it depends. Clearly, "I cannot be too willing to trump the collective decision in the name of individual rights if I haven't already moved some distance from the community which makes these decisions".[45] Elsewhere Taylor spells out the implications of neutralism's tendency to implosion: a free agent cannot "be concerned simply with his individual choices and the associations formed from such choices to the neglect of the matrix in which such choices can be open or closed, rich or meagre...".[46] Given the interdependence of persons and their autonomy, individualism in seeking our ends and the means to them is self-defeating, since much of what persons seek for their well-being can be neither supplied nor enjoyed individually, as my closing chapter will maintain.

I hope to have shown by now, by cumulative theoretical argument and practical illustration, serious defects in a purely negative conception of freedom which demands—from other individuals or from society through the state—nothing more than abstention from interference with the autonomous preferences of persons in whose lives social conditions are seen as the backdrop to agency. Once it is accepted that we have each to be concerned not just with our individual choices but also with the social matrix which makes them the choices that they are, it becomes clear that our autonomy can be neither secured nor protected by purely individual means. Taylor argues convincingly for the interdependence of autonomous persons in the exercise of free agency. When we add a more fundamental kind of interdependence to the picture—that resulting from the dialectical relation between what is internal and what is external to the person in the course of development—then autonomy can be clearly seen, not as something which sets individuals at a distance from their social context, but as a capacity which enmeshes them with it: not as an attribute owned by atomistic individuals, but as a profoundly social good. The maintenance and development of that good then becomes one of the *social* purposes of public education. And that has necessary implications for the role of a liberal state as much in proper oversight of education's distribution as of its provision.

CONCLUSION

That there has been debate from the beginning over how liberalism's ideals might best be realised is well known. Debate has concentrated, however, on how the separate freedom of each to pursue his own good in his own way might accommodate the equivalent freedoms of others. In the nineteenth century, a kind of 'trickle down' theory of rational and moral autonomy underpinned the inviolability of individual preferences and the neutrality of the public sphere. Public action was required only to 'level the playing-field' on which autonomous preferences were expressed, with education looked to to nurture autonomy individually. In the course of this book I have related the fortunes of attempts to realise the liberal ideal of equal liberty through the extension of educational opportunity to all. In attempting to untangle today's unresolved problems of public liberal education (which neo-liberal policies claim to address but do not), I turned to an examination of the philosophical assumptions which justify its aims. In this and the preceding chapter I have tried to show that matters are more complex than those neutralist liberal assumptions allow, with the prime locus of the problem being the "view of the person" which Sandel, rightly I believe, charges with both inspiring and undoing (pervading interpretations of) liberalism.

Having, in earlier chapters, characterised many key disputes over the provision of education in a liberal society as reflecting long-standing tensions between the good of each and the good of all, I turned in chapter five to the conflict which encapsulates those tensions in theory and reflects them in practice. I argued that whereas liberty and equality have seemed conflicting values for liberals, that clash results from too negative a concept of freedom and too thin a conception of equality. Since those commitments have rightly been defended by liberals against over-positive concepts of freedom and over-thick conceptions of equality which are indeed potentially illiberal, I needed to show that the standard choice in each case offered a false alternative. I thus traced the roots of that dichotomous choice to liberalism's problematic view of the person—a view which sees the individual as self-contained and self-defining, interacting with others in a social world comprised of similar others. This chapter has offered arguments to challenge that view. I began by outlining a view of persons in which what is internal and what is external to them at any given time is in a process of dialectical interaction: a view of the self as in continuous evolution as long as learning continues. I then sought to support that view by analysis of the complex sources of individuality, with the focus on persons uncontroversially in process of development. Individual abilities, traits, understandings, tastes and values were seen to evolve through processes in which social relations, arrangements and structures are enmeshed at all points with what is 'inherent' to the self. For further support, I turned to the respective rights and roles of the family and the state in the formation of persons, and showed that neutralist liberal fears about interference in that process from the public sphere generate a host of contradictions. These alert us to the fact that questions of how autonomy and the preferences issuing from it are to be protected have been inadequately posed.

The conception of the self which I have criticised—with its curious dualism—has never accommodated a convincing account of autonomy, most particularly concerning how persons develop that valued capacity. The conventional construal (in which frameworks of understanding, principled commitments and emotional attachments cannot but be taken on board unreflectively in order that they can then be subjected to rational appraisal, as if from without) fails to take account of the complex sources of individuality, and casts a cloak of invisibility over the complex ways in which we are all 'members of one another'. The thicker conception of autonomy I have sketched above has clear implications for how individual development should be fostered in a liberal society, particularly through the institutional fostering of autonomy in the provision and distribution of education. Less obviously at first sight, it has implications for how the good of each relates to the good of all, and for how certain social practices—and most particularly public education—are fundamental to the realisation of liberal ideals. It is to those matters that my concluding chapter now turns.

NOTES AND REFERENCES

1. See Williams, B. (1962), *op. cit.* and discussion in chapter five above.
2. Locke, J., *Second Treatise of Civil Government*, para 27.
3. i. e. 'to each whatever he/she has acquired by fair means'.
4. i. e. 'to each according to her/his need/ merit/ desert/ contribution to society', etc.
5. Flew, A. (1983), Competition and co-operation, equality and elites, *Journal of Philosophy of Education*, 17. 2, p. 267.
6. See chapter five.
7. See Dworkin, R., *A Matter of Principle* (London, Harvard University Press, 1985).
8. *Ibid.*, p. 229.
9. *Ibid.*
10. No references are given here since these debates constitute a whole industry in education and psychology. For key references see bibliography to Jonathan, R. (1986) *Giftedness and Education* (Edinburgh, Scottish Office Education Department).
11. Nor indeed as they appear in disputes about the extent and origins of gender differentiation in traits, abilities and inclinations; see Jonathan, R. (1983), Education, gender and the nature/culture controversy, *Journal of Philosophy of Education*, 13 2, pp. 3–10, and Jonathan, R. (1989), Gender socialisation and the nature/culture controversy: the dualist's dilemma, *Educational Philosophy and Theory*, 21.2 Special Issue, pp. 40–48.
12. Representative of expert advice of this sort, among many hundreds of relevant publications, might be Hall, E. G. and Skinner, N., Somewhere to turn; strategies for parents of gifted and talented children: in Tennenbaum A. J. and Neuman, E. (eds.), *Perspectives on Gifted and Talented Children* (New York, Columbia University, Teachers College Press, 1980).
13. Galton, F., *Hereditary Genius* (London, Macmillan, 1869).
14. Binet, A. and Simon, T. (1908), Le dévelopment de l' intelligence chez les enfants, *L'Année Psychologique* 14, pp. 1–94.
15. Terman, L., *Measuring Intelligence* (Boston, Houghton-Mifflin, 1937).
16. i.e. according to a 'Bell curve', where the fraction of a population at any given point on the curve is inversely proportionate to its distance from the median point.
17. Thoday, J. M., Geneticism and environmentalism: in Neade, J. E. and Parkes, A. S. (eds.), *Biological Aspects of Social Problems* (London, Oliver & Boyd, 1965) pp. 92–106.
18. These arguments are more fully presented in my (1988) The notion of giftedness—or, how long is a piece of string?, *British Journal of Educational Studies* 26. 2, pp. 111–125.
19. Plowden Report *Children and their Primary Schools* (London, HMSO, 1966).
20. See Hirst, P. H., Liberal education and the nature of knowledge: in Peters, R. S. (Ed.), *The Philosophy of Education* (London, Routledge and Kegan Paul, 1973) and Hirst, P. H., *Knowledge and the Curriculum* (London, Routledge and Kegan Paul, 1974).
21. See MacIntyre, A., The idea of an educated public: in Haydon, G. (Ed.), *Education and Values* (Institute of Education, University of London, 1987); Carr, D., *Educating the Virtues* (London, Routledge, 1991); Jonathan, R. (1993a), Educating the virtues: a problem in the social development of consciousness, *Journal of Philosophy of Education*, 27. 1, pp. 115–124; Jonathan, R. (1993b), Education, philosophy of education and the fragmentation of value, *Journal of Philosophy of Education*, 27. 2, pp. 171–178.
22. Jonathan, R. (1995b), *op. cit.*, from which p. 179 here is adapted.
23. Berlin (1969), *op. cit.* p. 124.

24. *Ibid.*
25. Hayek, F. A. (1960), *op. cit.* p. 3.
26. It incidentally directly controverts Rawls's distinction, discussed in chapter five above, between the individual-as-person and the individual-as-citizen .
27. Rawls, J. (1971), *op. cit.,* p. 73.
28. Pareto, "Suffragio Universale", in *L'Italiano Gazzetta del Popolo,* 12. 10. 1872, p. 3.
29. Some libertarians have recently begun to challenge this in publications by right-wing 'think-tanks'; see, for example, Tooley J., *Education Without the State* (London, Social Affairs Unit, 1996).
30. MacIntyre, A., *After Virtue* (London, Duckworth, 1981).
    MacIntyre, A., *Whose Justice? Which Rationality?* (London, Duckworth, 1988).
31. Taylor, C., *Hegel and Modern Society* (Cambridge, Cambridge University Press, 1979), p. 157.
32. There is of course a much longer ancestry, from Aristotle through Marx and Hegel to Dewey, critical theory and various types of communitarianism of the present day, but that is outside the scope of this analysis.
33. de Tocqueville, A. (1843), *Democracy in America* (New York, Doubleday, 1969) p. 508.
34. See Rawls, J. (1985), Justice as fairness: political not metaphysical, *Philosophy and Public Affairs* 14, pp. 223–251.
35. Ackerman, B. A., *Social Justice in the Liberal State* (New Haven, Yale University Press, 1980), p. 156.
36. *Ibid.,* p. 141.
37. As elucidated in Mendus, S. (1987), Liberty and autonomy, Proceedings of the Aristotelian Society, Vol. 87.
38. MacIntyre, A. (1981), *op. cit. p. 119.*
39. See MacIntyre, A. (1987) and (1988), *op. cit.*
40. Dworkin, R. (1986), Autonomy and the demented self, *The Milbank Quarterly* 62, p. 8.
41. See Raz, J., *The Morality of Freedom,* (Oxford, Clarendon Press, 1986).
42. Raz, J., *op. cit.* p.155.
43. *Ibid.*
44. *Ibid.* (see pp. 110–164 for exposition and rebuttal of arguments against 'perfectionism'; pp. 245–266 for difficulties with rights-based conceptions of individual freedom; pp. 369–399 for the case that a 'thicker' conception of autonomy, far from being antithetical to pluralism, requires it.)
45. Taylor, C., Alternative futures: legitimacy, identity and alienation in late twentieth century Canada: in Cairns, A. and Williams, C. (eds.), *Constitutionalism, Citizenship and Society in Canada* (Toronto, University of Toronto Press, 1986), p. 211.
46. Taylor, C., *Philosophical Papers II: Philosophy and the Human Sciences* (Cambridge, Cambridge University Press, 1985), p. 207.

Chapter 7
Liberalism and Education

In the course of this analysis I have moved from educational theory to social and political philosophy, from philosophy of education to policies and practices for education, from present day debates in social and educational theory and policy to their roots in earlier circumstance—and back again. It is now time to draw those threads together in this concluding chapter. The two preceding chapters here may seem to have strayed a long way from my opening focus on relations between education and the social order and my practical interest in the particular re-ordering of society represented by a neo-liberal deregulation of public education. It may also have seemed surprising that what began with scrutiny of claims for the virtue of libertarian policies and the soundness of neo-liberal theory gradually widened in scope. The reasons for this should now have become clear. Following a number of contemporary social theorists to whose work I have referred, I regard the re-orderings of society and of education which are the focus of this book as symptoms of what Taylor has called "the hardening of an atomistic outlook"[1]. I have not, however, sought simply to draw on that work in social and political philosophy in order to enrich philosophy of education or to find powerful additional ammunition for a critique of policies which take atomism to new lengths. Rather, I have set out to show that atomism in relation to education, whether in theory or in policy, exacerbates the hardening of that outlook.

This book is entitled *Illusory Freedoms...*, and there are two reasons for that use of the plural. One, of course, is to signal the atomistic individualism of resurgent theory and recent policy which promises particular freedoms to each at the cost of broader freedom to all. The other reason for recourse to the plural is that I am interested in more than one source of illusion. It is unremarkable to note that an atomistic outlook has "hardened" in recent times and is evidenced in neo-liberal theory and its policy ramifications. I hope to have taken that point further by giving some account (of necessity only in outline) of how and why an atomistic view of the person has been a strong thread running through liberalism from its beginnings. In other words, I hope to have indicated that that hardening has merely taken on a turn of speed in neo-liberalism: that the neutralist liberalism dominant through most of this century, with its priority for the right over the good, its suspicion of public action as interference by the state, its concern with freedom as immunity from interference, and its view of persons as rationally autonomous definers of ends and bearers of preferences, itself arises from (and reinforces) an atomistic world-view.

The relation of that world view to the social practice of education is rather curious, as I have already indicated. At one level, the democratisation of public education has, in policy and practice, sought both to realise its aims and to mitigate its effects. At another level, a liberal philosophy of education has found itself caught between two stools; pulled on the one hand by the neutralism which informs the philosophical framework to which it makes reference and pushed on the other to explicate and inform a social practice which—in its un-deregulated form—seemed to many to be at variance with certain of neutralist liberalism's basic tenets. This strange disjunction, I believe, can be turned to useful account. For our understanding of the social world it helps us to see why, on matters of education, the deregulators found themselves pushing at a door which, if not open, was certainly ajar. For the advancement of theory, its usefulness can extend much further. I suggested above that today's revitalised social and political theory should not be seen by philosophers of education as simply a body of work on which they can draw. Rather, I have tried to show that enquiries of both sorts would be more fruitful if brought together, given the present concern with liberalism's view of the person. One reason for that—that persons and their autonomy are in part formed through education—has been sufficiently elaborated. A second is that educational reforms throughout this century (until the radical revisionism of recent years) have been the practical manifestation of key elements of a substantive thesis which liberalism requires and with which neutralism claims it can dispense. A third is that the proper maintenance of public education, by public action, is indeed crucial to the maintenance of a liberal society in the modern world—as none but neo-liberals deny. That this is so in practice, combined with the facts that education serves both public and private interests and that in so doing it has moral as well as instrumental purposes, presents a serious challenge to any neutralist interpretation of the liberal ideal.

Three things need to be done then in this final chapter. A first section will outline the arguments required to redeem those last two claims. I shall indicate some of the features of education as a social good, pointing up relations (both logical and contingent) between its constitution and its distribution, as well as its significance not only for the formation of preferences but also for the range of options across which freedom can be exercised. This will suggest that only an ethical interpretation of liberalism can accommodate the realities of personal development and social evolution. In the light of that and of earlier argument I shall then sum up the case that a neo-liberal approach to education cannot be defended in theory, and that when carried into practice it offends not only against goals which neo-liberalism repudiates but also against those it explicitly endorses. A third section turns briefly to theory and practice for a liberal education. What is regarded as 'a liberal education'—the formation of persons in a liberal order—clearly differs in its policies and practices depending on how liberalism itself is understood. Here I indicate that an ethical re-interpretation of liberalism is needed to bring the problems of practice and the puzzles of theory into congruence with each other and to support, through education, the liberal ideal of an equality of freedom for all. These considerations, taken together, highlight the centrality of the conduct of public education to the social order, bringing this analysis back to where it began. I hope by that point to have established at least the outlines of a case to show that education is not just one social practice among others—still less just one public service—with which persons, citizens and theorists should be concerned. I hope rather to have shown that this practice is of unique significance for the freedom of the individual in a free society. And if that is accepted, then any defensible interpretation for liberalism must provide a framework within which the aims of public education can be explicated without internal contradiction.

EDUCATION AND THE LIBERAL IDEAL

At the start of this analysis I characterised the cumulative reforms of public education over a century-long period as offering ever widening access to an increasing proportion of the population. Though the pace of change at different times and the shape of particular policies has varied between one society and another, it would be a reasonable generalisation to say that this trend has been common to western liberal democracies. I have also emphasised that such democratising measures for education were animated by the liberal ideal in two respects. On the one hand, education was seen as freeing individuals from internal constraints on their future freedom—constraints which result from ignorance, prejudice or unfamiliarity with possible ways of life and sources of satisfaction or commitment. Additionally, it was seen as empowering individuals to resist external constraint by enabling them, through the social opportunities to which education was the key, to improve their position within the social structure. I have also suggested that public education has had a unique place among social practices in that it is not simply animated by the liberal ideal but that a special role in realising that ideal has been delegated to it. In its aim of freeing the individual from internal constraints, it represents society's institutional arrangements for fostering autonomy in the rising generation. And in reforms to bring ever greater numbers of the population within that the ambit of that aim—to replace socialisation and training for less privileged sections of society with liberal education for all—it has represented a liberal society's attempts to extend the preconditions of freedom to all.

I have referred throughout my argument to 'public education'. What is at issue is not simply the education of the public (which logically might be furnished as in earlier days by a philanthropic few or by sectional interests) but the education of the public, by the public. Education for all, by public action, is an accepted feature of modern liberal democracies: where dispute arises is over the proper limits of public regulation. In theory, at least, a hallmark of such democracies is the scrupulous neutrality of the state with respect to particular religious or moral values and ways of life: it is for individuals to determine how they should live, with the state ensuring that, subject to the harm condition, the views and preferences of none are privileged over those of others. Public action is permissible for strictly limited purposes whose common feature is their even-handedness towards the free agency of all citizens. This neutralist liberalism is thus not devoid of moral content, but that content is restricted to procedural principles such as impartiality, tolerance and respect for individual freedom. These procedural principles are essentially negative, to do with refraining from judgement about or interference with personal identity and agency. The one area of exception, where public action has a substantive end in view, is public education. There is, of course, a standard accommodation of that for the neutralist liberal. Active intervention in the development of persons through public education is seen not to compromise neutralism in so far as that education is liberal. To comply with that requirement, its primary aim must be the achievement of autonomy and its content and procedures must be even-handed between alternative religious and moral values, ways of life and so on. I have already cast doubt on the feasibility of those requirements, which presume an untenable view of development and an atomistic conception of the self. (I shall not rehearse again the theoretical incoherence and empirical implausibility of standard rejoinders based on the saving power of self-definition through critical reflection.) What I wish to highlight here is that *neutralist liberalism, in which the public sphere must eschew all but procedural values, has long been reliant for the realisation of its ideals on the public provision of a social practice which cannot—either empirically or logically—itself instantiate neutrality.*

One important upshot of recasting liberalism's "view of the person" is therefore to challenge the coherence of the neutralist interpretation of liberalism which until recently has been dominant as theory. At the same time, that neutralism has long been belied by the realities of political life where policy-makers in all fields are well aware that any social arrangements have substantive and differential implications for varying ways of life. (The most obvious example being fiscal and other measures of relevance to couples which, whether by their existence or their absence, cannot say nothing about favoured patterns of life.) The object here of denying the possibility of neutralism is to defuse certain hackneyed objections to an ethical interpretation of liberalism. And the purpose of insisting that an ethical (or 'perfectionist') interpretation is no threat to liberal ideals but rather is essential to their realisation is threefold. Firstly, it enables us to explicate the aims of the project of liberal education for all without constantly falling into contradiction. Secondly, it enables philosophy of education to escape from the curious position where a theory of practice apparently stands aside from the messy business of prescription by confining itself only to what education should avoid or refrain from. Thirdly and most importantly for my purposes here, it allows a defence of public action in maintaining principles for the distribution of education as well as for its conduct—a defence which is fatal to the justifications propounded for recent neo-liberal deregulatory policies.

Before going further, the hold which neutralism has on so much of our thinking may require me to distance an ethical interpretation of liberalism from that illiberal encroachment by the state on the freedom of the individual which neutralism is designed to hold at bay. The three standard objections to an ethical interpretation of liberalism are well-known. It is argued that to allow substantive ideals into politics is to privilege certain values and beliefs when all such are controversial. Such partiality, it is added, leads to the coercive imposition of certain ways of life and is thus incompatible with pluralism. This offends against the liberty of the individual, as pluralism is both a fact of life and a liberal good. It is the first of these objections which would be devastating if sound and which is also of greatest pertinence for education. (The two consequential objections need not detain us. They require not only that the first be sustainable—which I shall shortly indicate to be false—but that the practicalities of social life be ignored and the condition of democracy be discounted. There is no entailment between substantive values in public life and coercion. If, for example, there are fiscal advantages to marriage, that coerces no-one into marrying. That one choice rather than the other may have different costs and benefits is simply a fact of life: social arrangements could always be otherwise—and should be democratically negotiated—but they can never be no-wise.) On respect for pluralism, there is no reason to conflate the (inescapable) inclusion of substantive ideals into politics with state-sponsored monism. Liberal respect for pluralism demands not that every way of life be respected in the public sphere—that would be state-licensed relativism—but that all ways of life compatible with the liberal ideal be so respected. For the ethical liberal, only substantive ideals compatible with an equal distribution of freedom are candidates for inclusion in politics. (A full rebuttal of the contemporary notion that perfectionism is hostile to pluralism cannot be given here. I believe, with Raz, that fidelity to the tenets of Millian liberalism implies a conception of personal freedom constituted by *twin* commitments to personal autonomy and value pluralism. On a socially-sensitive understanding of autonomy, those two commitments are internally related.)

It might therefore be asked what it is that an ethical interpretation adds to liberal theory and in what respects this perspective is an improvement on neutralism. Even more to the point for the analysis here is to ask what difference it makes to an understanding of how social practices, education in particular, can reflect and contribute to the liberal ideal. I have already indicated that the value of an ethical interpretation is as much in what it removes as in what it adds. It removes a host of contradictions and insoluble puzzles as well as the need to rely on an ontology which is at odds with both logic and experience. What it adds is in some respects a moot point. Critics of neutralism in recent years have denied that it can be sustained in theory, on grounds both logical and ontological. I have claimed that as an ideal for social life, neutralism has always been more apparent than real (and not by default but of necessity). I have further suggested that we see this most clearly in the contexts of educational theory and practice. Those contexts, I believe, demonstrate not only that liberalism *can* be interpreted in ethical terms without betrayal but that this is *the only interpretation which fidelity to its ideal admits*.

I shall try to show that public education, if it is to be liberal in character—promoting the autonomy of the rising generation and ensuring an open future for society—cannot dispense with, indeed presupposes, publicly endorsed substantive values. I shall argue first that the content and process of education require this and then, more controversially, that the mechanisms adopted for its distribution do so as well. I shall present both of these cases not merely in terms of benefit to the individuals whose current experiences are at stake, but also in terms of benefit to the public as a whole, and not on instrumental grounds but in terms of the availability of a range of options which make up the context in which preferences are formed as well as exercised. In echoing the truism that the proper maintenance of public education is the key to the health of a liberal society, I shall claim that what counts as such maintenance can only be explicated on an ethical interpretation of liberalism. I hope thereby to indicate that more is required of the liberal state than a procedural framework for regulating the (competing) rights and (conflicting) interests of its members. *A fortiori*, therefore, more is required from the state for public education than an adequate range of provision and some procedural framework for whatever is deemed 'fair competition' (screening, selection, market activity) for its private benefits.

It is obvious that in practice, judgements of worth about what are appropriate understandings, tastes and values to put before the rising generation cannot be avoided. Curriculum content, pedagogy, institutional arrangements and so on must either be selected or be left to chance by design on good grounds. The neutralist liberal philosopher of education accommodates this by reference to abstention from undue influence, the power of critical reflection and the aim of eventual autonomy. I called that rationale into question at length in the last chapter. There I insisted that whatever selection is made, the commitments it implies cannot be devoid of effect, whether by commission or omission, on the development of the individuals concerned. What should be added here is that it cannot plausibly be claimed that the selection and commitments in question are publicly endorsed (and publicly provided) only to serve the goal of autonomy. After all, if they were subsequently comprehensively rejected by all or even most with the benefit of hindsight, however autonomously, that would not be a matter of indifference to either practitioners or providers of education. In such a circumstance either the process of education or its content would be deemed to be in need of drastic revision. If, on the contrary, outcomes were indeed a matter of indifference, provided only that autonomy were achieved, then neutralist liberalism would be no more than an endorsement of relativism and a set of procedural principles designed to allow subjectivism to flourish—and liberal education would be no more than the "cafeteria" of values and experiences which MacIntyre rightly pillories.[2]

What seems to be causing confusion here is ambiguity in what is understood by the achievement of autonomy. Ostensibly, it is a matter of nurturing rational appraisers who will define ends for themselves and in combination take the future of society wherever they will. Given that very thin conception, it should be noted that there is a certain logic to the elevation of consumer-power in education, where individual endorsements sum to unspecifiable effects. That this sits ill with the commitments of a liberal philosophy of education is one indicator that underlying the priority for individual autonomy there are assumptions at work which sustain an implicit thicker (substantive) conception. These are the remnants of those nineteenth-century beliefs about causal connections between freedom, reason and the good to which I have sufficiently referred. Autonomy is to be fostered through liberal education, not because we are *indifferent* to the understandings, tastes and values of the next generation provided that they choose them freely but because we believe that, given an education which places a range of worthwhile options before the young, and provided that these are offered rather than imposed, *they will freely choose what is worthwhile.* (An analogous rationale informs liberal upbringing in the home. When we say to young people "You must do what you think is right" it is not that we line up to endorse whatever they choose to do just because they have chosen it. It is rather that we have a sneaking (though sometimes misplaced) confidence that the range of options they are considering— on the basis of what we have put before them and the critical disposition we have encouraged—are broadly acceptable, and that deliberating about them adds to the likelihood of wise choice.)

Just as any parent (and any child) needs no alerting to the very different degrees of licence offered by "Do what you like" and "Do what you believe to be right", so any educator has substantive aims in view for learners, and any system of public education has substantive hopes for both the individual and the social outcomes of provision. And to assert that is not to endorse any of the bogeys of indoctrination, socialisation-in-place-of-emancipation for the individual, or reproduction-rather-than-open-evolution for society. All of these are clearly incompatible with liberalism. But equally incompatible, I am arguing, is a 'look no hands' neutralism which relies on hidden philosophical beliefs which cannot be sustained. What matters here is that this is not an esoteric argument about how education should be explicated, of interest to theorists but of little significance for the real world. The point of labouring it is that just as the terminus of neutralist liberalism as political theory may well be, in Macedo's words, a world "like California",[3] so the terminus for public education may well be just that destructive consumerism which has been the practical concern of this book. These states of affairs in the social world are vaunted in terms of a very thin conception of autonomy, seen to be required in the name of individual freedom. In respect of public education, I have argued that they risk being destructive of freedom in multiple respects.

Of course, the case recounted in this book of half a century of educational change in one liberal society shows that this need not be the fate of public education. It is only in the past two decades that neutralism has taken on its turn of speed, handing over to the forces of the market—to the aggregate choices of individuals—the future evolution of the social practice whose primary role is to foster the personal prerequisites to free agency and whose collective outcomes constitute the framework within which the liberty of all is exercised. Under the earlier consensus settlement, though neutralism was dominant as theory, substantive commitments (to increasing equality of opportunities and a particular conception of social justice) mitigated its effects and disguised its implications. Those sustaining values were accommodated within a neutralist framework by the belief that the measures they prompted were basically corrective: that they would gradually bring about social conditions (the 'level playing field') in which neutralism would permit a self-sustaining liberal order. I will not repeat the antecedents of those hopes nor rehearse again how the hidden social thesis of twentieth-century neutralism ran into the sand. I refer to it here only in order to back my claim that there have always been more than procedural values at work, in social theory as in social practice. And more than procedural values are required for public education if the thoroughgoing neutralism, which neo-liberal policies now represent and reinforce, is to be replaced by arrangements for education which are less damaging to a liberal polity.

The case with respect to the *social distribution of individual liberty* was presented in chapters five and six. There I emphasised education's salience not only for the individual's opportunities to exercise free agency but also for his/her opportunities to develop its prerequisite capacities. Here I wish to focus on the public dimension of freedom from a different aspect and to stress the salience of education for *the public availability of a range of worthwhile options*—for the social conditions which constitute the parameters of free agency for all. And once again, it is not just a matter of the exercise of preferences but also of their development, since social conditions structure the formation of preferences as surely as the actual conditions of society place differing price-tags on preferences when they are exercised. Without a range of options for personal commitment, satisfying pursuits and rewarding ways of life, freedom for anyone is constrained as well as hollow. Since the conduct of education has direct and deliberate significance for the construction of the social future, and its distribution has substantive effects on that future, then it is clearly of fundamental importance for the freedom, not just of each, but of all. As such, a liberal society must be committed to public action for the guidance of public education in whatever respects are necessary to optimise the public availability of freedom and its preconditions, social as well as individual. Once it is accepted that we have each to be concerned not just with our individual choices but also with the social matrix which makes them the choices that they are, it becomes clear that, collectively, our autonomy can neither be secured nor protected by purely negative means. As Raz puts it: ". . . if autonomy is an ultimate value, then it affects wide-ranging aspects of social practices and institutions. . . . The provision of many collective goods is constitutive of the very possibility of autonomy and it cannot be relegated to a subordinate role, compared with some alleged right against coercion, in the name of autonomy".[4]

Those collective goods, of course, comprise far more than the 'public goods' long recognised by liberals of all descriptions; they also encompass many social activities, institutions and structures without which goods standardly thought of as 'private' can be neither constituted nor enjoyed. Pre-eminent among these is a liberal education for all, publicly provided and publicly distributed, with both provision and distribution fit subjects for democratic negotiation and public action. Since both aspects of education policy have salience for the constitution of society, both are of public concern. The point of careful oversight of the provision of education is that each individual be enabled to construct a personal life which they find worthwhile. It is also, however, in the hope and expectation that their individual choices will combine to form a social future which secures worthwhile possibilities for all. Public oversight also of its distribution is not simply an acknowledgement that the formation of each affects the future of all, indirectly: it is also recognition that all are directly affected by the social options which thereby ensue.

An ethical interpretation of liberalism, unlike neutralism, accommodates the fact that the outcomes of education, for society as well as for the individual, are not a matter of indifference provided only that they are freely individually chosen. It can therefore dispense with faith that worthwhile social options will result by some mysterious process from the aggregate preferences of autonomous individuals. *Once that (ungrounded) assumption is set aside, public action to ensure that a liberal education is provided and distributed to all becomes not merely permissible but indispensable.* It then becomes inescapable that substantive judgements of value enter into deliberations about the proper distribution as well as the proper provision of education. This follows from the fact that a liberal education is designed precisely to secure the social conditions for judgements of worth to be publicly instantiated and continually revised. That the spectre of illiberalism seems to be raised for neutralists by the fact that these judgements are public judgements seems frankly odd. They are presented publicly, in order that they may be appraised through the use of capacities for autonomy which are socially achieved. That achievement and its role in social and personal evolution is publicly endorsed and publicly provided for. And if the appraisal which autonomous individuals then carry out is to mean anything, the modified judgements which result are in turn publicly instantiated in our public aspirations for society and education, and so on. The alternatives before us are straightforward. Either the existence of worthwhile options for the formation of preferences and the exercise of freedom is important or it is not. If this does matter, then either private, individual choices are thought to sum to an availability of worthwhile options, or public action is required. In educational matters, that public action cannot be confined to concern that provision reflect publicly endorsed values, since it is clear that distributional questions also have substantive consequences for the social future and the parameters of freedom for all.

Across the liberal spectrum, neutralists tend to accept that worthwhile options matter, but they evince an untenable agnosticism about what these might be and an unwarranted optimism about their equal availability, provided only that they come into being through the exercise of 'thin' autonomy. In public education this leads to the contradictions for theory and the impasses for practice which I have elaborated, and to a pervasive neglect of distributional questions. Neo-liberals either maintain, on the grounds that what is worthwhile is simply whatever individuals happens to endorse, that free choice does away with any problem, or they mount an ethical justification for the market which resurrects key elements of the nineteenth-century social thesis. (This position can be seen in Hayek, where the market is claimed to secure not only the negative freedom of non-interference, but the positive good of worthwhile options for choice.[5]) In public education this either delegates judgements of worth to current consumers or reflects a concern with 'standards' which is fundamentally instrumental. (Differing criteria of quality are appropriate to different social groups in accordance with their 'potential' and corresponding prospects.) Distributional questions are left to the market since worthwhile options from this perspective are seen in doubly individual terms. Whereas the liberal educator is over-sanguine about the *provenance* of worthwhile options for all, assuming that they will result from individual autonomy, the libertarian educator is uninterested in their *social availability:* not only are they properly matters for purely individual decision; they are seen as having only individual effects. Across the policy spectrum, then, all perspectives neglect distributional questions, if to different degrees and for differing reasons. (Even advocates of common provision for all justify this practical solution on grounds of private benefit and the welfare of individuals.) And distributional matters, as this enquiry into public education has indicated, have relevance beyond the usual questions of social justice, concerning the relative availability of freedom and choices to individuals across society. Given the relation of education to the formation of persons and their autonomy, and through this—in an open society—to the social future, the matter of *how opportunities in education are distributed is of profound importance to the constitution of socially available goods: to the prior consideration of what options for the development of preferences and the exercise of freedom are available for anyone.*

In earlier chapters I tried to show the general relation between schooling policy and practices and the ranges of culture, knowledge, taste and skill in the society served, arguing (against strong neutralists) that this range is significantly altered by its differentiation across society. There I noted that judgements about what individuals are capable of understanding, appreciating, enjoying and creating are reflected in educational practices which then become partially self-fulfilling prophesies. Where those judgements assume ranges of abilities which require only the removal of external constraints for their proper realisation, it is not so much that a cultural elitism results which is politically offensive (the usual objection to that position and the practices based upon it) as that what count as—and what become—the interests and pursuits of only a minority is the reflection in the social world of those very judgements. It is thus not that 'elitism' is a celebration of what is worthwhile backed by a realistic acknowledgement of a given human diversity: it is rather that it amounts in practice to a decision that some options are not relevant to the generality of citizens—a decision which in turn becomes a self-fulfilling prophesy, altering the range of social goods by stratifying it.

Of course, hypotheses about individual capacity can no more be avoided in educational practice than can substantive judgements of value about the worth of understandings, tastes and values. And hypotheses about the range of capacity across society necessarily underlie public policies for education along with public judgements of what is worthwhile. What I wish to stress is that these two kinds of judgement, though conceptually quite separate, are functionally related. Policies and practices which advocate a liberal education for all, where what is judged worthwhile is deemed educationally appropriate for all, support the availability in the social world of those commitments, pursuits and forms of life whose worth is publicly endorsed in society's arrangements for public education. On the other hand, policies and practices which advocate offering different ranges of experience to individuals, not all of whom are thought capable of benefiting from what is judged to be intrinsically valuable, do not only risk short-changing some of those individuals (as argued earlier). Their consequence is more widespread than this, in that they work against the availability in the social world of commitments, pursuits and forms of life which embody public judgements of intrinsic worth. In so doing, they thwart and reinterpret those judgements, changing for all the meanings and forms of life available to them. Hence such policies for education detract from the freedom not just of some but of all. They do this in two ways, each of which potentiates the other. Certain options cease to be common currency in the social context where preferences are exercised. And with changes in that context, differing options present themselves as pertinent to the educational context where preferences are formed.

It seems that the more we attempt to restrict the role of the state in the distribution of education (in the name of individual liberty), the more we risk compromising the range of worthwhile options available to all—a range which in part constitutes the preconditions of freedom. Where the strongly neutralist liberal educator opposes intervention by the state to regulate education's distribution beyond providing a framework for 'fair competition', the results are as described. Where the neo-liberal policy-maker retreats even from that regulatory framework, replacing openly meritocratic competition (whose shortcomings have been sufficiently detailed above) by the workings of market forces, the consequences for the social availability of worthwhile options become more severe. For the market is left to set in train a quasi-Darwinian process whereby, according to polemic, the weaker among options go to the wall and only those which are popularly endorsed survive. What makes this ostensibly democratic solution to the problem of judgement so damaging for the social range of worthwhile options is that judgements are made severally by individuals, on the basis of what they perceive as their private interests.

It would require another book to describe and analyse the manner in which a market distribution of education alters the nature of its content and process and in consequence changes the social frame-work in which preferences are formed and exercised. Here I can do no more than point to how this distribution mechanism, which does indeed appear to absolve the state from any decisions of value, delegating these to individuals, changes the nature of a good which is inescapably social. That education fits neatly into neither discrete category of public nor private goods is to cast doubt on that categorisation, as I argued in chapter three. That it has a place in both categories—on both the private and the public dimensions of benefit—goes some way towards explaining the conflicting expecta-tions that private citizens have of it, for whilst they have private interests they are nonetheless citizens. That it can be conceptualised on either dimension of benefit explains the neo-liberal impulse to exert tighter control over content and process, whilst at the same time deregulating access to diversified provision. That it cannot be understood unless it is conceptualised on both dimensions, which are in continual interaction, indicates that it is a social or collective good.

Although neo-liberal policy-makers pay greater attention to the social outcomes of education than liberal educators traditionally have done, this does not reflect recognition on their part that education is a good which is social in the sense I am stressing. Though part of the persuasive force of their proposals is that they have public as well as private interests clearly in view, the former are seen essentially as economic, with the relation of education to the social order understood in instrumental terms. Their position, briefly, is as follows. It is in the private interests of individuals that they receive education (or schooling and training) which fits both what they are thought capable of and also the future to which they might reasonably aspire. And it is in their interests as citizens that all should be prepared in this manner—that is to say, differentially—with the best way to ensure an efficient differential distribution of experience being the particular kind of open competition which market arrangements are claimed to represent. This interest in the public outcomes of education, therefore, is not cause for celebration (except by those who happen to endorse the neo-liberal vision of the good society in which questions of value in education are instrumentally relative to anticipated social role, and the value of what is intrinsically worthwhile somehow 'trickles down' to the benefit of all), for the social vision of neo-liberalism brings with it a serious underestimation of *relations between* the private and public benefits of education. (In other social spheres, advocates of a much-reduced role for the state are beginning to warn that "The exercise of free choice has most value when it occurs in a public space that is rich in options and amenities, and its value dwindles as that public space wanes."[6] It seems extraordinary that so little attention is paid to the role of education in maintaining and renewing that 'public space' and its 'options and amenities'.)

I have already explored the roots of the neutralist liberal educator's insensitivity to both logical and contingent connections between the public and private benefits of education. The neo-liberal insensitivity is additionally explicable by a general hostility to distributional questions, which appear in neo-liberal thinking not as matters of justice (whose distributional aspects are denied) but as matters of prudence (for the protection of social stability). I hope to have shown in this analysis that, prudence aside, no polity can be liberal, maintaining conditions in which all can equally develop autonomy, to be later exercised over a range of worthwhile options, unless distributional questions in the key social practice of education are a matter for democratic deliberation and public action. Support for that contention has been produced at several points in my analysis. I described in chapter two how, when access is deregulated, 'quality' is seen as something all have a right to compete for, rather than something to be assured for all as of right. I also described there how what is educationally worthwhile is conflated with the aggregate choices of current consumers.[7] I noted in chapter three that such choices obscure the fact that choosers have interests as citizens as well as private interests. In chapter four I analysed how choices based on private interests are doubly structured by circumstance, pressing individuals to respond to what they see as the contingencies of the moment and pre-empting broader political choices—with significant effect on the structure of the polity. In chapters five and six I examined how what education offers to the individual contributes to making them the persons that they become. It need scarcely be added that those persons then in combination construct the future that each will inhabit and which in turn will provide the context for the freedom of all.

To be concerned about the distribution of education is therefore not to prefer the good of some illiberal collective to the freedom of the individual. On the contrary. Only such a concern can secure individual freedom if that is to be more than the ability to choose between whatever options are thrown up by the aggregate choices of individuals exercising their several preferences. To insist, further, that the distribution of education is a matter for public action, on the grounds that—like the content of education—it reflects and modifies public judgements of worth, is decisively to reject the neo-liberal approach where outcomes for all are produced by non-co-operating individuals responding to what they currently see as the exigencies of the moment—exigencies produced in part by the market model of distribution itself. It is claimed that this serves 'the needs of society' as well as those of individuals, by giving the young a 'realistic' preparation for life, but this sits uneasily with the commitment to an open future to which a liberal of any stripe must subscribe. When the rising generation cannot but comprise the future, delegating judgements to the market risks predetermining the future in the guise of preparing for it, by privileging social possibilities which happen to cohere with the present private hopes and fears of education's current consumers or their proxies. That stance over-looks the reciprocal relation of education to society, emphasised in my opening chapter, whereby education produces and modifies aspirations and realities for persons and the social order at the same time as it responds to those which are currently in evidence. Thus if options for all are to be kept open, choices for all in the future cannot be circumscribed by the present need for each to jockey for position with other competing individuals.

Finally, if there is virtue in having options between which free agents can make autonomous choices, this must surely be because exercising freedom is a means to personal commitment, satisfying pursuits and rewarding ways of life. That in turn requires that the options which are socially available to citizens be themselves worthwhile, unless liberalism is no more than a framework for relativism in which the mere fact that something is chosen is believed to invest it with value. I have argued at length that the social availability of options—worthwhile or otherwise—is more open to influence by public education (intentionally or by default) than by any other social practice or institutional arrangement. I hope to have shown that a market distribution of educational opportunity actively militates against the necessary public maintenance of options for the exercise of freedom which cannot but be socially constructed. I hope also to have shown that the neutralist perspective as a whole lacks coherence, relying on the legacy of a discredited social thesis or on unexplicated philosophical assumptions to sustain a rationale for education within which substantive values are to be avoided except, curiously, as a *means* to 'thin' autonomy. If those arguments are tenable, and my (too brief) recommendation of an ethical (perfectionist) interpretation of liberalism is persuasive, then liberal respect for autonomy has more far reaching implications than the individualist emphasis of traditional liberal theory for education suggests.

When autonomy is understood as a capacity which is socially achieved, and freedom is understood as valuable for what it brings, then education is unambiguously a collective good as well as a private benefit. As such, its distribution as much as its content and process must be carefully and deliberately designed to maximise its power to advance the liberal ideal of equal opportunities for all to exercise personal choice from among a range of worthwhile options. Arguments for public action to ensure collective goods are well summed up by Raz when he insists that "personal autonomy depends upon the persistence of collective goods, and . . . therefore the notion of an inherent general conflict between individual freedom and the needs of others is illusory. Though an individual's freedom, understood as personal autonomy, sometimes conflicts with the interests of others, it also depends on those interests and can be obtained only through the collective goods which do not benefit anyone unless they benefit everyone. This fact, rather than any definition, undermines the individualist emphasis on rights".[8] That is as good a note as any on which to turn to a brief summing-up of the practical implications of my arguments.

AN EDUCATION FOR CONSUMERS

This analysis set out to offer an explanatory framework for a watershed in policies for public education which was reached some twenty years ago in several western liberal democracies. It has taken the UK as prime example of a process whereby a 'hardening of the atomistic outlook' brought deregulation to many social practices and public services which had formerly been considered best served by democratically negotiated public oversight of both provision and distribution. Both aspects of oversight were then designed to ensure that individuals, who unavoidably began life with varying levels of personal and social advantage, did not embark on their adult lives with discrepancies in their social opportunities unaddressed, or worse still compounded, by their experiences of education. In other words, the provision and regulation of public education, along with its instrumental role in schooling and training the next generation, had a moral purpose. That purpose was to realise the ideals of a liberal society in which each person had equal opportunities to develop autonomy and exercise liberty. Despite that, the 'radical reforms' of education which began in the late 1970s, changing the climate of debate, were themselves propounded and sold to the public also in the name of liberty.

A series of questions are prompted by this state of affairs, questions which my analysis has sought to address. How did this radical revisionism come about? What were the sources of its public appeal? What conceptions of liberty, of the person and of the good society are at work in these contrasting approaches to education? What differing empirical assumptions about the nature, purpose and function of education, and about the capacity of individuals across society to benefit from education, does each approach carry with it? To what extent are any of those two sorts of premises common to the two dispensations? What clues about unresolved difficulties, in both the theory and the practice of liberal education, can we gain from an enquiry into these matters? All of these questions are of interest for our understanding of the principles which have informed the evolution of public education. They are of obvious importance to educational theorists and also, I believe, to social and political theorists. A second series of questions are of urgent concern to educational practitioners and to the beneficiaries of education. These latter, as the previous section stressed, are not only those members of society who are currently engaged in their own or their children's education: they are also the public at large—the body of citizens in a liberal polity. Such questions include the following. Is that nebulous good thing 'the quality of education' improved by policies under-pinned by a basically neo-liberal rationale, and what are the criteria of quality at work? What are the benefits to individual consumers? Do all individual consumers benefit equally? What are the concomitant losses to individuals? What are the gains and losses for society as a whole from this radical shift in arrangements for a fundamental social practice? Is the liberal ideal of maximising an equal distribution of liberties advanced or retarded by such policies for education? And what do our answers to all of those questions suggest for education policy and practice in the future?

At this point I shall not attempt a full summary of my efforts throughout this book to throw light on each of these (interconnected) issues. On the practical questions, I have tried to show that the benefits promised to 'the consumer' are vitiated by a multi-layered individualism. The appeal is to individuals, who are offered deregulatory means of maximising their private benefits. They are on one level addressed as direct beneficiaries of educational experiences, competing with others seeking similar benefits. On another level they are addressed as indirect beneficiaries of the schooling and training of the rest of the population, thought to be generally enhanced by the virtuous operation of market forces. On a third level they are addressed as individual citizens in a polity where the education of all should serve global economic competitiveness and the education of each is a means to securing an advantageous individual slice of a (growing) social cake. It is not difficult to see that all of this adds up to conditions ripe for the classical economist's 'market failure'.

Its origins were explored in early chapters here which recounted how, in a society where expectations had been (properly) fuelled by enhanced educational opportunity, a watershed in the social consensus prompted two reactions. Politicians were initially exercised by anxiety that education was not adequately serving society's economic interest but was over-emphasising individual aspiration. A political belief that the discipline of the market was required to shake up the preserves of professionals led to the scapegoating of a system claimed to be impervious to the needs and legitimate demands of its consumers. The public were thus invited to blame professionals and bureaucrats for the non-delivery of a conflicting series of expectations which each citizen has of public education. And while individual 'winners' of direct benefit endorsed claims about a shortfall in their indirect benefit, many of the rest echoed disaffection with arrangements which in their case had still not met personal expectations of direct benefit. The way was thus paved for a right-wing backlash with populist appeal—supported by a championing of the rights of the individual—and for the dismantling, in the name of individual freedom, of a consensus settlement on education which had seen a role for public action as much in its distribution as in its provision.

It is a fact of political life that the complex task of any system of public education is the delivery of public benefit—social, cultural, economic—consistent with the meeting of private expectations from all those who combine fiscally to provide for education. The tricky problem in a liberal democracy, in which all so combine, is to balance public benefit against the equitable fulfilment of the diverse aspirations of all. At the heart of that doubly complex problem lies the fact that *public education is the site where aspirations, private and public, are formed as well as realised.* This makes the accommodation of competing demands a moral as well as a political question. The proposed neo-liberal solution to these exigencies (as with other, less logically complex social practices) has been radically to individualise the whole enterprise, making each consumer, willy-nilly, one of the blind puppeteers of the hidden hand which promises to bring about beneficial outcomes from market discipline and market freedom. Defences of this radical revisionism in social policy are various and often conflicting. It will punish lax, incompetent or arrogant providers and thus benefit all consumers. Alternatively, it will align poor providers and poor consumers, so that desert on both sides is at a premium. It will be more democratic, giving people what they show that they want. Or it will be more socially productive, giving the polity what it actually needs. It can be recommended and defended pragmatically, by its consequences. Or, whatever the (unknown) effects, it is an overdue change required to respect individual rights and restrain an over-weening state. The list of justifications (often conflicting) could be extended.

As I hope to have shown in the course of my argument, the promises to empower all by placing each individual's future in his/her own hands whilst simultaneously delivering public benefit cannot be redeemed. In reality the changed ethos sends a slow trend towards increasing equity into reverse, exacerbating for many their previous discontents rather than addressing them. On the public dimension, the consequences are if anything more damaging. If we take those questions for practice which I listed above, the following summary points can be made. We would agree without further ado that 'quality' is improved only if what is worthwhile were co-extensive with the aggregate judgements of current consumers; and the flaws in that conflation are legion. In chapter two, I detailed the effects on provision for all consumers of the sticks and carrots of market pressures. In chapter four, I showed that as market competition— between providers as well as consumers—increases 'product diversity', so the chances of given individuals obtaining 'quality', even on the approved definition, depend on the market-acuity of their proxies. In the previous section of this chapter, I have stressed that we are all 'consumers of education', and not merely as regards our private interests in a healthy level of GNP. When that neglected consideration is included in an assessment of the quality of public education, we would only agree that quality was improved if all of my arguments about the intellectual, moral and cultural role of education in the formation of persons and the social future, together with all of my claims about the role of education in supporting a range of worthwhile options for personal and social life, were unfounded.

The less complex questions of private benefit to individuals were examined in chapter four. There I concluded that what looks simply like a retreat (in the curious name of individual rights) from earlier commitments to an extension of social equality brings about in reality an overall reduction not only in equality but in socially available freedom. Even leaving aside the interests of those who clearly lose out from heightened competition for private benefits which are in part positional, we saw that the immediate gainers themselves had a hidden hand twisting their apparently autonomous arms. For individual consumers (*and producers*, wherein lay a compounding problem) new individual rights at best increase choice whilst curtailing negotiation on options for choice, and increase control over personal position in the social future whilst forgoing democratic collaboration to negotiate the structure of that future—the social framework which will give currency in the future to whatever choices are made in the present. On the gains and losses to society as a whole, effects are much more far-reaching and correspondingly difficult to summarise.

It is clear at least that when the concept of the citizen as individual consumer is extended to the one social practice which provides the site for the formation of preferences as well as for their satisfaction, this results in a fragmentation of interest and action which denies the public that most basic social good of all: some shared notion of what the good of society consists in. Far from placing us in greater control of our fate, this individualised conception of citizenship simply releases each of us individually to obtain the best deal that we can within circumstances we have ceased to try and optimise together. To ignore the fact that we are all social actors, affecting and affected by the choices and actions of others—which in their turn modify us, our society and the subsequent choices available to all—is not to *solve* the intractable clash between individual aspiration and societal demands; *it is merely to abdicate responsibility for trying to resolve that tension by democratic means.* The result of that abdication is not that one set of demands will be fulfilled at the expense of the other (though in the short term it may seem so to better-placed individuals) but that both sets will be frustrated. There lies one aspect of the 'market failure' which results when individuals are urged to adopt 'utility maximising' strategies in circumstances where their welfare and interests are inextricably bound up with those of others.

I noted earlier that literature on markets abounds with instances where agency intended to maximise individual utility cannot serve even the good of each. Sen cites many situations where the market makes "rational fools" of agents[9] when what each in fact requires in order to secure her own interests is that she collaborate with others in a situation where private interests are *by the logic of the situation,* and irrespective of personal moral commitments, inseparable from the private interests of her fellows. Standard examples, moreover, are of situations where only private interest is at stake: such market failures are compounded when private and public interest are inextricably linked—as they are, more than in any other social activity, in education. It is a commonplace that the complexity and mutual interdependence of individual interests in the contemporary world multiplies the conditions for 'rational folly', with "powerful mechanisms of social life" prompting individuals not only to act in ways which are in fact contrary to their material interests but also in ways which confound their experience and commitments: "A manager in spite of her own orientation may be forced by the conditions of the market to adopt a maximising strategy she feels is destructive. A bureaucrat may be forced . . . to make a decision he knows to be against humanity and good sense".[10] The maximin reasoning produced by heightened conditions of competition in a market thus impels agents to act in ways which can be clearly foreseen as damaging, not just to some, but to all. This is a particularly serious criticism when a major virtue of deregulation is claimed to be the capacity of markets to embody accumulated knowledge and wisdom.[11]

Whatever the merits of markets in *private* goods as repositories of what Hayek terms 'social epistemology', we see that where the goods are social, a market may as easily place knowledge and wisdom at a discount. It seems ironic that when the need to collaborate to secure our own and others' interests is even more pressing than in the past, we should now turn away from the common-sense expressed in de Tocqueville's much-quoted observation that "Knowledge of how to combine is the mother of all other knowledge".[12] That we should turn away in relation to public education, the social practice which should both instantiate and realise the liberal ideal, has particularly serious consequences for the public interest. For collaboration is not a purely instrumental device to enable each the better to achieve personal goals in a complex world. It can also be seen as a social value in itself and a vital underpinning for a liberal democracy. By collaborating to secure private interests, habits of collaboration develop: "Men chance to have a common interest in a certain matter . . . those concerned meet and combine; little by little in this way they get used to the idea of association."[13] In this way "social capital"[14] is built up, mutual trust is augmented, and the resources available for further social co-operation are increased. A reverse process is set in train by the individualising of control over social processes, and *nowhere more*

so than when the practice in question retains as one of its functions the
moral and social development of its 'consumers'.

When we focus, therefore, on those public benefits which are sought
from public education—social cohesion, cultural richness, economic
prosperity—we see that at least the first two of these are placed in
jeopardy by policies which licence, indeed encourage, a scramble for
immediate personal interest. Then only the economic argument
remains. And on that, even if all the discredited supporting empirical
claims were true, it would remain entirely implausible to suppose that
in a modern liberal society the economic well-being of all could be
entirely divorced from social and cultural considerations. Nor can
there be any liberal (or even neo-liberal) warrant for an elevation of
economic goals at the expense of the social and cultural prerequisites to
a society in which all have equal opportunities to develop autonomy
and exercise liberty. As Dworkin noted, consumerism does not
necessarily extend options, but it does, necessarily, alter them. Being
". . . self-fuelling and irreversible, and [making] a way of life found
satisfying in the past unavailable to future generations, the process is
not neutral amongst competing ideas of the good life, but in fact
destructive of the very possibility of some of these."[15]

In the course of the arguments summarised here I hope to have
made good my claim that public education represents the limiting
case for the virtue of the market. I have tried to show that those
commentators who have drawn attention to the neo-liberal impulse
to tighten centralised control over content and process in provision,
whilst deregulating access to a diversity of experiences within it, are
right to see these two features as significant and in tension. Where I
depart from them is in my analysis and response to that tension. The
rationale for curriculum prescription and public influence on process
can only be that this social practice, with its substantive input to the
formation of persons and their preferences, should be under
democratic control. One might criticise how that control is effected
(noting for example that it cannot be realised only through the views
of a governing party in a political system which is adversarial in
character), but the locus for such control must surely be public when
the development of autonomy in citizens—their future liberty—and
the formation of the social future is at stake. The rationale for
deregulated distribution of education is none other than the hallowed
liberal argument that once preferences have been formed, it is not the
state but only private citizens who have the right as individuals to
make choices, resulting in whatever aggregate outcomes their choices
will produce. Those outcomes are seen as representing the public's
judgement of what is worthwhile, with each choice acting as a vote
for a particular option. There would be no clash between those two
positions if the processes of forming and exercising preferences were

functionally separate. The theoretical arguments in this book (most notably in chapters five and six and in the first section of this concluding chapter) are intended to show that this cannot be the case.

Once we reject the atomistic view of the person which lies behind so much liberal theory and which is foregrounded in neo-liberalism, and move away from the curious dual conception of a discontinuous selfhood which it requires, we reinstate the social context as dialectically involved in personal development and social evolution. When we add to that revision in our premises, the role of education in both aspects of the future's evolution, and keep in view the fact that the manner in which that social good is distributed produces fundamental changes both in its constitution and in our conception of it, then the sources of contradiction in neo-liberal policies for education appear in a even more serious light. For it is not merely(!) that they are offensive to long-standing aspirations to increased social equality through educational means, or simply(!) that they are damaging to education in purely educational terms. More devastatingly for policies which have an ideological provenance and an ideological purpose, they offer a programme prioritising the liberty of the individual which is plainly self-contradictory under democratic conditions.

Though no project to re-form society can neglect education—and indeed any social order requires a broad and approximate alignment between its policies and practices for education and its political principles—the deregulatory impulse meets a fatal difficulty in arrangements for the education of the public. For this is the one social practice which cannot both instantiate the values of individual choice for utility-maximising individuals and also bring about a social order in which the autonomy of such individuals and the functioning of markets in all but 'public goods' (of the traditionally restricted sort) is assured. Precisely because the outcomes of the hidden hand are, on principle, quite open for neo-liberals, education for them requires careful state attention, part prescriptive, part deregulatory. However, since, in education, deregulation alters constitution, then *if* access to this social good is governed by the market *and if* choices in that market are truly free, giving rise to whatever outcomes arise, there is no reason at all to suppose that outcomes will maintain in good order those understandings, attitudes and cultural institutions on which the market—and a neo-liberal order—themselves depend. Conversely, if choices are not truly free, then deregulated governance of education loses its justification and the project loses its rationale even on its own terms. If my case has been persuasive, it offers a transcendental argument against the extension of priority for the liberty of the individual *atomistically conceived* into the governance and distribution of education. This is an argument which needs no (easily supplied) references to damaging consequences for learning and for equity. Furthermore, as I announced at the start of this exploration, if neo-liberal principles can be shown incompatible with the governance of the one social practice without whose alignment no vision for the ordering of society can be realised, then the vision itself is thereby called into question.

EDUCATION AND THE LIBERAL ORDER

Throughout this analysis I have emphasised the reciprocal relation between education and the social order. I began by arguing that the notion that politics and education are practically separable was a pipe-dream, seductive only in periods of broad consensus about the basic constitution of society. The examination of neo-liberal policies for education, their rationale and their intended role in reconstructing social relations, leaves no doubt that educational policy and practice both reflects and produces social values and circumstance. In itself that is a rather uninteresting observation. A key social practice cannot but reflect prevailing circumstance and value: what is of interest is how educational policies and practices mediate both. Even more obviously, education cannot but produce values and circumstance: what is of interest there is the nature of the linkage between existing and future conditions. In an unambiguously illiberal regime, indoctrinatory practices seek a congruence between input and output. An intended reproduction of values is designed to bring about circumstances desired by those in charge of the process. (This should not be conflated, as it was by certain neo-Marxist critics of education in Britain and the US during the 1960s, with practices which have no such intention but which fail—for reasons many of which are outside the purview of education—to bring about significant changes in the social structure.) It would be wholly unjustified to charge neo-liberal policies with a deliberate and substantively specified linkage between input and output such as that. It would also be very odd, since the avowed intent of neo-liberalism is the shrinkage of the state and the encouragement of an open future to be produced by the virtuous consequences of free-contracting between sovereign individuals.

However, whether or not particular policies for education are to be judged as liberal is a question not only of intent but also of effect. There are two aspects to that judgement. To be so judged, we would expect policies and practices to instantiate liberal commitments—to reflect a commitment to developing the capacity for autonomy in each individual. We would also expect them, moreover, to be at best contributory to, and at least supportive of, a liberal society—one in which the autonomy of all was equally nurtured and the freedom of all equally respected: a society where a range of worthwhile options for personal commitment, satisfying pursuits and rewarding ways of life was socially available and where structures and institutions were democratically negotiated to allow the development of an open future which nonetheless maintained that framework of procedural principles. By these criteria, as I have sought to show, market-inspired policies for education can scarcely be judged as producing a system of public education which is liberal. They fall short of that on several counts. I shall refer to some of these briefly first and then make the much more controversial claim that the principles and policies which they challenged also fall short of that ideal—though to a much lesser degree—and that they do so for reasons which in some respects exhibit a worrying family resemblance.

Throughout this analysis I have stressed five key kinds of (interconnected) considerations that lie behind prescriptions for education which are purportedly liberal. There are particular conceptions of persons and their development, assumptions about the relation of persons to the social context, beliefs about the relation of education to the social future, understandings about the permissible role of the state in endorsing values and structuring social conditions, and a view of the good society. (I am not including those kinds of considerations which necessarily underpin policies for education of any sort, about the nature of knowledge, the role of the teacher and so on, even though these also vary with the philosophical perspective and moral and practical intents of those programmes, for I am restricting my argument, for brevity, to those issues which are most germane to the matter in hand.) Whether or not an education which is liberal in intent meets the criteria I have suggested (somewhat schematically) for being liberal in effect depends on the tenability of key philosophical assumptions and empirical beliefs. And one of the many features which marks education off from other social practices is the strength with which interacting assumptions, well- or ill-founded, are causally operative in the construction of values and social conditions.

With respect to the policies of the deregulators, I have argued that relevant assumptions are dubious on many counts and false on several. The conception of persons and their development assumes a range of individual ability to which education should respond, rather than a spectrum of achievement which it partially creates; when this is allied to consumer choice rights in the name of individual freedom and responsibility, and the consumers thought apt to exercise those rights are the proxies of learners within a tightly-defended private sphere, then the results for individuals are strongly socially reproductive in the sociological sense, passing advantage and disadvantage from one generation to the next. In a broader sense they are not *re*-productive at all, but lead to particular kinds of social change. In terms of social advantage and disadvantage, they exacerbate disparities rather than merely reproducing them (empirical evidence is now amply available to bear out what time was not needed to tell). This occurs in part as a result of discrepancies in cultural capital and the diversification of experience described earlier: it is further compounded by the perceptions, the hopes, fears and expectations, of consumer-citizens themselves. For when deregulation in education increases the climate of competition for whatever form of it seems to have highest exchange value, individuals tend, in inverse proportion to their cultural capital, to underwrite whatever understandings and skills seem to be at a premium in the evolving situation. Where there is widespread labour-market insecurity (resulting to a significant degree from other social deregulation), the devolution of choice to consumers ensures not that consumers have a freer choice in determining the nature of the product, but that 'rational' consumers will seek (and thereby help to bring about) a product in line with the 'enterprise culture' and its values—in which individualism and conformity are curiously entwined. I have analysed at length elsewhere how value-change becomes self-fuelling under the social conditions that ensue[16]; all that I wish to draw attention to here is that deregulation of the social good which is productive of value and circumstance has a momentum of its own which ratchets the social competition, placing an increasing premium on self-interest and an increasing cost on solidarity and altruism. With the focus firmly on individual rights and freedoms comes a privatising of political interest, a loss of faith in public action and a decreasing interest in the significance for individuals of the wider social framework. Relations with fellow-citizens and the social environment become instrumentalised, and in so far as politics is about framing and deliberatively re-framing the rules of the game, rather than merely presiding over them (the manage-rialism which in a market society stands as a substitute for politics) political apathy increases and democratic values are placed at a discount. In one sense the state has retreated, though it is less the power of central government that wanes—indeed technological development and political apathy combine to increase state surveillance over citizens—than the power and influence of intermediate institutions whose political function is to provide checks and balances to central control. With the weakening of institutions which also functioned to protect the vulnerable, *cultural capital is not merely regressively redistributed between individuals: it is also globally reduced.*

The rationale for the resulting social order, and for the education policies and practices which play a considerable role in bringing it about, is clearly 'liberal' in the sense that it gives priority to the rights and freedoms of individuals, reinforces the agency of the private sphere and constrains the interventionist role of the state, and is avowedly agnostic about the futures of individuals and of the polity provided that the first of these results from personal preferences, choices and actions, and the second from the aggregate outcomes of those private decisions. The education of the public according to this rationale, however, can scarcely be described as liberal according to the criteria I set out above. I have argued at length in earlier sections that untenable empirical and metaphysical assumptions about learning and development combine with a blindness to relations between the individual and the social to ensure that whilst the development of personal autonomy (thinly conceived) is certainly made possible for some and even for many individuals, it is not carefully nurtured for all. As to the social purposes of education, the intended retreat of the state from public judgements on all but instrumental values has effects which are contradictorily socially determinist: the 'ends vacuum' which results for social life may well distance the public sphere from judgements of worth, but it nonetheless produces a moral climate which we all come to inhabit although none of us may have chosen it individually and all of us are affected by it collectively.

It is a long time since Aquinas observed that "if a great number of people were to live, each intent only upon his own interests, such a community would surely disintegrate. . . .".[17] In this, he was warning against what Sandel identified six centuries later as the social consequences which result from the continual interplay of ideas and circumstance—of the world and our beliefs about it—when certain philosophical premises form cornerstones of the prevailing world-view. He points out: "Only if the self is prior to its ends can the right be prior to the good. . . . What is denied to the unencumbered self is the possibility of membership in any community bound by moral ties antecedent to choice; he cannot belong to any community where the self *itself* could be at stake. Such a community—call it constitutive as against merely co-operative—would engage the identity as well as the interests of the participants, and so implicate its members in a citizenship more thoroughgoing than the unencumbered self can know."[18] I argued earlier in this chapter that only such a community is consistent with the liberal ideal of equal liberty for all members of society. I therefore do not quote Sandel in order to advocate one of the many versions of 'communitarianism' currently proposed by some moral and political philosophers and by politicians of both right and left (and critique of the implications for education of those positions lies outside the scope of this book). I cite his claims because they identify the key premises which, I believe, have long presented difficulties for both the theory and the practice of what philosophy of education standardly refers to as 'a liberal education'.

Disclaimers are needed if my closing remarks here are not to be misunderstood. I am emphatically not tarring with the same brush the commitments of what for a century now have been called 'liberal educators' (nor indeed of liberal philosophers of education of the past forty years) and neo-liberal proponents of deregulation in what they dub the 'public service' of education. Nor am I suggesting that there is little to choose between the outcomes of neo-liberalism and of neutralist liberalism respectively for the good conduct of public education, the prospects for individuals, or the character of the polity. To do so one would need to be not only cavalier or confused about theory, but also, as regards education and society, completely blind. However, among the themes running through this book, two make repeated reference to family resemblances in key philosophical premises underlying those contrasting approaches. Though these ontological commonalities are disguised by their conjunction with quite disparate aspirations for individuals and visions of the good society, they are nonetheless real. And for neutralist liberals they stand, I believe, as obstacles to the explication and realisation of the aims and rationale of public liberal education. The first of those commonalities is a shared individualist emphasis, as if policies and practices for public education should ideally instantiate on a very large scale just those requirements that a single learner might require for personal emancipation and private benefit. (This, of course, is how individual citizens tend to judge such policies and practices but, as I argued earlier in the case of policy-makers, social arrangements for education demand more of theorists than this.) The second is the determination to remain scrupulously agnostic about ends, whether they be those which autonomous individuals espouse for themselves or those which ensue for society from the aggregation of their choices.

It would be otiose to set out here the tenets of what counts, within the neutralist liberal paradigm, as a liberal education—tenets referred to throughout my argument, and with which readers are thoroughly familiar. In aims, content and procedures whose purpose is to free each developing person from the constraints of "the present and particular",[19] the intent with respect to individuals could not be more faithfully liberal. And the same is true about intent for society as a whole, since the aims concerned are thought proper for all individuals, whatever the initial 'natural' and 'willed' inequalities between them.[20] The problems with this impeccable programme become very evident when we make serious attempts to put it into effect in the real world. The obstacles to its realisation have been detailed at length in earlier chapters. They include, among others, the fact that education has public as well as private purposes, that those purposes in both cases involve interests in both intrinsic value and instrumental benefit, that the goods of education sought on all four dimensions are to varying degrees positional, that the obstacles to the development of free agency are internal as well as external, that upbringing in families and education in publicly-provided institutions often have non-compatible aims though the latter requires the allegiance of the former—the list could go on. The list of theoretical puzzles, several or which have been explored above and many of which mirror the practical obstacles thrown up by experience, is similarly long.

The most crucial, I believe, revolve around the concept of autonomy which is central to this rationale (causing such difficulties in addressing the role of the school in spiritual, moral, social and political development and understanding, and indeed in dealing with the role of teachers, the status of learners and the cultural content of the curriculum) and the supporting conception of how development proceeds—how persons become individuated in part through the process of education. There, the tensions examined in chapters five and six between the needs both to respect the differences between individuals (in abilities, attributes, motivation, etc.) and also to compensate for what are seen as socially produced deficits, lead equality and liberty to seem in conflict with each other, despite the fact that the former is constitutive of the latter. And to cap all of this, the public purposes of education—a high standard of public culture and civility, a satisfactory level of social cohesion established not through conformity but through genuine allegiance, and a healthy economy (in which economic roles are functionally related but differentially rewarded)—are to be achieved without directive public action (for that would contravene the neutrality of the state on ends and values) but only by individuals exercising rational and moral autonomy, with each making their own decisions on the basis of essentially private commitments. The good society then becomes no more and no less than the aggregate outcomes of all of those (interacting) preferences.

I have had three main purposes in this book. The first was to offer a sustained critique of the neo-liberal impulse in educational theory, policy and practice. The second was to explore why a neutralist liberal rationale for educational policy and practice seemed ripe for challenge after several decades of increasing success in achieving at least some of its aims, and to argue, more controversially, that its theoretical rationale simply does not add up in several important respects. Given that the aims of the programme for practice underpinned by this rationale are impeccably liberal in intent, it remains to ask whether it is indeed liberal according to the criteria I applied to its challenger. And on these criteria I find myself obliged to claim that it, too, though to a much lesser degree, falls short of that ideal through inadequacies in its premises. Where there is a conception of constraint which comprehends what is internal as well as what is external to the individual, the neutralist programme does indeed instantiate the liberal *commitment* to developing the capacity of autonomy in each individual. What frustrates realisation of that commitment is an underestimation of the enmeshment of autonomy's development in any individual with its development in their fellows. On the second criterion, that of at best helping to bring about and of at least maintaining a liberal society—one in which the autonomy of all is equally nurtured and the freedom of all equally respected—I will simply make reference to three arguments I have already advanced. Firstly, given the asymmetrical relation between education and social equality, the belief of the post-war period that education could of itself realise the liberal ideal was as chimerical as the nineteenth-century belief that free-exchange and democratisation would of themselves achieve that aim. Secondly, on the lesser aim of at least supporting a liberal society, there is good reason to suppose that the principles of liberal educators might well maintain a liberal society, given a generous conception of constraint and given, in addition, a better understanding of how persons become individuated, if such a society already existed. The problem, of course, is that such a society—animated by an equal distribution of personal freedom—is not one we already enjoy (unless we agree to define societies in terms of their formally endorsed aspirations rather than their actual conditions). Indeed, the problems which a liberal philosophy of education meets with in the real world arise in part from the very unequal distributions of free agency which the real world exhibits, just as its theoretical precepts imply that aspirations to liberal ideals need only individual autonomy for their realisation.

Those inequalities in liberty result, to be sure, from a whole series of causal factors, many of which are not directly connected with education (this, together with the positionality of many educational goods, is what burdened challenged policies with overblown expectations). I have indicated, however, that a rationale for education which is fundamentally neutralist has an inbuilt tendency to unwarranted optimism about the social outcomes of its individualist aims. That claim might be countered by the neutralist rejoinder that educational aims cannot, if they are to be liberal, make reference to substantive socio-political goals. I tried to show earlier in this chapter that a distinction between educational and socio-political aims cannot be so neatly maintained. Since our practices for forming individuals have substantive implications for the socio-political future, since that context in turn is a powerful component of their development (not just through its reflection in educational policy, but in its manner of distributing both internal and external constraints to the development of autonomy and the exercise of freedom), the education of the rising generation is a political matter in multiple respects. To give due recognition to that fact is not to open the door to coercion, oppression, or party-political dominance, as I explained above. Provided that the political ideals which I claim cannot be excluded from education's aims and the policies and practices they justify are *liberal aspirations for the polity*, their inclusion in educational theorising is no betrayal of liberal ideals. On the contrary, when they are excluded as a matter of principle, then theory or philosophy for education, with its undue confidence that the emancipation of the individual, times *n*, amounts to a liberal ideal for the polity, does not give rise to an understanding of education which stands above and apart from the hurly-burly of political argument and the pressing realities of social life. Rather, policies for the education of the public reliant on these self-denying ordinances have substantive consequences for the development of individuals and of the social world—consequences which belie that agnosticism about the outcomes of education which is an article of faith for neutralist liberal educators.

Two examples may help illustrate this point. If we take, say, the neutralist liberal stance on moral education, this warns against undue influence by educators in the development of moral commitments. Their role is to foster eventual moral autonomy by developing young people's capacity and concern for rational evaluation and by presenting contending commitments to them with as much objectivity and impartiality as possible. That this scrupulous open-mindedness relies on a conception of persons and their development which cannot be sustained was argued in chapter six. That conception, moreover, downplays the potent role of the social and material worlds in the construction of consciousness. Since personal outlooks—understandings, values, tastes and preferences—arise from a dynamic interaction between thinking and feeling selves and their contingent circumstances, the principled agnosticism of educators risks ceding the place for contingent circumstance to become the engine in the dynamic of development. Education is thereby disempowered as a force for individual and social emancipation, with the result that procedural neutrality in education has far from neutral effects in the social world. With a revised conception of how persons develop and of how personal and social development are each implicated in the other, on the other hand, moral autonomy presents itself less as an individual right than as a social value. We see that it is a capacity which is achieved socially and whose exercise by any individual is constitutive of its achievement by others. On such a view of autonomy, then in the development of values and commitments education has a broader transformative purpose than the emancipation of the individual. The enduring ideal of liberal philosophy of education—of the emancipation of persons from the constraints of their contingent circumstance—becomes inseparable from a socially transformative purpose for education. For it is only if the structures and conditions of circumstance themselves become educative that general emancipation is possible. To elaborate the implications of this claim for the content, process and distribution of public education offers a task for educational philosophy and theory over many years. My purpose in this analysis has been largely diagnostic, intended to establish that that task needs urgently to be pursued.

A second example can be drawn not from the conduct of education but from its distribution. Again the key issues are the concept of the person and the permissible role of public action in securing educational arrangements which actively foster the liberal ideal. The implications for public education of a view of the person which understands development to be a continuous feedback loop between the internal and the external, the personal and the social, consist firstly in alerting us to what arrangements we should avoid. The most obvious way to overdetermine the consequences of unverifiable beliefs about the talents and traits of individuals would be to diversify the public schooling system in terms of type and quality of available experience, to consign individuals to elements of that system at a relatively early stage in the developmental process, and to compound all of that by making parental acumen a decisive factor in who got what. That, of course, is a fair description of the educational policies reported in chapter two and examined in chapter four. It is not surprising that neo-liberalism, which compounds liberalism's theoretical shortcomings, should accordingly compound their damaging consequences for the social practice of public education. Liberalism, on the other hand, has long sought means to serve individual development by making reference to individuals' inherent attributes, rather than to inherited economic or cultural capital. Chapter three chronicled successive educational policies which aimed to identify 'potential' as objectively as possible, to provide differentially for it with as little damage to social esteem as possible, and to put in place mechanisms for rectifying 'mistakes'. There is no need to rehearse again here how such policies fell foul of experience nor how subsequent changes, designed to delay or disguise the identification of individual attributes, led to deadlocked debates about common curricula and mixed ability methods versus tracked curricula and streaming or setting. The point to be emphasised is that, given the view of the person that lies at the heart of neutralist liberalism, these debates present themselves as practical matters of pedagogy, to be decided not on grounds of principle but on the basis of empirical judgements (which tend to be vitiated by the same dubious metaphysics). And the force of those judgements in educational debate is vulnerable to swings in political mood. Such swings and their consequences for the distribution of educational experience may cohere with or offend against the personal pedagogical convictions and political commitments of individual philosophers of education: within the neutralist paradigm, however, they are not the business of philosophy of education itself. That remains centrally the explication of liberal aims and of educational content and process consistent with those aims.

With a revision of the twin premises which liberalism has long exhibited and which a neutralist interpretation requires and reinforces, all of that appears in a very different light. What looked like matters for pedagogy and practical politics become *internal to a defensible rationale for the liberal education of the public, and that rationale has substantive implications for practice.* With an untenable view of the person set aside, neither traditionally contending position can be sustained. With development continuous and the individual's attributes understood as those they currently possess (including motivation to develop them further), a common system of schooling is indicated for all, for as long as the society concerned can or will afford it during the period of compulsory attendance. Within that system, individual differences require to be taken into account, but in a manner which closes the fewest possible options for future change either in the direction or rate of development. Of course, the later that individuals are categorised, the larger the number of categories, the fewer the members of each category, and the more complex the pathways between categories, the greater will be the call on resources of expertise, time and finance which such policies demand. I am not attempting here to put a political case for such arrangements; merely to argue that *the further actual arrangements diverge from that ideal, the more our policies for public education are clearly driven by considerations which are at variance with the liberal ideal of the equal development of individual freedom.*

Though this is a case which has to be *argued for* in the arena of practical politics (for the down-to-earth reason that it has resource implications in competition with other social demands) it is nonetheless not one which should be *consigned to* that arena, for it is not a matter extraneous to a liberal rationale for public education. Properly understood, it is a matter of liberal principle—a matter with which a liberal philosophy of education, or a philosophical explication of educational aims and procedures consistent with fostering the liberal ideal, must be centrally concerned. It is a truism of philosophy of education that its focus of enquiry has a fundamentally moral purpose. These two indicative examples, together with the cumulative arguments of the case I have presented, may give support to my claim that both the explication and the achievement of that purpose seem inconsistent with a principled reliance on purely procedural values—a reliance which, throughout the history of liberalism, has always been more apparent than real.

Highlighting that issue has been my third purpose in this book. I have tried to show that the neutralist interpretation of liberalism, dominant for much of this century, is seriously theoretically flawed and that by extension a neutralist philosophy of education runs into contradiction when it explicates a theory of education designed to reflect the liberal ideal of equal liberty for all. I have suggested, in company with a growing number of political philosophers and social theorists, that liberalism requires an ethical interpretation, since it is a mirage to suppose that we can build either a social theory or a key social practice productive of values and circumstance on purely procedural values. I argued earlier that there have always been substantive values at work, although these have seemed to be both prohibited and redundant when causal connections are assumed between individual freedom, right reason and the good. Neither philosophical argument, nor the lessons of experience, give us good reason to cling to that latter belief. Without it, there is no escaping judgements on ends, and these cannot be purely matters for the individual, for a series of connected reasons explored throughout this analysis. Nowhere are those judgements more inescapable than in the theory, policy and practice of education, for in that practice we are not simply educating individuals, but constructing a social future. This third purpose is one I have only gestured towards here: to explore the implications of an ethical reinterpretation of liberalism for the theory and practice of education is a very large research programme of its own. From that perspective, familiar analyses, say, of authority, equality and autonomy would appear in a different light and the perennial controversies, say, of moral and social education might be more effectively addressed. The programme would not be merely revisionist, however. It would foreground a series of neglected relational questions such as arise between the distribution of educational goods and the nature of those goods themselves, between the constitution of those goods and the parameters for our social options and personal freedom, and between these latter and available forms of citizenship. The present period of contestation in both social theory and educational policy might be expected to encourage that enquiry. I have emphasised throughout my arguments that education is unique among our social practices. As the one social practice which both reflects and produces social circumstance and values, with its practices changing the parameters for the further evolution of the social world and our aspirations for it, it is a particularly fruitful site for studying how our beliefs and commitments about human possibility and defensible social principles cash out in the real world.

CONCLUSION

This book has been driven by two preoccupations, one practical and one theoretical, with the second arising from the first. For almost two decades now I have been dismayed, as an educational theorist and practitioner, as a parent and as a citizen, by the political, social and moral fall-out from the steady "privatisation of the public sphere".[21] At the start of that period, like many commentators, I responded to various proposals and policies for the 'reform' of education on what I saw as their own merits, analysing lobby-group proposals to restrict traditional liberal education to a minority of the public as an affront to equity, seeing the rise to prominence of industrial and commercial interests in education policy debate as epistemologically unsound as well as socially short-sighted and divisive, and regarding initial government measures to deregulate the distribution of education as a political device to sweeten those sections of the public who were most likely to demand a better resourced public education service.

In the course of those analyses, however, I found time and again that the rationale advanced for revisionism, and its appeal to the public in polemic and debate, relied on crude versions of the very taken-for-granted assumptions that I had found problematic for a much longer time. These concerned the relations between the individual and society, between education's intrinsic value and its exchange value, between educational opportunity and social equity, between public education and the social order, and most of all between the liberal social ideal of an equal distribution of freedom and the coherence (or otherwise) of society's educational arrangements with that ideal. My unease with these assumptions had long pre-dated the rise of neo-liberalism in academic debate (at one end of a spectrum of revitalised social and political theory) and the (to some extent associated) advent of libertarianism in the practical politics of several democracies, Britain notable among them.

That unease had begun during time as a school teacher in the heady early days of common schooling provision—educational arrangements which attempted to delay and/or disguise the merito-cratic features of the openly competitive policies they had replaced. In those reformed conditions two things sat uneasily together. The role of any teacher was to serve the interests of the young people in her/his charge (by producing, in today's strange terms, as much 'value-added' as possible), just as teachers had always tried to do. As a professional group, the role of teachers was to serve all of the young, and to serve them in similar ways in an education system now thoroughly democratised. Teachers who saw themselves (as many then did and many still do) as engaged in a social project whose aims extend further than cognitive 'value-added' sensed a latent contradiction there. For the better a teacher served the interests of her own charges, the more she necessarily placed at a discount the similar interests of youngsters elsewhere—learners who, but for accidents of fate, might just as easily have been her own immediate concern. Of course that was not something to be fretted over daily in staff-rooms; indeed the prevailing social optimism of the 1960s tended to see it as a self-resolving problem. A better educated public would be disposed to endorse extra-educational social arrangements whereby the unavoidable differences in exchange value which attended educational outcomes (themselves now to result from the appropriate realisation of differing 'potentials') would permit equal freedom for all to live satisfying lives of dignity and mutual respect.

Now the schooling policies and practices this vision justified seemed then, to a majority of practitioners and citizens (this writer included), more faithful, for more individuals, to the emancipatory aims of education than any that they had replaced. Nonetheless, a nagging awareness that the larger vision was founded on faith remained. That disquiet was not allayed by the analyses of the neutralist liberal philosophy of education which had risen to institutional prominence at about the same time. For although the analyses of philosophers of education of the 1960s and 1970s seemed to offer cogent insights into, say, teacher authority, a defensible epistemological curriculum framework, the logical implications of child-centred pedagogies, or the implications of key moral principles—equality, liberty, respect for persons—for the emancipatory education of the individual, the primary focus of interest was unambiguously the education of the individual in a liberal society. It was as if such a society were no more than the sum of autonomous individuals, with their autonomy mysteriously safeguarding the substantive social features which it presupposed. That research paradigm was not apt to address those problematic assumptions, some of which I listed above, which are concerned not so much with the aims and principles internal to education as with the relational properties of that social practice: relations, for example, between the individual and the social aspects of emancipatory education, and between education's role—for good or ill—in the enmeshment of the good of each with the good of all in a liberal society. (The range of questions which philosophy of education then saw as its remit was consistent with the neutralism dominant in anglophone philosophy at the time of that revival. Of course, philosophy of education has since moved on, with growing—and welcome—heterogeneity aiding its renewal. Nonetheless, emphasis tends to remain on education as a process for the emancipatory development of individuals.[22])

As I set to work (at the start of the new 'reform' period) in a changed role—as theorist enquiring into education and its aims from the outside rather than practitioner trying to realise those aims from the inside—I found it no easier to get a metatheoretical purchase on the tools at my disposal than I had previously found it possible as a practitioner to accommodate both my immediate duties to my charges and the larger social vision those duties were also meant to advance. Quite soon my analyses of libertarian 'reforms' seemed to develop common themes. In training a searchlight on the dubious claims of neo-liberalism which backed reform, problems of longer standing seemed also to be illuminated. These could be traced to some of the basic tenets of modern neutralist liberalism—tenets which provide the framework both for much contemporary liberal philosophy of education and for the policies and practices which for fifty years have sought to realise the emancipation of steadily increasing numbers of individuals by educational means. It seemed necessary to look at the history of these tenets and to examine the hot debates which now surround them in contemporary reinterpretations of liberalism. Revision of those tenets—a conception of persons and their autonomy, the relation of public action to personal well-being, the priority of the right over the good, etc.—is, I have argued, basic to progress in our theoretical understanding of education as a social practice. It is also a precondition to resolving the perennial conflicts between the good of each, of others and of all which arise at so many points within and as a consequence of that practice.

I should not need to insist again here that I am not tarring with the same brush the quite different social understandings and educational arrangements associated respectively with neo-liberalism and contemporary neutralist liberalism. Nor need I deny again any temptation to conflate those two (far from homogeneous) theoretical perspectives themselves. In the course of my argument I have sought only to bring out the fact that, in both theory and practice, it is not so much that the sea-change I have described puts an entirely new set of problems before us as that it brings out into the light of day—and compounds—*an interconnected set of very old problems indeed*. In much less stark form, related ontological and metaphysical beliefs are part of the liberal legacy and have long bedevilled attempts to explicate what is implied by the liberal ideal of an equal distribution of liberty. Moreover, they have frustrated efforts to develop educational and social policies and practices which can at least accommodate and at best further that ideal. My initial target for analysis was the libertarian push to establish consumer sovereignty over aspects of education previously considered fit matters for democratic negotiation and public regulation. That targeting, however, produced a widening circle of ripples which resulted in the concentric claims I have advanced in this book.

There would have been little point in lengthy argument to counter infrequent polemic urging the wholesale retreat of the state from the provision of education. Such proposals are as incoherent in principle as they are chimerical for practice. This analysis has therefore not sought to knock down what is clearly a 'straw man', except by implication. Few serious neo-liberals fail to regard the provision of at least schooling and training as a public good, with a liberal education, at least for some, recognised as essential to the maintenance of an open and civilised society. Where they depart from neutralist liberals is not that they urge this good be *provided* by the market, but that it is best *distributed* by that mechanism, giving reasons which I have sufficiently reported and countered. In so doing I hope to have refuted universalist claims to the effect that all goods (except those, like lighthouses or national defence, from which none can be excluded) are best distributed by the market. I hope to have done so by establishing that in respect of at least one good which admits of personal exclusion and private benefit, a market distribution cannot bring the virtuous consequences claimed. In education, the market model of just distribution is not just destructive of some aspects of the good itself, it also represents, not the fulfilment of priority for individual liberty as regulating principle for political association, but the frustration of that aim. Education therefore is the one good which consistent neo-liberals should themselves see as representing the limiting case for the market's claimed virtues. To the more modest claim, on pragmatic grounds, that whatever the case with other goods, however categorised, education happens to benefit from market forces, I believe I have shown that there are no gains ensuing which could not be achieved by other means and hence without the accompanying (often necessary) losses.

The wider implications of my analysis arise from the claim that the recent sea-change in aspirations for the social order, to be seen ranging from neo-liberalism in political theory to libertarianism in education policy, gain considerable impetus from long-standing and unresolved difficulties in the ontological premises of liberalism. I hope to have said enough on that subject to fulfil two purposes. One aim has been to bring together unresolved problems and contemporary disputes in political and social theory on the one hand and in philosophy of education on the other, so that each can alert the other to promising cases for (collaborative) treatment. In that respect this book may well amount to little more than (overdue) 'talks about talks'. The second aim is both more practical and more personal, taking me back to where I began. As parent and teacher in my early days in education, I was often 'pulled both ways' by the apparently conflicting interests of my own charges and the interests of others. Now, as parent of parents and teacher of teachers, I see others still wrestling with contradictions which in the intervening period have only been compounded in perception and exacerbated in practice. Further attention to relations between the good of each and the good of all seems urgent. Recognition that we are 'all members of one another' is most particularly overdue in relation to the social practice of public education. To insist on this is not to be the 'bleeding heart' liberal of current popular scorn. On the contrary: to ignore or to deny the profound interdependence of free persons is to make an important intellectual mistake, to champion illusory freedoms—and to be no liberal at all.

NOTES AND REFERENCES

1. Taylor, C., *The Malaise of Modernity* (Concord Ontario, Anansi Press, 1991), p. 96.
2. MacIntyre, A. (1990), *op. cit.*
3. Macedo, S., *op. cit.* (1990), p. 278.
4. Raz, J., *op. cit.* (1986), p. 207.
5. See Hayek, F. A. (1960), *op. cit.,* p. 126.
6. Gray, *J., op. cit.,* p. 60.
7. In this, my caveats about education echo Mill's about the capacity of the market to reward merit in individuals. He warned that "success . . . depends not upon what a person is, but upon what he seems: mere marketable qualities become the object instead of substantial ones." Mill, J. S., *Civilisation* in *Collected Works XVIII* (Toronto, 1977), p. 119.
8. Raz, J., *op. cit.* (1986), p. 250.
9. For example, "When prices of crops fall, a farmer may well try to produce more to generate more income. Unless he is one of a minority who so act, his action is self-defeating. Not only does it not ameliorate his situation except in the very short-term; in the medium term it doesn't help, and in the longer term it makes things worse." Sen, A., *On Ethics and Economics* (Cambridge, Blackwell, 1982), p. 84.
10. Taylor, C. (1991), *op. cit.*, p. 7.
11. See refs. 44–47, chap. 2.
12. de Tocqueville, A. (1843), *Democracy in America*, Mayer, J. P., (Ed.) (New York, Doubleday, 1969), p. 517.
13. *Ibid.*, p. 520.
14. See Coleman, J., *Foundations of Social Theory* (Cambridge Mass., Harvard University Press, 1990), pp. 300–321.
15. Dworkin, R. (1981), What is equality? Part 2, *Philosophy and Public Affairs*, 10, p. 287.
16. Jonathan, R. (1995b), *op. cit.*
17. Aquinas, *Selected Political Writing*, d'Entreves, A. P., (Ed.), trans. Dawson, J. G., (Oxford, Blackwell, 1959), p. 3.
18. Sandel, M. (1984), The procedural republic and the unencumbered self, *Political Theory* 12, pp. 81–96.
19. Bailey, C. (1984), *op. cit., passim.*
20. See the discussion in chapter six of this distinction of Dworkin's.
21. MacIntyre, A. (1990), *op. cit.*
22. Among recent exceptions is Carr W. and Hartnett A., *Education and the Struggle for Democracy* (Buckingham, Open University Press, 1996).

Bibliography

Ackerman, B. A., *Social Justice in the Liberal State* (New Haven, Yale University Press, 1980).

Almond, B. (1991), Education and liberty, *Journal of Philosophy of Education*, 25. 2.

Anscombe, E. (1978), On the source of the authority of the state, *Ratio*, 20.

Aquinas, *Selected Political Writing*, d'Entreves, A. P. (Ed.), trans. Dawson, J. G. (Oxford, Blackwell, 1959).

Aristotle, *Nicomachean Ethics*, trans. Ross (1980).

Avineri, S. and de-Shalit, A. (eds), *Communitarianism and Individualism* (Oxford, Oxford University Press, 1992).

Bailey, C., *Beyond the Present and Particular. A Theory of Liberal Education* (London, Routledge and Kegan Paul, 1984).

Bellamy, R., *Liberalism and Modern Society* (Polity Press, London, 1992).

Berlin, I., *Four Essays on Liberty* (Oxford, Oxford University Press, 1969).

Binet, A. and Simon, T. (1908), Le dévelopment de l'intelligence chez les enfants, *L'Année Psychologique* 14.

Bloom, H., *The Western Canon: The Books and School of the Ages* (New York, Harcourt Brace, 1995).

Bowles, S. and Gintis, H., *Schooling in Capitalist America* (London, Routledge and Kegan Paul, 1976).

Bradley, F. H., *Ethical Studies* 2nd edn. (Oxford, Oxford University Press, 1927).

Braybrooke, D. (1984), Preferences opposed to the market, *Market Failure, Social Philosophy and Policy*, Vol. 2.1.

Buchanan, J. (1993), Asymmetrical reciprocity in market exchange: implications for economics in transition, *Liberalism and the Economic Order, Social Philosophy and Policy* , 10. 2, 1993.

Campbell, T. D., Markets and justice, *Justice and the Market, Occasional Paper 21* (Centre for Theology and Public Issues, University of Edinburgh, Edinburgh, 1991).

Carr, D., *Educating the Virtues* (London, Routledge, 1991).

Carr, W. and Hartnett, A., *Education and the Struggle for Democracy* (Buckingham, Open University Press, 1996)

Cohen, G. A., Capitalism, freedom and the proletariat: in Miller, D. (Ed.), *Liberty* (Oxford, Oxford University Press, 1991).

Coleman, J. L., *Markets, Morals and the Law* (Cambridge, Cambridge University Press, 1988).

Coleman, J., *Foundations of Social Theory* (Cambridge Mass., Harvard University Press, 1990)

Colquhoun, P., *Treatise on Indigence* (London, 1806).

Cooper, D., *Illusions of Equality* (London, Routledge and Kegan Paul, 1980).

Cox , C. B. and Dyson, A. E. (eds.), *The Black Papers on Education 1–3* (London, Davis-Poynter, 1970).

Cox , C. B. and Dyson, A. E. (eds.), *The Fight for Education: Black Paper 1975* (London, Dent, 1975).

Cox , C. B. and Dyson, A. E. (eds.), *Black Paper 1977* (London, Temple-Smith, 1977).

Lord Devlin (1959), The enforcement of morals, response to *The Wolfenden Report on Homosexual Offences and Prostitution* (London, HMSO, 1957).

Dowding, K. H., *Rational Choice and Political Power* (Sussex, Edward Elgar, 1991).

Dunn, J., From applied theology to social analysis: the break between John Locke and the Scottish Enlightenment, in: Hont, I. and Ignatieff, M. (eds.), *Wealth and Virtue: the shaping of political economy in the Scottish Enlightenment* (Cambridge University Press, 1983).

Dworkin, R., *Taking Rights Seriously* (London, Duckworth, 1977).

Dworkin, R., *A Matter of Principle* (Oxford, Oxford University Press, 1985).

Dworkin, R. (1986), Autonomy and the demented self, *The Milbank Quarterly* 62.

Flathman, R., *Toward a Liberalism* (Cornell University Press, Ithaca, 1989).

Flew, A., *A Dictionary of Philosophy* (London, 1979).

Flew, A. (1983), Competition and co-operation, equality and elites, *Journal of Philosophy of Education*, 17. 2.

Galton, F., *Hereditary Genius* (London, Macmillan, 1869).

Gibbbard, A. (1985), What's morally special about free exchange? *Social Philosophy and Policy*, 2.2.

Gray, J., *Liberalism* (Milton Keynes, Open University Press, 1986).

Gray, J., *Beyond the New Right* (Routledge, London, 1993).

Green, T. H. (1883), *Prolegomena to Ethics*, Bradley, A. C. (Ed.) (1924) (Oxford, Oxford University Press).

Green, T. H., *Liberal Legislation and Freedom of Contract*, in: *Works of T. H. Green* (London, Longmans, 1888).

Hall, E. G. and Skinner, N., Somewhere to turn; strategies for parents of gifted and talented children: in Tennenbaum A. J. and Neuman, E. (eds.), *Perspectives on Gifted and Talented Children* (New York, Columbia University, Teachers College Press, 1980).

Harris, K., *Education and Knowledge* (London, Routledge and Kegan Paul, 1979).

Lord Harris, The morality of the market, in: *The New Right and Christian Values, Occasional Paper 5* (Centre for Theology and Public Issues, University of Edinburgh, Edinburgh, 1985).

Hayek, F. A., *The Constitution of Liberty* (London, Routledge and Kegan Paul, 1960).

Hayek, F. A., *Law, Legislation and Liberty, Vol. 2, The Mirage of Social Justice* (London, Routledge and Kegan Paul, 1982).

Heald, D., *Public Expenditure* (Oxford, Martin Robertson, 1983).

Hirsch, E. D., *Cultural Literacy: What Every American Needs to Know* (Boston, Houghton-Mifflin, 1987).

Hirsch, F., *The Social Limits to Growth* (London, Routledge and Kegan Paul, 1971).

Hirst, P. H., Liberal education and the nature of knowledge, in: Peters, R. S. (Ed.), *The Philosophy of Education* (London, Routledge and Kegan Paul, 1973).

Hirst, P. H., *Knowledge and the Curriculum* (London, Routledge and Kegan Paul, 1974).

Hollis, M. (1982), Education as a positional good, *Journal of Philosophy of Education*, 16. 2.

Hollis, M. (1989), Atomic energy and moral glue, *Journal of Philosophy of Education*, 23. 2.

Hollis, M. (1990), Market equality and social freedom, *Journal of Applied Philosophy*, 7. 1.

Jonathan, R. (1982), Two concepts of education? *Journal of Philosophy of Education*, 16.2.

Jonathan, R. (1983), Education, gender and the nature/culture controversy, *Journal of Philosophy of Education*, 13 2.

Jonathan, R. (1983), The manpower service model of education, *Cambridge Journal of Education*, 13.

Jonathan, R. (1986), *Giftedness and Education* (Edinburgh, Scottish Office Education Department).

Jonathan, R. (1986), Cultural elitism explored, *Journal of Philosophy of Education*, 20. 2.

Jonathan, R., The Youth Training Scheme: an educational initiative? in: Holt, M. (Ed.), *Skills and Vocationalism* (Milton Keynes, Open University Press, 1986a).

Jonathan, R., Education and the 'needs of society' in: Hartnett, A. and Naish, M. (eds.), *Education and Society Today* (London, Falmer Press, 1986b).

Jonathan, R. (1986c), Education for democratic participation, *Education and Community* (Centre for Theology and Public Issues, University of Edinburgh, Edinburgh).

Jonathan, R. (1988), The notion of giftedness, or how long is a piece of string?, *British Journal of Educational Studies*, 26. 2.

Jonathan, R. (1989), Choice and control in education: parental rights and social justice, *British Journal of Educational Studies*, 37. 4.

Jonathan, R. (1989), Gender socialisation and the nature/culture controversy: the dualist's dilemma, *Educational Philosophy and Theory*, 21. 2 Special Issue.

Jonathan, R. (1990), State education service or prisoner's dilemma: the 'hidden hand' as source of educational policy, *British Journal of Educational Studies,* 38. 2, and *Educational Philosophy and Theory,* 22.1.

Jonathan, R. (1990), The curriculum and the new vocationalism, *Journal of Curriculum Studies,* 22. 2.

Jonathan, R. (1993), Onderwijsvandering in het Verenigd Kononkrijk in de jaren tachtig: Over het inperialisme van de instrumentale rationaliteit, *Pedagogische Tijdschrift,* 18, 1.

Jonathan, R., Parents' rights in schooling, in: Munn, P. (Ed.), *Parents and Schools: Customers, Managers or Partners,* (London, Routledge, 1993).

Jonathan, R. (1993a), Educating the virtues: a problem in the social development of consciousness", *Journal of Philosophy of Education,* 27. 1.

Jonathan, R. (1993b), Education, philosophy of education and the fragmentation of value, *Journal of Philosophy of Education,* 27. 2.

Jonathan, R. (1995a), Liberal philosophy of education: a paradigm under strain, *Journal of Philosophy of Education,* 29. 1.

Jonathan, R. (1995b), Education and moral development: the role of reason and circumstance, *Journal of Philosophy of Education,* 29. 3.

King, D. S., *Politics, Markets and Citizenship* (London, Macmillan, 1987).

Knight, F. *The Ethics of Competition and Other Essays* (London, Allen and Unwin, 1935).

Kymlicka, W. (1989), Liberal individualism and liberal neutrality, *Ethics* 99.

Laslett, P. (Ed.), *Patriarcha and Other Political Works by Robert Filmer* (Oxford, Oxford University Press, 1959).

Lavoie, D., *Rivalry and Central Planning: the Socialist Calculation Debate Reconsidered* (Cambridge, Cambridge University Press, 1985).

MacCallum, G. C. (1967), Negative and positive freedom, *The Philosophical Review,* 76.

Macedo, S., *Liberal Virtues: Citizenship, Virtue and Community in Liberal Constitutionalism* (Oxford, Clarendon Press, 1990).

MacIntyre, A., *After Virtue* (London, Duckworth, 1981).

MacIntyre, A., The idea of an educated public, in: Haydon, G. (Ed.), *Education and Values* (Institute of Education, University of London, 1987).

MacIntyre, A., *Whose Justice? Which Rationality?* (London, Duckworth, 1988).

MacIntyre, A. (1990) The privatisation of good: an Inaugural Lecture, *Review of Politics,* 52. 3.

Marx, K., *Capital, III* (London, Harmondsworth, 1978).

Mill, J. S., *Utilitarianism, On Liberty and Considerations of Representative Government* (London, 1972 2nd edn.).

Mill, J. S., *Civilisation* in *Collected Works XVIII,* (Toronto, 1977).

Mueller, M., *Public Choice* (Cambridge, Cambridge University Press, 1989).

Murdoch, I., *The Sovereignty of Good* (London, Routledge and Kegan Paul, 1970).

Nozick, R., *Anarchy, State and Utopia* (New York, Basic Books Inc., 1974).

O'Connor, D. (1982), Two concepts of education, *Journal of Philosophy of Education,* 16.2.

O'Neill, O. (1979), The most extensive liberty, *Proceedings of the Aristotelian Society,* 80.

Oakeshott, M., Education: the engagement and its frustration in: Dearden, R. F., Hirst, P., Peters, R. S. (eds.), *Education and the Development of Reason* (London, Routledge and Kegan Paul, 1972).

Pareto, V., Suffragio universale, in *L'Italiano Gazzetta del Popolo,* 12. 10. 1872.

Peters, R. S., The justification of education, in: Peters, R. S. (Ed.), *The Philosophy of Education,* (Oxford, Oxford University Press, 1973).

Plant, R., *Equality, Markets and the New Right* (London, Fabian Tract No. 494, 1984).

Polanyi, M., *The Logic of Liberty* (Chicago, University of Chicago Press, 1951).

Ranson, S., From 1944 to 1988: Education, citizenship and democracy, in: Flude, M. and Hammer, M. (eds.), *The Education Reform Act 1988, its Origins and Implications* (Falmer Press, Basingstoke, 1990).

Rawls J., *A Theory of Justice* (Cambridge Mass., Harvard University Press, 1971).

Rawls, J. (1980), Kantian constructivism in moral theory: the Dewey Lectures 1980, *Journal of Philosophy*.

Rawls, J. (1985), Justice as fairness: political not metaphysical, *Philosophy and Public Affairs*, 14.

Rawls, J., Social unity and primary goods, in: Sen, A. and Williams, B. (eds.), *Utilitarianism and Beyond* (Cambridge, Cambridge University Press, 1982).

Rawls, J., *Political Liberalism* (New York, Columbia University Press, 1993).

Raz, J., *The Morality of Freedom* (Oxford, Clarendon Press, 1986).

Rocco, A., The political doctrine of fascism: in *Readings on Fascism and National Socialism* (Chicago, University of Colorado Press, 1952).

Rorty, R., *Contingency, Irony, and Solidarity* (Cambridge, Cambridge University Press, 1989).

Rorty, R., *Objectivity, Relativism and Truth* (Cambridge, Cambridge University Press, 1991).

Sager, L. G. (1980), Pareto superiority, consent and justice, *Hofstra Law Review*, 8.

Sandel, M., *Liberalism and the Limits of Justice* (Cambridge, Cambridge University Press, 1982).

Sandel, M. (1984), The procedural republic and the unencumbered self, *Political Theory*, 12.

Schoeman, F. (1980), Rights of children, rights of parents, and the moral basis of the family, *Ethics*, 91.

Self, P., *Government by the Market? The Politics of Public Choice* (Basingstoke, Macmillan, 1993).

Sen, A. (1985), The moral standing of the market, *Social Philosophy and Policy*, 2.2.

Sen, A., *On Ethics and Economics* (Oxford, Blackwell, 1987).

Simon, B., *Intelligence, Psychology and Education* (London, Lawrence and Wishart, 1971).

Smith, A., *The Wealth of Nations*, (annotated edition, Callan E., London, 1904).

Smith, A., *The Theory of Moral Sentiments*, (annotated edition, Callan E., London, 1904).

Taylor, C., Alternative futures: legitimacy, identity and alienation in late twentieth century Canada, in: Cairns, A. and Williams, C. (eds.) *Constitutionalism, Citizenship and Society in Canada* (Toronto, University of Toronto Press, 1986).

Taylor, C., *Hegel and Modern Society* (Cambridge, Cambridge University Press, 1979).

Taylor, C., What's wrong with negative liberty? in: Ryan, A. (Ed.), *The Idea of Freedom* (Oxford, Oxford University Press, 1979).

Taylor, C., *Philosophical Papers II: Philosophy and the Human Sciences* (Cambridge, Cambridge University Press, 1985).

Taylor, C., *The Malaise of Modernity* (Concord Ontario, Anansi Press, 1991).

Terman, L., *Measuring Intelligence* (Boston, Houghton-Mifflin, 1937).

Thoday, J. M., Geneticism and environmentalism, in: Neade, J. E. and Parkes, A. S. (eds.), *Biological Aspects of Social Problems*, (London, Oliver & Boyd, 1965).

de Tocqueville, A., *Democracy in America,* Mayer, J. P., (Ed.), (New York, Doubleday, 1969).

Tooley, J., *Education Without the State* (London, Institute of Economic Affairs, 1996).

Virgo, P., Learning for change, training, retraining and lifelong education for multi-career lives, Bow Paper, Nov. 1981.

Walzer, M., *Spheres of Justice* (New York, Basic Books, 1981).

Williams, B., The idea of equality, in: Laslett, P. and Runciman, W. (eds.), *Politics and Society* (Second Series) (Oxford, Blackwell, 1962).

Young, M. F. D., (Ed.), *Knowledge and Control* (London, Collier-Macmillan, 1971).

1944 Education Act, England and Wales, HMSO.

1945 Education Act, Scotland, HMSO.

1966 Children and their Primary Schools (Plowden Report) London, HMSO.

1988 Education Reform Act, England and Wales, HMSO.

1989 Self-Governing Schools etc. Scotland Bill , HMSO

The Citizen's Charter, Command 1599, London, HMSO, 1991.

The Parent's Charter, Edinburgh, The Scottish Office, HMSO, 1991.

The Parent's Charter, London, Department of Education and Science, HMSO, 1991.